# The Devil in the Details

# The
# Devil
## in the
# Details

## Cuban Antislavery Narrative
## in the Postmodern Age

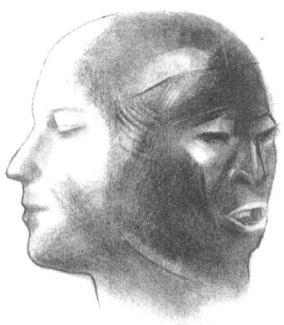

# Claudette M. Williams

UNIVERSITY OF THE WEST INDIES PRESS

Jamaica • Barbados • Trinidad and Tobago

University of the West Indies Press
7A Gibraltar Hall Road    Mona
Kingston 7    Jamaica
www.uwipress.com

CATALOGUING-IN-PUBLICATION DATA

Williams, Claudette.
The devil in the details: Cuban antislavery narrative in the
postmodern age / Claudette M. Williams.

p. cm.

Includes bibliographical references.

ISBN: 978-976-640-231-0

1. Cuban literature – 19th century – History and criticism.
2. Slavery in literature. I. Title.

PQ7382.W543 2010                 863'2

*Cover illustration:* George Rodney, untitled.

Book and cover design by Robert Harris.
Set in Fairfield Light 11/15 x 24.
Printed in the United States of America.

# CONTENTS

# PREFACE

THIS IS A BOOK about breathing new life into texts from the past. Slavery in the Americas, a popular theme for many a historian, literary artist and political ideologue before emancipation, continues to provide a minefield for investigation. Scholars worldwide have viewed the subject from every imaginable standpoint. A desire to promote a homogeneous view of the practice and institution of slavery has led many to speak about it in monolithic terms. With the passage of time and the availability of new lenses, however, more nuanced perceptions and interpretations have been emerging in the postcolonial era. I begin this appraisal of nineteenth-century Cuban antislavery narrative by acknowledging the many enlightened and enlightening readings that my predecessors have generated over the years. Those who laid the groundwork for this exploration include both Cuban literary critics and historians and traditional and revisionist Caribbean historians, as well as the many scholars who have been studying and writing about the theme of the diasporic African experience in Hispanic literature since the 1960s. Without the insights they have provided, this book would not have been written; I cite many of those to whom I am indebted at different points in the following pages.

Cuba's literature of slavery is almost by definition antislavery literature. Self-respecting nineteenth-century writers of fiction who saw themselves and were seen as liberal did not write in conscious support of slavery. Although there was a healthy output of poetry in the period, narrative fiction was the vehicle of choice for the literary expression of dissent from proslavery dogma. Quite apart from its contribution to developing that country's distinct literary tradition, antislavery fiction is highly valued as an alternative source of historical information about colonial Cuba. This literary activity was seen for what it was: no less powerful a threat to the establishment than the more active expressions of resistance.

But why return to this subject, one might ask, when it has been treated almost to exhaustion by scholars inside and outside of Cuba? The most obvious response is that we have come to realize that no reading of a work can exhaust its store of meaning. Meaning in the universe of art, to repeat a truism, is neither coherent nor monolithic, not fixed but volatile, contradictory, plural, unsettled and sometimes unsettling. Each novel, each poem, each painting has room for multiple interpretations. It is this view of art as a potentially infinite fount of meaning that allows a twenty-first-century reader to arrive at new understandings of this narrative tradition whose heyday dates back more than one and a half centuries. The new life with which this book seeks to infuse such an old topic is testimony to this time-defying attribute of creative literature.

Moreover, the subject of slavery, its nature, representation and legacy, continues even today to inspire national debates; slavery is one of the defining historical experiences that must inform any proper understanding of the contemporary reality of the Caribbean and the Americas. For those of us who inhabit the spaces that were once its arena, slavery is an emotional and emotive subject. The revival in recent years of the demand for reparation and apologies for the forced transfer of Africans across the Atlantic, and the subsequent exploitation of their labour in Europe's empire-building, is one indication of the presentness of the past in the Americas.

Rather than seek to discredit existing interpretations, this book suggests other ways of thinking about and understanding these Cuban narratives in the light of contemporary ideas about the art of representation. My selection of texts will also bring little-known or -studied compositions out of the shadows and into the spotlight while giving a new gloss to the iconic novels. In addition, important details of these texts, some of which commentators have overlooked or given inadequate attention, will be unearthed to support alternative readings or expand existing ones.

# ACKNOWLEDGEMENTS

FIRST AMONG THE contributors to the writing of this book is my home institution, the Mona campus of the University of the West Indies, which has supported my research and development efforts over the past thirty years. A two-year fellowship between 2006 and 2008 afforded me the time I needed to concentrate on advancing the research for this book. Librarians at the Biblioteca Nacional José Martí in Havana and the University of the West Indies Main Library, as well as University of Havana professor of history María del Carmen Barcia Zequiera, provided invaluable assistance in sourcing primary and secondary material. The priceless friendship of Mireille Milfort Ariza has been a wonderful source of comfort, reassurance and encouragement at every stage of the research and writing process. I am likewise grateful for the timely advice from two UWI colleagues, Professors Fay Durrant and Waibinte Wariboko, which gave considerable impetus to the research. Over the years University of Toronto professor emeritus Keith Ellis has inspired me with his own work and sustained me with his faith in mine. To him I owe a huge debt of gratitude. I am eternally thankful for my two daughters, Kamilah and Shari, who with loving firmness have kept me grounded in reality even while I have been grounding my research in the latest theory.

For their gentle polishing of the manuscript's rough spots I am indebted to the patient and accommodating editorial team of the UWI Press: Shivaun Hearne (managing editor), Gillian Watts (copy editor) and Amanda Mathis (proofreader). The staff of the Press, in particular Linda Speth (director) and Donna Muirhead (marketing manager), are also deserving of my gratitude. Their expert guidance has been indispensable to the completion of the publication process.

Finally, I extend appreciation to the editors who first published and have now agreed to the republication of revised versions of the following parts of the book: *Afro-Hispanic Review* (chapters 1 and 5), *Caribbean Quarterly* (chapter 2), *Bulletin of Latin American Research* (chapter 3) and *PALARA* (chapter 4).

# INTRODUCTION

THE NUMBER OF fictional narratives bred by slavery in nineteenth-century Cuba stands as one of the famous landmarks in the province of Hispanic Caribbean literature. As conspicuous as its prevalence in Cuban narrative is the scarcity of writing on this theme in the literature of the nearby island territories of the Dominican Republic and Puerto Rico. Indeed, no other geographical location in the Hispanic world boasts such a distinct body of writing on the slavery theme. Composed by progressive Euro-Creole writers, these narratives served as Cuba's formal induction into the anti-establishment mode that has come to be the signature of New World writing. Certain high-profile titles from this period, most notably Cirilo Villaverde's *Cecilia Valdés* and Gertrudis Gómez de Avellaneda's *Sab*, are now regarded as archetypes of the genre. In the general Cuban population these writers are household names and new editions of both novels continue to appear. Moreover, for the majority of Cubans in intellectual circles, they rank as monuments in Cuban letters. In addition to extended novels, the antislavery theme inspired shorter narratives, sometimes referred to as *noveletas* or novellas, whose value has been somewhat diminished by preferential treatment of the iconic works.

With the dearth of direct slave testimonies in Hispanic American literature, the autobiography of the Cuban slave poet Juan Francisco Manzano is a unique specimen in comparison with the US slave narratives, which constitute a genre. Cuban historian Gloria García has attempted to compensate for this absence by turning to an alternative source. In a volume entitled *La esclavitud desde la esclavitud* (Slavery Through the Eyes of Slavery), she has compiled transcripts of legal cases filed by slaves protesting against ill-treatment and injustice and seeking to improve their condition. Indirectly, these letters provide insight into the varied dimensions of the slaves' lived experience. Antislavery narratives may be viewed as a creative form of compensation for the shortage of first-hand accounts.

Collateral factors related to their historical and political contexts usually feature prominently in discussions of these narratives. Literature was only one battleground for the attack on slavery; at different historical moments, individuals of all racial and social sectors engaged in agitation against the institution. Antislavery authors formed part of a minority group of liberal intellectuals in Cuba's ruling class who represented the main opposition to both slavery and the slave trade, and who were thereby pitted against the sugar planters and merchants. Ideologically, they can hardly be said to have constituted a homogeneous group; much has been written about their diverse motivations. Propelled by dissatisfaction with Spanish colonial rule, a desire for independence, Christian humanitarianism or more self-interested motives such as class loyalties and negrophobia, writers promoted either systemic reform or gradual termination of slavery. International abolitionist movements and revolutionary ideas also influenced antislavery sentiment, and Cuban intellectuals collaborated closely with foreign advocates of abolition. Evidence from the period indicates that these narratives were viewed as threatening to the dominant values and existing relations of power. Strict political censorship by the Spanish colonial authorities at the time of their composition limited their circulation; after a clandestine first appearance, most remained unpublished until the first half of the twentieth century, and even later in some cases.

Inseparable from discussion of the early novels is the debate surrounding the modes and conditions of their production. Much of the debate has centred on the role of Domingo del Monte, famous patron of the literary arts in nineteenth-century Cuba, and the circle of writers and literary aficionados he gathered around him to engage in discussions of slavery and other social issues. Del Monte's literary *tertulias* (gatherings) served as an incubator for many of the antislavery narratives of the period. Another important figure during the early phase of the movement was Richard Madden, commissioner of the Mixed Court, which had been established by treaty between the British and Spanish governments in 1817 and was designed to enforce the decision to put an end to the Cuban slave trade. The main impulse behind the first fictional works, as well as Juan Francisco Manzano's autobiography, was Madden's request for compositions illustrating attitudes to Cuban slavery, for an album destined for dissemination in Europe to further his campaign against the slave trade. As a non-fictional text, Manzano's autobiography has been a source of some disappointment, if not controversy, because in it the slave presents himself more as a tragic victim than a conscientious rebel. In addition to a litany of horrors inflicted by typical slave owners, his account attests to various instances of good treatment at the hands of their benevolent counterparts. Manzano reiterates his desire for freedom, but he envisages it as a gift to be bestowed on him by the goodwill of the powerful, not as a right. Moreover, his concern with respectability and his reputation in the eyes of his superiors is as fervent as his desire for freedom.

Latin American writers' non-literary use of literature is not an uncommon phenomenon. The writers of Cuban antislavery fiction presented an early and blatant example of this practice. As a leader and mentor, del Monte greatly influenced the shape and content of the literary creations of the young and in some cases inexperienced writers in his group, whom he is said to have encouraged to present a moderate view of the slaves' response to their bondage. This has been used to explain the "victim" identity of some fictional slave characters. Del Monte's role as mediator and arbiter of the appropriateness of the writers' representations is undeniable, but it is also evident that his influence informed but did not completely control the literary creations. The absence of ideological unity within the group mirrored the diversity of views in the antislavery movement itself. Domingo del Monte was somewhat more conservative than some other group members, who parted company with their leader on important ideological issues. Though he recognized the African slaves' humanity, del Monte's antislavery stance had less to do with moral and humanitarian values and more to do with political and economic expediency. Furthermore, the compositions of the writers in his circle displayed none of the strident racism of his wish for the gradual disappearance of both slavery and blacks from Cuba. By 1843 del Monte had left Cuba and therefore no longer held sway over the minds of later writers. Yet, as long as slavery persisted as the basis of organization of Cuban society, criticism of the institution continued to exercise the imagination of white Creole writers.

The social and racial gulf that separated these writers from the slaves, and their need to establish the credibility of their undertaking, made presentation of enlightened self-images an integral part of their literary project. Under the constraints of their political purpose they also endeavoured to deploy strategies of effective persuasion in their compositions. Accordingly, the authors rarely left interpretation of their intent entirely up to the reader. Their anxiety manifests in the use of statements either inserted in an author's note preceding the text or encoded within the text itself.

Literary commentators are not the only readers from whom these narratives have drawn interest. Significant historical value has been invested in them, bringing to mind the hypothesis on which Roberto González Echevarría bases his study of the evolution of Latin American narrative: "The novel, having no fixed form of its own, assumes that of a given document endowed with truth-bearing power by society at specific moments in history."[1] University of Havana historian Digna Castañeda lends validity to this theory when she notes that the first works became primary sources of information on slavery in Cuba.[2] However, it is important to emphasize that, their historical usefulness notwithstanding, it is as literary creations that these narratives allow the slave experience to come alive for the reader.

Antislavery narratives also traverse the borders of different genres and discourses. Various commentators have captured their hybrid narrative lineage by referencing them as examples of Romantic realism or some variation of that style. A handy resource for many of these authors was the *costumbrista* sketch, popularized in the art and literature of nineteenth-century Europe and Latin America and dedicated to documenting the peculiarities of the time in which the artist or writer lived. In one manifestation it consisted of largely entertaining portraits of picturesque local scenery, traditional customs and popular character types. Side by side with this innocuous brand of *costumbrismo* were the satirical portraits painted by artists and writers who used the genre as an instrument of social commentary and criticism. Regarded in some quarters as a precursor of the Latin American novel, the *costumbrista* sketch thrived as a literary fashion in nineteenth-century Cuba.

Historically, a general discrepancy has existed in the critical responses to these narratives. The competing interpretations illustrate well the point that each reading of a literary text is in a sense a rewriting of it. As Terry Eagleton has reminded us, "a piece of writing may start off life as history or philosophy, then come to be ranked as literature, and then come to be valued for its archaeological significance . . . Breeding may count for more than birth. What matters may not be where you come from but how people treat you."[3] Antislavery literature occupied the forefront of intellectual discussions in Cuba from the early years of the nineteenth century. In fact, there is evidence that the business of members of the del Monte *tertulias* was as much to compose their own work as to appraise and edit the work of their peers. Their comments tell us much about the literary temper of the times and the thinking behind the writings. Among home-grown Cuban critics, interest in the genre peaked in the 1960s and 1970s. The period immediately following the Fidel Castro–led revolution of 1959 was a time of ideological fervour and cultural renaissance. Moved by the spirit of change, intellectuals and writers set about evaluating and reinterpreting their country's historical and cultural heritage. Slavery, as a formative historical experience and as a literary theme, became one of the most topical subjects for scholars in the immediate post-Revolution period.

Interest in this subject was equalled in energy only by the debates generated by and about the Revolution itself. Contributing to this renewed attention was the reprinting and dissemination of many nineteenth-century works of an antislavery nature. Cuban critics in their majority have credited the early writers with sincere intentions and ideological separation from the sugar planters. Using the new lens of the Revolution, twentieth-century writers such as Miguel Barnet (with *Biografía de un cimarrón* in 1966) and César Leante (with *Los guerrilleros negros* in 1977) sought to add other perspectives of the slave and slave society to complement the works produced by the nineteenth-century literary imagination. For Cuban historians too the subject of slavery has continued to provide raw material for new research. María del Carmen Barcia's *La otra familia* (2003), like Gloria García's *La esclavitud desde la esclavitud* (1996), is evidence that the topic continues to have considerable currency as a historiographical theme.

Outside of Cuba a sizeable body of critical commentary has also developed around these narratives. Members of the earliest generation of North American reviewers included them under the category of *costumbrismo*. In 1950 Roberta Day Corbitt described Anselmo Suárez y Romero's *Francisco*, one of the first and most robust denunciations of slavery, as "a picture of Cuban rural manners",[4] a view that is encouraged by the novel's 1898 subtitle: *El ingenio o las delicias del campo* (The Sugar Mill, or the Delights of the Country). Even a 1958 edition of Antonio Zambrana's *El negro Francisco* (1875) bears the rubric *"novela de costumbres cubanas"* (novel of Cuban customs). Tentative signs of an ideological critique of the genre appeared in the early 1960s. In 1962 Gabriel Coulthard opened his landmark comparative study, *Race and Colour in Caribbean Literature*, with an exposé on Cuba's antislavery novel. Anthony Castagnaro also included this body of work in one chapter of his 1971 book on the development of the early Spanish-American narrative tradition. The latter part of the 1970s saw added impetus being given to the study of these texts as North American and Caribbean scholars began to define the contours of what has now become the field of Afro-Hispanic literary criticism. One focus of this critical practice has been the ways in which writers in the Hispanic world have represented – and quite often misrepresented – people of African descent, their world, their historical experience and their culture.

External reviewers have been more wary than their Cuban counterparts in their judgements of these narratives. Even while recognizing the authors' desire to present themselves in a progressive and humanitarian light, these scholars have almost unanimously exposed the writers' hidden motives, and in particular their Eurocentric racism. For the most part, black nationalism and identity politics have set the agenda and provided the main ideological fuel for these analyses. From this perspective the appropriateness of the antislavery label has been questioned, because the authors espoused the lesser cause of reform rather than abolition. Also bolstering this case is the conservatism of the first wave of novelists and of Domingo del Monte himself, who had a vested interest in the continuation of slavery as a social and economic arrangement. Uneasiness with their inconsistencies and contradictions underlies much of the international scholarship on these texts. Critics have taken the authors to task for the perceived insincerity of their sympathetic posturing and the absence of genuine pro-black sentiments in their representations. In the second chapter of his seminal study *The Black Image in Latin American Literature*, noted pioneer of Afro-Hispanic literary studies Richard Jackson notes the recalcitrant anti-black sentiment undermining the antislavery project of these novels. He concludes, quite defensibly, that the authors' argument against slavery was largely sabotaged by this failure to portray black people in a favourable light.

Dissatisfaction with these narratives has also centred on their supposedly inadequate recognition of slave resistance and their portrayal of the slave actors as compliant and lacking in courage.[5] This perceived flaw has become particularly irksome in the postcolonial era, when physical *marronage* and open revolt are the preferred forms of slave resistance; the story of such resistance is the master narrative to which all others are subordinated. It is this search for stories of slave heroes that has induced some reviewers to privilege the reported testimony of the runaway slave Esteban Montejo, in Miguel Barnet's *Biografía de un cimarrón*, over the autobiographical testimony of the compliant house slave Francisco Manzano. Such a view has prevailed despite the fact that in his re-presentation of Montejo's life, Barnet's mediation as interviewer, transcriber and reporter is more intrusive than del Monte's interference in the compositions of his club members. While partiality towards slave heroes is necessary and natural, it has led to discounting of the literary accounts of other slave responses that do not meet this expectation. As I hope to show by exploring these writings, the theme of slave resistance receives a somewhat more nuanced treatment than previously believed.

New perspectives continue to emerge in scholarship on the Cuban antislavery narrative tradition. Various scholars of the post-1970s era have been enlarging the subject through valuable books, essays and journal articles. One of the most comprehensive studies to date is William Luis's *Literary Bondage: Slavery in Cuban Narrative* (1990), which explores the theme in works from the late 1830s to the post-Revolution era. Luis's book contains a wealth of historical information about the political, social and cultural scenario that had an impact on the production of these narratives. This critic unravels the two sides of the slavery debate and explains the complexity of the ideological conflict and the multifaceted and sometimes ambivalent attitude of white Creole groups to the colonial government and to slavery. Although there is no need to rehearse his findings here, information in Luis's study serves as a useful reference point for the textual interpretations I propose in this book.

Terry Eagleton's remark about the variability of successive interpretations of a work is a useful backdrop for my reading of these narratives: "We always interpret literary works in the light of our own concerns. Different historical periods construct different versions of a particular text for their own purposes and find in them elements to value or devalue . . . All literary works are 'rewritten' . . . by the societies which read them."[6] Since the 1980s there has been a concerted effort to articulate the new set of values in Western artistic and intellectual culture that have been replacing the long-standing traditions of modernity. These traditions have remained dominant since the 1750s, the date frequently taken to mark the beginning of the Age of Enlightenment. The concept of the postmodern age, or postmodernity, which is the optic I have chosen for viewing these narratives, is a vague and slippery but convenient and widely used umbrella term for this new ethos. Often referred to as postmodernism, the phenomenon has been difficult to pin down as a hard and fast "theory" (the one label that some who have enunciated its values seem to want to avoid). The broader term *postmodernity* (rather than *postmodernism*) is the one favoured by those who wish to steer clear of the connotations of conceptual rigidity conventionally associated with a theory. Linda Hutcheon, who uses the adjectives *postmodern* and *postmodernist* interchangeably, sums it up neatly: "the postmodern is, if it is anything, a problematizing force in our culture today: it raises questions about (or renders problematic) the common-sensical and the 'natural.' But it never offers answers that are anything but provisional and contextually determined."[7]

The answer to the question "What is postmodernity?" might very well be "Different things to different people." To some extent the term has been applied retrospectively and, as implied by Hutcheon, postmodern practice may even have predated attempts to theorize the postmodern. It is in the very nature of this cultural phenomenon that it is dogged by debate without being beset by anxiety for resolution. There is, for example, no consensus on the exact term limits of the postmodern paradigm. However, the 1980s is most frequently taken as the period that marked its entry into intellectual discourse. Other denominations of *postmodern* include *post-industrial* (following the designations of the preceding agricultural and industrial ages) and *post-ideological* (signalling the movement's unease with the truth claims of traditional theories and ideologies).

Without venturing into the turbulent waters of the theoretical and political debate surrounding the phenomenon, one can still identify recurring themes and premises of postmodern discourse that may be usefully applied to the interpretation of the texts selected for this study. Like other belief systems, the postmodern world view may be defined both by what it seeks to avoid and by what it proposes and practises. As first articulated by post-structuralist thinker Jean-François Lyotard in 1979, the "postmodern condition" – or postmodernity – describes an ethos that draws attention away from consecrated master narratives (of modernity) as sole truth-bearers and towards the diverse range of small and often forgotten stories and their versions of truth.

Another sign of the postmodern sensibility is a high tolerance for formerly outlawed events such as chaos and ambiguity. Rather than privilege the hallowed principles of homogeneity and consensus, postmodern discourse embraces diversity, whether of human experience or theoretical approaches. It promotes peaceful coexistence of different and even contradictory ways of being, thinking and seeing. As an enemy of hierarchies and polarities, the postmodern perspective is concerned with shades and nuances.

While it may be said to have superseded some of the values of modernity, the postmodern paradigm does not claim novelty for itself; instead it may be thought of as a convenient label for a package that subsumes pre-existing theories and methods. Its very looseness and the fluidity of its borders facilitate interpenetration of different disciplines and discourses. In the field of the arts, postmodernity manifests in the ascendancy of recent theories of art, most famously post-structuralism, a theory that places the burden of meaning-production as much on the reader as on the author, whom Benítez-Rojo prefers to think of as the "performer".[8] The postmodern approach refuses to either fetishize or discredit artistic products. It promotes not preferred but rather *possible* interpretations that take into account all the elements in the process of production and reception: author, text, context, consumer.

Accordingly, I draw on an eclectic blend of contemporary approaches and conceptual tools to extend the range of possible interpretations of the selected narratives. This process will be enabled by models of analysis developed by postcolonial theorists such as Frantz Fanon and his ideas about the effect of colonialism on the psyche of the colonized. It will also profit from the work of Edward Said, with his groundbreaking treatise on orientalism and his critique of Western narrative fiction as a part of the imperialist project. Coming out of an earlier intellectual tradition, Russian formalist Mikhail Bakhtin, one of the most influential theorists of the twentieth century, has elaborated a theory of narrative discourse that lends itself readily to analysis of texts from any historical period. Although he formulated his ideas in the early twentieth century, before talk of postmodernity, they are in line with postmodern thought. Bakhtin perceives a tension between conflicting impulses as an inextricable part of virtually all aspects of human experience, including language and ideology. He theorizes that a centripetal tendency towards coherence and unity must always contend with a centrifugal movement in the opposite direction of disunity and dispersion.[9]

Bakhtin's ideas are not idiosyncratic; they are akin to the psychoanalytical theories of Swiss psychologist Carl Jung, who in the 1930s put forward the notion of the divided personality as a normal fact of human life rather than a pathological condition. The idea also finds an echo in the confluence of opposing tendencies that Deepak Chopra, a leader of the New Thought Movement, sees in the rhythm of life. Indeed, before them, Aristotle's poetics of tragedy and epic also revolved around the idea of a battle for supremacy waged between opposing forces. The difference, however, is that where the Greek philosopher required resolution to the struggle (in the form of the superior force's triumph), postmodern thinking tolerates unresolved and unresolvable conflicts and contradictions. This notion is the centrepiece of the postmodern world view.

Postmodern critical practice has also benefited from application of the methods of deconstruction theory, premised as it is on the assumption that since meaning in a literary work or other cultural product is constructed rather than given, it is open to being *de*constructed, or disassembled. Deconstructive analysis of the ideological processes that shape antislavery narratives can prove worthwhile whether or not they conform to established standards or conventions. Moreover, since every process of cultural production involves selection, meaning can be sought in the literary work's emphases and gaps alike, in utterance as well as in silence. What remains in the shadows is of no less interest to deconstructive criticism than what is clearly highlighted.

The postmodern sensibility can be claimed as part of Europe's patrimony, but its transhistorical and transcultural relevance has been masterfully demonstrated by Antonio Benítez-Rojo's adaptation and comprehensive application of postmodern ideas to the study of the Caribbean and its culture in *The Repeating Island*, a project that Vera Kutzinski has felicitously described as seeking to "graft a branch of postmodernism onto the tree of Caribbean postcoloniality".[10] Benítez-Rojo references the analysis of the enslaver–enslaved relationship as an object lesson to illustrate postmodern pluralism:

> If we want to study, for example, planter-slave relations of some place in the Caribbean, we now see that we can't keep our analysis within, say, a strictly socioeconomic language, which by itself does not suffice for a reading of those relations. We must resort, in addition, to certain later nomenclatures which might allow us entry into areas that were thought until a very short

time ago to exist at the margin of socioeconomic phenomena, areas which we might see as inhabited by desire, sexuality, power, nationalism, violence, knowledge, or culture – and all of these seen from such varied perspectives that it's not rare to come upon analytical models combining the psychoanalytic model with that of political economy, or the philosophical with the feminist, or the jurisprudential with the literary-theoretical.[11]

While ideological studies of these narratives abound, the scholarship has paid rather less attention to the strategies that the authors use to convey their vision. Most commentaries gloss over the subject by describing the works as having scant aesthetic worth. One possible explanation for this apparent consensus is that the critical assessments that have prevailed since the time of their first appearance have been based mainly on age-old ideas about literary value, derived initially from the stylistics of poetry. In his seminal essay "Discourse in the Novel", Bakhtin bluntly challenges the nebulous notion of a separable "literary" quality in a novel.[12] Noting the analytical inefficiency of traditional stylistics as a way of thinking and talking about novels, he reconceptualizes narrative art as one of many forms of social discourse, similar to "discourse in the open spaces of public squares, streets, cities and villages, of social groups, generations and epochs".[13] For Bakhtin, narrative discourse operates on different levels simultaneously; it is a dialogic or polyphonic affair, that is, a combination of different and sometimes competing voices. Bakhtin's theory is also premised on the idea that the tensions between a novel's competing discourses may coexist without resolution.[14] Among the important implications of this view is its subversion of the belief in a single authoritative voice in the text, be it of the author, the narrator or a character.

By turning attention away, then, from the ideologically problematic notion of literary merit, the reader can usefully focus on the literary text as discourse – a way of writing that is underpinned by ideological values. Signs of interest in this technical dimension of Cuba's antislavery fiction have grown since the latter part of the past century, as has the tendency towards readings that broaden the black nationalist approach. Published in 1986, Jill Netchinsky's "Engendering a Cuban Literature: Nineteenth-century Antislavery Narrative" explores the link between what she calls "antislavery plot" and "antislavery poetics" and offers a positive reinterpretation of some of the alleged flaws of the novels. Her interest in these narratives centres less on their function as ideological constructs and more on the process of their becoming literary texts. To develop her thesis, Netchinsky chooses the iconic narratives and identifies the thematic motifs that recur in their plots, as well as their "autobiographical incursions and discursive manipulations".[15] As will be shown in this book, the less well-known narratives also lend themselves to the deconstructive analytical approach. An elegantly executed full-length study of the subject is Lorna Williams's 1994 book *The Representation of Slavery in Cuban Fiction*. Like Netchinsky, this scholar carefully unravels the process of construction of these texts. Other, more recent essays reflect the concerns of contemporary critical theory and practice. Carlos Alonso's brief analysis leads him to the conclusion that, in addition to their common reformist purpose, these novels were engaged in "the construction and circulation of a discourse that is founded on the categories of strangeness, perversion and opaqueness".[16]

Although Jackson chides the authors for devoting too much time to the cruelty of the masters and too little time to slave rebellion,[17] most studies of this type of narrative turn the spotlight on the fictional slave portraits, leaving the white enslavers mainly in the shadows. Yet the latter were of equal and in some cases greater interest to the antislavery writers. Gordon K. Lewis's observation, though made in respect of the advocates of slavery, is apposite. Referring to the value of the vast and diverse body of colonial literature (travellers' reports, pamphlets, colonial assembly debates, metropolitan state papers, local newspaper publications), Lewis notes that it enables the student "to catch glimpses of the self-image of the plantocracy and the images that class entertained of the other actors in the *dramatis personae* of the colonial scene". "For the essence of ideology," he maintains, "is perceived self-image, how any societal group sees its function within the general matrix of the social structure, how it sees other groups, and what particular arguments it produces as a means of self-justification."[18] H. Orlando Patterson argues along similar lines when he declares that "an examination of the lives of the slaves must begin with an understanding of the socio-economic order of their masters, since within this wider framework the slaves were only one element, albeit the most important, in the total structure and functioning of the slave system".[19] Representation of the slave and the slave owner is the equal focus of the analysis undertaken in this book.

A deconstructive reading method will illuminate certain blind spots in earlier appraisals of the novels, including the varied menu of discourses used to communicate meaning and the dialogic manner in which the ideologies generated around slavery are articulated. To this end I have selected both the well-known narratives and those that have been dwarfed by them, and will examine the ways in which their authors pressed narrative discourse into ideological service. In the spirit of postmodern enquiry, a nuanced notion of *antislavery* will be invoked. Any sign of a will to destabilize or subvert slavery's ideological foundation, however tenuous or indirect, will be seen in this light. Literary expressions of opposition to slavery did not end with abolition. My interest in this study, nonetheless, is those fictional works written during the nineteenth century but before abolition, that articulated antislavery sentiments as a political instrument. Some works on the slavery theme have been omitted from this study, Francisco Manzano's autobiography being most conspicuous among them. This seminal work – the only known slave autobiography in the Hispanic Caribbean – cannot be treated in the same breath as the fictional narratives, despite the fact that it seems to have provided the writers I have selected with some real-life fodder for their fiction.

In his commentary on the Cuban antislavery project, Carlos Alonso characterizes the fictional compositions as "structured on ambiguity and ambivalence" and notes their deeply complex significance. However, by his own admission, he only skims the surface of the novels, studying them "through indirection and suggestion rather than through the marshalling of fact and textual quotation".[20] The analysis that follows will show how attention to these very textual details can lead us to a deeper understanding of these works.

Chapter 1 examines Félix Tanco y Bosmeniel's *Petrona y Rosalía*, a novella written in 1838, which has been largely sidelined by the preferential treatment accorded iconic narratives on the same theme. By engaging theories of deconstruction and discourse analysis, this chapter lays bare the work's covert narrative signs and the paradox of the author's liberal and conservative sentiments.

Traditional readings of Anselmo Suárez y Romero's *Francisco* (1839) have represented it as a fundamentally conservative novel, primarily because its slave actors have been deemed totally compliant. An overview of the critical appraisals of the novel suggests that many of the statements about its ideological significance have been based on the partial evidence provided by some of the work's dominant features. Using the insights offered by postcolonial theory, chapter 2 demonstrates the subversive potential of various unobtrusive signs in the novel. To uncover its subtle and frequently indirect expressions of opposition to slavery, the chapter pays attention to the inner voices of the characters, fathoming their deeper selves and taking account of the ambiguities and contradictions of their relationships.

Gertrudis Gómez de Avellaneda's *Sab* (1841) is celebrated as much for its literary importance as for its radical combination of antislavery and feminist ideas. Yet it has been the subject of very divergent interpretations. Chapter 3 draws on ideas from the postcolonial scholarship of Edward Said and Frantz Fanon as well as those of Mikhail Bakhtin for a reading of this novel. The analysis considers the implications of nationalist, racial, sexual and feminist politics for *Sab*'s antislavery meaning and provides a possible accommodation for the conflicts between the novel's various interpretations.

*Romualdo, uno de tantos* (1869), Francisco Calcagno's little-known and eccentric novella, is the subject of the fourth chapter. In this story the author engages the satirical *costumbrista* method to document and denounce some of the hidden illegal practices of slavery, filling in gaps left by narratives from and about the 1830s. While acknowledging the novelty of this depiction of *marronage*, my review of the work will focus on what his account of slavery both reveals and conceals about the author and his subject.

For an alternative interpretation of Antonio Zambrana's novel *El negro*

*Francisco* (1875), the fifth chapter invokes the postmodern concept of parody to account for the areas of convergence and divergence in its intertextual relationship with its model, Anselmo Suárez y Romero's *Francisco* (1839). In exploring the author's dramatization of the Cuban slave experience and his articulation of his antislavery opinions, I argue that the second novel is neither mindless mimicry nor reckless rejection of the first, and that neither novel can claim ascendancy over the other.

Cirilo Villaverde's depiction of slavery and slave society in his encyclopaedic novel *Cecilia Valdés* (1882) is complex, ambiguous and filled with a chorus of different voices. The final chapter teases out the tragic, ironic and dialogic facets of this representation that give the novel its distinctive mark.

My ultimate aim in this book is neither to glorify nor to discredit this body of narratives, but rather to open up a space to salvage their subversive value without ignoring their counterproductive features. The analytical procedures used to achieve this purpose reflect Bruce King's recommended approach for the study of Caribbean literature. "Caribbean literature", he posits, "needs to be examined 'piece by piece', for large generalizations will not take us very far because generalizations have inscribed within themselves, within the theories on which they are based, the results they claim to investigate".[21] The devil, King seems to say, is in the details.

# · 1 ·

## "PIG-REARING PEASANTS TURNED MARQUISES AND COUNTS"

### *Félix Tanco y Bosmeniel's* Petrona y Rosalía

AMONG THE EARLY expressions of opposition to slavery that appear in Cuban narrative is the little-studied *Petrona y Rosalía,* a long short story written in 1838. Its Colombian-born, Cuban-bred author, Félix Tanco y Bosmeniel (1796–1871) was a prominent member of the del Monte group. Not content to confine his politics to intellectual discussion, Tanco translated his ideology into practical action. His activism and abolitionist views led to his arrest and imprisonment as one of the white Creoles implicated in the 1844 "Conspiración de la Escalera", an alleged plot by free blacks and mulattoes to liberate Cuban slaves and declare independence from Spain. Published for the first time in 1925, in the journal *Cuba Contemporánea,* Tanco's story was conceived as one in a collection of *costumbrista* depictions of the local scene for which he proposed the title *Escenas de la vida privada en la isla de Cuba.* Although he later published other works – *Refutación al folleto intitulado Viaje a la Habana por la condesa de Merlín* (1844), *Los jesuitas en la Habana* (1862) and *Probable y definitivo porvenir de la isla de Cuba* (1870) – *Petrona y Rosalía* seems to be the only part of that original project that has been published. The less tendentious title of the larger project that he envisaged has somewhat overshadowed the political significance of this story, but the publishers of the 1980 Letras

Cubanas edition claimed that it was Cuba's first fictional work of protest against slavery.

Tanco y Bosmeniel was among the white Creole literati who, like Juan Francisco Manzano, the slave poet, were commissioned by Domingo del Monte to produce compositions for Richard Madden's antislavery album. Compared with the full-length novels on the slavery theme, this work, perhaps because of its brevity and limited scope, has received no more than a passing mention in studies of antislavery texts. Tanco's *noveleta* relates the experiences of Petrona, a black slave in the family of Doña Concepción Sandoval Buendía and her husband, Don Antonio Malpica y Lozano. As punishment for her pregnancy, she is sentenced to work on the sugar estate and to receive fifty lashes. The father of Rosalía, the mulatto child born of this pregnancy, is none other than her master, Don Antonio. Because of her adolescent beauty, Rosalía is sent to the city to work in the master's house, where the cycle of sexual exploitation repeats itself: she is impregnated by Fernando, her half-brother. Don Antonio's death shortly after hearing news of her pregnancy is precipitated by the thought of the incest he believes his son has committed. Rosalía subsequently dies in childbirth, soon after her mother. In the meantime, it is revealed in a surprising final twist that Fernando is the product of Doña Concepción's extramarital affair with a family friend, the Marqués de Casanueva.

Although its intention is to oppose slavery, *Petrona y Rosalía* stands apart from Suárez y Romero's *Francisco,* for example, in the nature and expression of its dissent. Tanco turns the spotlight more on the conduct and customs of the master class than on the travails and tribulations of the slave community. As important as the view that he affords the reader is the lens through which that view is refracted. This view is neither neutral nor transparent, for it bears traces of the thinking of a particular sector of Cuban society. A close look at the strategies deployed by the author to reveal or conceal his viewpoint can expand and deepen our understanding of the work. In examining its overall narrative approach, one cannot but notice that Tanco puts in an occasional brief, undisguised appearance in the story. Overt signs of the author's involvement with the historical situation about which he writes are inserted strategically as authenticating strategies to boost the truth-bearing value of the text. For the most part, however, the author seems to clear the stage for the performances of his characters and the interpretations of an ostensibly autonomous narrator. Less obvious are the more covert signs of the author's influence on the work's meaning: at different moments the narrator's words seem to merge seamlessly with the author's perceptions.

Within the narrow boundaries of the genre, the author contrives to create a broader social framework for the classic short-story situation. Notwithstanding the expectations raised by its title (Tanco follows the tradition of creating eponymous slave characters) and the contrapuntal narrative structure that gives the impression of equal focus on slave and slave owner, the story's axis is the private life of the latter rather than the obvious theme of the recurring sexual abuse of female slaves by their masters. Tanco's revelation of the behaviour and psychology of the slave-owning class is a significant but not fully explored dimension of this and other narratives in the genre. By choosing slave characters for the story's title while giving the central role to the slave-owning family, he tacitly acknowledges the impossibility of non-whites' being real protagonists in the drama of slavery. And since both the black slave and her mulatto daughter suffer the same fate, he avoids that other notion of the mulatto woman's improved social status deriving from her "whitened" blood. The brutal treatment of the slave that fuels outrage in other narratives does not provide a flashpoint for Tanco's story; rather, the author's dissidence surfaces tangentially in his criticism of the slave-owning class. Moreover, he reduces his concern to those problems of slavery that he attributes to the morally decadent ethos of a specific category of slave owners.

While the uneasy cohabitation of white master and black slave was the dominant, overarching feature of nineteenth-century Cuban society, it did not represent the sum total of social relations. As race and class combined to provoke tension between master and slave, certain antagonisms likewise divided whites. Though united by race, they were separated by issues of class and political ideology. Some of those rivalries are brought to bear on Tanco's depiction of this slave-owning family. With the following comment about their origins and status, the narrator locates them in place and time:

> These were two members of a noble and rich Havana family, although with respect to their nobility, their predecessors were said to be upstarts who had belonged to the Spanish lumpen and not to any noble house. But be that as it may, we . . . will consider them one of the most ancient blue-bloods of the monarchy; their membership of one social class or another will be of little or no importance to our story. [*Eran estos dos personajes de familia noble y rica de la Habana, aunque, respecto de lo primero, se hablaba de sus mayores como de gente advenediza que había pertenecido al vulgo de España y no a ninguna casa solariega. Pero sea de esto lo que fuere, nosotros . . . los tendremos en el concepto de los más rancios linajudos de la monarquía, importando muy poco o nada a nuestra historia que pertenezcan a tal o cual categoría de la sociedad.*][1]

As the first of the strategies to belittle the protagonists, the inclusion of this contextual detail merits special comment because of its multilayered significance. Most notable is the final disclaimer, by which the narrator seeks to avert any charge of class-based bias and to establish an exclusively political basis for his subsequent representation of his white protagonists. These characters, he leads the reader to think, are to be identified and discredited by their ancestral political affiliation to the Spanish monarchy, not by their social lineage. This anti-Spanish sentiment is not idiosyncratic; it represents a fledgling nationalism in the mental attitude of those *independentista* members of white Cuban Creole society who advocated political autonomy from Spain. Such a view does not, however, deny the general truth in Gordon Lewis's claim that the concept of nation was alien to the colonial world view of slave society, built as it was on the notion of the races as separate, different and unequal.[2]

Despite his valiant effort to conceal it, a class-inspired antipathy towards colonial Cuba's *nouveaux riches* lurks beneath the surface of Tanco's introduction of the family. During that period, white Creoles who traced their bloodline back to the Spanish *conquistadores* assumed a privileged social status and guarded it fiercely against the attempts of newcomers who threatened to usurp their position. Included among the *arrivistes* were, of course, Spanish *peninsulares* who had become wealthy barons in Cuba's sugar kingdom. The epithets "noble" and "rich" are paired initially in a manner that seems to give them equal objective value. But the nobility first ascribed to the family is immediately called into question. Of greater import than their undeniable wealth is the speciousness of their aristocratic pedigree. Ultimately, it is implied, the family lacks the elite social status that cannot be bought or compensated for by material wealth. The comment serves, therefore, as a device to mask the author/narrator's class prejudice. Even though they belong to the moneyed class and have bought noble titles, the slave-owning couple still bears the stigma of social upstarts.

Proof of this underlying but irrepressible class anxiety resurfaces later. The narrator cannot resist returning to the issue of class origins. In a declaration redolent with contempt, he extends his disquiet to include other slave-owning families of similar provenance, whom he describes as "Spanish pig-farmers turned Cuban marquises and counts". Even the vocabulary – the initial plosive descriptors of the pig-rearing peasants, "*porquerizos y patanes*"[3] – is deployed strategically to place the imposters on the Madrid side of the battle line between Havana and Spain. Thus another apprehension emerges, this time about the perceived threat to the social order posed by Cuba's sugar-based wealth, which was eroding the notion of elite status as conferred only by inheritance. In the mind of those Creoles who constitute themselves as traditional aristocracy, individuals such as Don Antonio and Doña Concepción cannot escape their historical origins and the stigma of being interlopers. Having sprung originally from the popular classes, they lack the necessary breeding to lay legitimate claim to authentic nobility.

This comment in turn presents symptoms of a tribally motivated desire to hold on to the medieval idea of lineage's counting for more than wealth. Disguised beneath this chauvinism and thinly veiled resentment is the angst of the Euro-Creoles faced with the menace that Cuba's sugar wealth posed to their class supremacy. Tanco's alarm in the face of this threat seems as profound as the ubiquitous fear of abolition that the demographic superiority of blacks and mulattoes inspired in Euro-Creole advocates and critics of slavery alike. The social identity of the *arriviste* group, then, is represented in terms of illegitimacy, defined as inferiority to the traditional elite. Insistence on the illegitimacy of these upstarts obscures, of course, the more flagrant illegitimacy of slavery as a socio-economic system. These sneering comments also subtly correlate Cuba's increased sugar wealth with social disorder and moral decline. In its anti-materialistic implications, Tanco's representation is underlain by the Christian thesis at the heart of the biblical parable of Lazarus and Dives. The moral corruption of this class is a function of its wealth in a materialistic culture that has jettisoned traditional elitist values.

With such slurs on the class origins, material circumstances and political associations of this fictional family, the author paves the way for a subsequent onslaught upon their morals and mores. Having located them socially, he expands and deepens the portrait by focusing on family dynamics. Their values and lifestyle, Tanco would have us believe, are the natural opposite of the mores of the white Creole elite. In expressing his censure, the narrator has subtly connected their class origins to their beliefs and judgements. The discrepancy between their noble appearance and their lower-class origins subsequently becomes the touchstone of the family's portrayal. Their intellectual deficiency is the fount from which all their other failings flow. The author misses no opportunity to remind the reader of the nexus between their lack of education and their shallow values and flawed judgement.

Doña Concepción and Don Antonio, the implication goes, place a low value on education because of the intellectual deficit accompanying their low social status, which in turn makes them poor parents. To diminish the family even further in the reader's eyes, the author resorts to juxtaposition of the incongruous. The besotted parents' idolizing of their young son, so grossly disproportionate to his conduct and disposition, reflects their own intellectual inadequacy. Underlying this detail of the family picture is the thesis advanced by José Antonio Saco, one of the most vocal participants in colonial Cuba's slavery debate, that parents' neglect of their responsibility for the moral upbringing of their children was one cause of the country's social malaise. Thus the insufficiency of their parenting skills forms another basis for indicting the slave-owning pair. Moreover, since moral training, in Tanco's view, carries an even higher premium than formal education, Fernando's parents fall woefully short of being models of good values.

Tanco has painted a satirical portrait of this slave-owning family and their kind that coincides with the impressions of travel writers of the period, who noted, in reference to the British West Indian scene, a planter lifestyle full of "drinking, dancing, insipid conversation, gargantuan eating and sexual excess".[4] The image of this family fits the profile of the Other as posited in postcolonial and psychoanalytical theory. In both their actions and their thinking these slave owners are separated from and placed beneath an imaginary ideal self, which is represented by the author and his class. From his privileged position the author assumes the right to belittle these intrusive, uneducated slave owners and, inferentially, to hold up for the reader's endorsement his own cultural and intellectual superiority and that of the group for which he speaks.

One achievement of this story is its illustration of the role of gender in colouring master–slave relations. White slave mistresses are significant players in the fictional dramas of slavery. In *Sab, Francisco* and *El negro Francisco,* as well as in the autobiography of the slave poet Juan Francisco Manzano, they act as leading representatives of the traditional slave-owning class. Like the authors of the longer novels, Tanco gives a major role to the slave mistress in his story. Doña Concepción, embodying as she does the worst attitudes and behaviours of the slave-owning class, is virulently villainous and beyond redemption. In other narratives the slave mistress is shown to rationalize punishment of the slave by casting herself in the maternal role and the slave in the role of a child. Such punishment therefore becomes construed as a form of harsh but beneficial discipline meted out by a caring parent. Doña Concepción's naked brutality lacks this hypocritical veneer. She is the stereotypical slave owner: unrepentant, implacable and ruthless. By giving her this key role Tanco exposes what is now accepted as an integral dimension of the gender politics of slavery, with its double victimization of black and mulatto female slaves. They were the ones who found themselves at the mercy of both their white masters and their white masters' wives. As frequent as incidents of reputed good treatment of house slaves in general were the instances of ill-treatment of female slaves, victims of their white mistresses' displaced anger. Petrona's experience classically illustrates this phenomenon.

It is well-known that interracial sex involving white men and black or mulatto women was rampant in Cuban slave society. Tanco uses this unforeseen development in the colonial enterprise as a context for his exploration of the slave-owner psyche. Lewis explains how the negrophobia of the dominant white group set up an ideology of racial purity that was belied by the reality of colonial Caribbean society. Doña Concepción's actions speak to this dynamic. A dialogue in the story's opening pages is orchestrated to point up the difference between the thinking of the more benevolent slave master and that of his intransigently cruel wife, a difference that attests to the role played by sex(uality) and gender in narrowing the black/white divide in slave society. On the occasion of Rosalía's birth, Doña Concepción and Don Antonio engage in a conversation on interracial sex in which she berates the "shameless" slave for having seduced a white man. What remains unsaid but strongly intimated in this exchange is Doña Concepción's psychological dilemma, caught as she is between visceral awareness of the white slave master's sexual propensity towards the female slave and her own need to deny it. Faced with the horrifying implications of her husband's sabotaging of the rules of racial separation and unable to accept the discomfiting truth, she seeks reassurance in myth. She espouses a racist religion with its ideology of white purity and supremacy, its conviction of an unbridgeable divide between blacks and whites, and its belief in the inferiority of non-whites. Despite her efforts to hide her anxiety under a cloak of morality, the "bad example" she fears Petrona's pregnancy will provide for her son has to do not with any lesson about Christian ethics, but with the more crucial lesson about the need to maintain racial separation. As a slave mistress she defines her role as custodian of the socio-racial order, ensuring strict separation of white menfolk from black and mulatto slave women. Unable to ensure its observance in reality, her duty is to safeguard the spirit of the racist doctrine.

It is not hard to understand why the white female would feel most endangered by this cross-racial mingling. A combination of humiliation, fear and jealousy is what drives Doña Concepción's antagonism towards her erstwhile "loyal" house slave. Petrona, her social and racial subordinate over whom she claims absolute supremacy and control, is responsible, albeit unwillingly, for destabilizing the hallowed socio-racial order. Doña Concepción's physical chastisement of the slave is intended therefore to serve a compelling social end. Petrona is demoted to field-slave status on the sugar estate, where, in the words of her mistress, "she will have enough black suitors to court her" (*tendrá negros galanes que la enamoren*).[5] Doña Concepción's very language betrays her neurotic self-delusion. She seeks to reassure herself by tacitly invoking the proslavery idea of the sexually aggressive nature of the African. In denouncing Petrona's pregnancy she projects not only her husband's blame but also, unwittingly, her own sense of shame onto the slave woman. Hidden deep within her consciousness is her recognition of the inconceivable: the sexual desirability of the black female slave in the eyes of the white male. With the act of removing Petrona from her presence, she tries to wish and wash away this reality from her consciousness. Her response raises the spectre of the negrophobic proslavery ideologues who advocated banishing blacks from Cuba in the face of the demographic superiority of the latter and the pervasiveness of race mixing. Rosalía's birth, occurring as it does under extreme physical brutality, emblematizes the inexorability of creolization in defiance of those who made it their mission to thwart the process.

Illicit sex between white slave master and black slave woman is one of the recurring themes of antislavery narratives. In the context of white dominance, and frequently because of the master's assumed right to control the female slave's body, illegitimacy became the identifying impress of the mulatto sons and daughters of those unions. In *Petrona y Rosalía* Tanco varies this theme, treating illicit sex as a phenomenon within the white group as well. Doña Concepción's class background and pathological cruelty are not her only aberration from the slave mistress norm of other antislavery fiction. Her sexual immorality, itself a presumed function of her class origins, makes her an alien among Creole elite slave mistresses, each of whom is implicitly of impeccable moral standing in her sexual conduct.

Judged by nineteenth-century standards of sexual morality, the consensual illicit sex between Doña Concepción and the Marqués de Casanueva is of scandalous proportions. It also confers illegitimate status on her white son, Fernando, which she hides under the cover of her legitimate marriage to Don Antonio. This subplot ensures, of course, that as she was in history, so too in fiction the white female remains off limits to the black male slave. Other authors pit the love of the black male slave against the lust of the young slave master as they vie for the *mulata*. In this fictional work, however, the male slave figure is the missing party in a gender game played out between white male and non-white female on the one hand and white and non-white females on the other.

Curiously absent in much of Cuba's antislavery literature is the dominant slave master figure. In *Francisco*, as in *El negro Francisco*, the sugar estate falls under the control of a widowed slave mistress who delegates authority to her son. Varying this pattern somewhat in *Petrona y Rosalía*, Tanco presents a family scenario in which Don Antonio plays the role of slave master, but only nominally, for in no way is he fashioned to fit the historical slave master mould. In fact, the suggestion seems to be that in some ways he is, like the slave woman, a victim of his wife's tyranny. Therefore, Tanco's condemnation of Doña Concepción and Fernando, implacable co-conspirators in a vicious war against the two slaves, cannot be separated from his exoneration of the innocuous Don Antonio. The author paints a very grim picture of the slave mistress who emasculates her husband and destroys the slave. In other narratives the author puts some psychological and moral distance between the slave mistress mothers and their sons. No such subtle distinction is made between mother and son in Tanco's *noveleta*, nor does the author, like his contemporaries, give any weight to the influence of social environment on his slave mistress. Doña Concepción and Fernando form a deadly duo.

Fernando, who features as prominently as his mother in the cast of characters, is no less reprehensible. Caricature is the representational method chosen for his portrayal. In addition to his profligacy and indolence, the cosseted Fernando is a semi-literate simpleton, and the reader cannot miss the barbed irony of the incongruous title "don" repeatedly bestowed upon him. Making Fernando of such low intelligence is a way of totally diminishing him and his class. He is denied not just education but also the educability that would have been a redeeming quality. His illegitimate birth, which is disclosed at the end of the story, echoes both the implied illegitimacy of his family's social status and the unrecognized illegitimacy of slavery as an institution. With such a self-validating gesture Tanco once again ensures the symbolic exclusion of Fernando and those of similar ilk from the intellectual class of the educated bourgeoisie to which he belongs.

If one justification of slavery was the African's non-humanity, then slavery's effect, Tanco shows, was equally to convert members of the slave-owner class into brutes. Nowhere in the portrait of this household are there signs of the conviviality between Cuban house-slave children and the children of their masters that was remarked on by nineteenth-century travel writers. In fashioning Fernando's image, Tanco overturns long-standing convention by his wholesale transfer to Fernando of the stereotypical attributes of the slave found in this era's proslavery rhetoric: "lazy, irresponsible, . . . sexually aggressive, mentally inferior, biologically retarded".[6] He achieves his satirical purpose with repeated cacophonous references to *Don* Fernando as barbaric. In Tanco's world view, an uneducated white (title notwithstanding) is a veritable savage. At age ten, Fernando shows all the signs of a cruel slave master in the making, and he eventually becomes an irredeemable sexual predator. In this role he is similar to the sons in other narratives, who represent the younger Euro-Creole generation of slave owners and who bear direct blame for the brutality visited upon the slave. Although Fernando perpetrates the final acts of brutality, the reader is not allowed to absolve his parents, and in particular his mother, as we have seen, for his degeneracy. "Morally repulsive" describes not the enslaved but the enslavers.

One point of agreement in the vast scholarship on Caribbean slavery is a general similarity in the belief systems that gave birth to and sustained slavery across the region. Also acknowledged are the specific variations arising from differences in the methodology, temper, politics and modus operandi of the different colonizing powers and from differences between individual slave masters. While the very foundation of the system, as well as the overwhelming experience of slavery, was cruel treatment of blacks by whites, there is also evidence of good treatment and less hostile relationships between master and slave. Operating within the confines of this short narrative, Tanco manages to expose some of the diversity of master–slave interactions.

What little benevolence exists in Tanco's fictional universe is vested in Don Antonio. A telling indicator of the author's view is the absence of direct reference to Antonio's sexual exploitation of Petrona, which belongs to a period shortly before the start of the narration; on its details, the text is silent. However, one can read into this silence Tanco's lack of interest in what could be regarded as the less extreme aspect of the slave woman's experience of sexual abuse, for fear of diluting the impact of the message. Unlike Fernando, whose treatment of Rosalía is blatant and crude, Don Antonio's presumably more discreet sexual relationship with Petrona may be inferred from his token regard for her humanity. Their relationship is a fictional illustration of one of the ways in which the miscegenation process, according to Lewis, "took the edge off the endemic hatred between white master and black slave".[7] One can assume that their unequal relationship derived primarily from his sexual interest, yet in their interaction he is not completely heartless, nor does he seem to see her as a mere sex object. Though weak and totally under the yoke of his wife, Don Antonio shows compassion towards Petrona in his initial efforts to intervene on her behalf and to lessen her punishment. It is true that he ultimately abandons her to the whims of his sadistic wife, but this seems to be a function more of his weakness than of malice, and it has the effect of further demonizing Doña Concepción.

Petrona's response to him also signals the special character of her relationship with Don Antonio. In a world that normalizes abuse of the slave, Don Antonio is the lone figure of dissent. This he expresses through a more lenient attitude towards Petrona and his verbal opposition to the harshness of his wife's treatment of the slave. Not only is he more favourably disposed towards her, but she perceives him as a kind of saviour, thus reinforcing the idea of a less brutal if not more humane form of master–slave engagement. Two themes of slavery are reiterated in this detail. First, the distinction between Don Antonio on the one hand and Fernando and Doña Concepción on the other drives home the point that the slave master should not be thought of as a single individual, that the master class was not homogeneous in character and temperament. Second, it underscores the instrumentality of sex in making some masters less virulently opposed or more kindly disposed to the female slave. Such a perspective is a reminder of the historical evidence of the master's dealings with the slave woman not as a monolith but as a continuum of sexual encounters ranging from the coerced to the consensual. This dimension of their relationship also explains why it is to Doña Concepción rather than to Don Antonio that the enslaved woman represents a racial threat.

The significance of Don Antonio's cursory interventions, his perfunctory attempts to intercede on Petrona's behalf, pale in the face of the violence inflicted by Doña Concepción and Fernando. Through Antonio's deference to his wife's authority and his complacent denial of his autonomy, the author implies the inconsequentiality of the more benevolent slavers and maintains the view of the dominant mode of black/white coexistence as that of merciless master and suffering slave. Though Don Antonio speaks in defence of the slave, his voice is not heard, and the final shroud of silence covers him in death. While not denying its existence, through this silence the author minimizes the significance of the much-advertised benevolence of slave masters in the Spanish colonies. Don Antonio's capitulation to his wife, his inaction and his eventual death all indicate the relative weakness of the forces of moderation. His good intentions notwithstanding, the feckless Antonio earns only slightly less contempt than his wife and Fernando.

Turning to Tanco's representation of the slaves, one notes that they remain voiceless for much of the story. He paints a picture of the slave woman's overwhelmingly brutal existence, in which the dominant atmosphere of violent oppression eclipses the few glimmers of relative good treatment and benevolence. Moreover, Petrona appears in the story without a past; unlike the white family, she is not placed in time. Silence in this instance is not only an index of the importance of master and slave to the author's thesis but also a reflection of the real power relations in slave society. Nevertheless, Tanco manages to give the reader a glimpse of the slave mentality. In the same way that he reveals the animus in the Creole elite attitude to the *nouveaux riches* among the sugar barons, he sheds a passing light on the clash of views within the slave ranks, albeit in a more disinterested manner. A cameo discussion between Rosalía and the other, nameless house slaves discloses the particular predicament of the female slave whose companions view her suffering as just retribution for consort-ing with the enemy (the slave master). Petrona's victimhood is thus com-pounded by three hostile forces arrayed against her, personified by her master, who exploits her as sexual property; her master's wife, who blames her as an evil temptress; and her peers, who brand and revile her as a trai-tor. If Petrona and Rosalía represent the tame slave response, in this exchange their companions strike a more radical note of resistance.

In order to grasp the full significance of narratives such as *Petrona y Rosalía*, it is useful to view them as written against the grain of proslavery thinking. Myths and stereotypes about Negroes disseminated by Western philosophers of the stature of Kant and Hegel appealed to the Caribbean proslavery imagination. Negrophobic themes such as the non- or subhu-man status of Africans, their savagery, immorality, lawlessness and lack of feeling lent themselves readily to bolster the arguments of slavery's advo-cates. Tanco's representation of the slave in this story indirectly invokes these inventions and goes a short way towards dismantling them. The story features one of the egregious iniquities of slavery, namely the policy of discouraging the formation of permanent slave family units and the fre-quent separation of spouses and of children from their parents.[8] As a reminder of the other side of the fabled good treatment of mulattoes who were co-opted as house slaves, Tanco points to the emotional price paid by the black slave mother who was thereby deprived of the meagre joy achievable under slavery. He highlights Petrona's anguish and Rosalía's sorrow to pre-empt any positive interpretation of the separation of mother and daughter, first by the overseer's wife and then by Doña Concepción. By juxtaposing the strong attachment of Petrona and Rosalía to each other with Doña Concepción's callous disregard for their mother–daughter

bond, Tanco challenges the age-old stereotype of the black person as individualistic, asocial and without feeling, and as an enemy of community.
Likewise, Petrona's love for Rosalía, despite the circumstances of her con-
ception, stands starkly opposed to the ineptitude and misguided
overindulgence of Fernando's parents. Extending the comparison to
the offspring of the two women, the author uses the warmth of Rosalía's
affection for her mother to counter Fernando's chilly alliance with Doña
Concepción.

Somewhat paradoxically, the author ascribes to both slave women
attributes that were the mainstays of proslavery essentialist discourse. Of
Petrona the narrator says:

> Petrona's natural strength, like that of all members of her race, made her
> withstand the work and ill-treatment she endured for three months, at the
> end of which she gave birth to a baby girl. [*La natural fortaleza de Petrona,
> como la de todos los de su raza, la hizo triunfar de los trabajos y malos
> tratamientos que experimentó en tres meses, al cabo de los cuales dio a luz una
> niña.*][9]

It is a comment that reverberates with the sounds of the original rationalization of African slavery (espoused even by priests of the Dominican and
Franciscan religious orders such as Las Casas), on the grounds that Negro
slaves would be better able to withstand the rigours of plantation life than
their more fragile native Indian counterparts. In this instance, however,
Tanco's appropriation of the notion of the African's natural hardiness does
not serve a clear proslavery end, nor does it detract from the subversive
implications of the author's message. Rather than justifying slavery, it has
the effect, if not the intention, of celebrating the slave woman's survivor
abilities while simultaneously denouncing the cruelty of her treatment.
Celebration is also the underlying motive in the author's insistence on
Rosalía's strong, healthy constitution despite the wretched circumstances
of her birth and early life. Endowing both female slaves with strength,
deriving, we may infer, from their African heritage and enabling them to
survive acute physical adversity, may be interpreted as mere reproduction
of the African stereotype. But the kernel of truth in this essentialist cliché

may be seen equally to be borne out by the historical reality of the Africans' survival of the hell-world of slavery.

The converse of this validation of African-descended women through their association with good health is the correlation of physical and psychological infirmity in the lives of the whites. With his ill health, the epileptic Don Fernando is a weakling and a foil for the healthy Petrona and Rosalía. Doña Concepción, in spite of her social advantage, can produce only physically feeble stock, and that with some difficulty. Her slave, despite the brutality visited upon her, conceives and gives birth to a strong, robust baby. By normalizing the slave women's fertility, the author comes perilously close to reproducing one of the staples of proslavery ideology, which compared black women's reproductive capacity to that of animals. However, he cleverly sidesteps this danger by imposing a more positive meaning on the cliché, turning it against the white overlords. In his eyes, the slave mistress's sterility is a curse. The failed bids to abort the pregnancies of Petrona and Rosalía by Don Antonio and Doña Concepción, respectively, not only serve to bolster the sturdy image of these individual slaves but are a poignant reminder of the enslaved Africans' survival to later become the bedrock of Caribbean society. Similarly, when Don Antonio succumbs to the sudden illness brought on by the shocking news of Fernando's impregnation of his sister Rosalía, compared to the length of Petrona's suffering before her death, it again creates a sense of the constitutional fragility of whites as opposed to the physiological stamina of blacks.

In his portrayal of the two slave women, Tanco, perhaps inadvertently, bears witness to the nuances in the Caribbean slave experience. While their shared experiences and similar physical fortitude imply equitable narrative attention to both women, Tanco's preferential treatment of Rosalía tacitly mirrors the different location of black and mulatto women in colonial Cuba's racial hierarchy. Miscegenation confounded efforts to maintain white racial purity in colonial society. One of the concessions made in the face of that unstoppable trend was the ultimate accommodation of mulattoes at a kind of midpoint in the racial hierarchy. The mixed-blood mulattoes, by virtue of their affiliation to the white race, enjoyed a social advantage over racially pure blacks, who were relegated to the bottom of the social ladder. White slave masters often bought the freedom of their mulatto children. Moreover, the mulatto woman's perceived beauty, and her sexual allure in particular, became a notorious cliché in the social discourse of the period. In this we see the beginning of the discriminatory practice of favoring the *mulata* over the black woman in the Cuban literary tradition.

Commensurate with the social perception of her blackness, Petrona's portrait is a bare sketch; the narrator hardly tarries to describe her, for she is no more than a workhorse-cum-sex-object. The silence regarding her physical appearance creates a glaring contrast with the deliberate attention paid to her mulatto daughter. Struck by Rosalía's seductive beauty, the overseer's wife takes her as her handmaid. Doña Concepción likewise values her as "a decorative appendage" (*un dije de adorno*).[10] In light of this differential treatment, Fivel-Démoret's reference to Petrona and Rosalía as two black women implies an alien frame of reference, for it elides the shade gradation that is fundamental to Caribbean racial discourse, and which is at the heart of the text's discrimination between the two slave women.[11]

Despite his ostensibly enlightened stance, Tanco is still locked into orthodox thinking as he mindlessly appropriates the *mulata* stereotype and applies it to his depiction of Rosalía. If Fernando at age ten is an anticipation of the cruel slave master, Rosalía at an even more tender age is seen as the promise of the sensual *mulata* stereotype: "A charm typical of her class could be seen in her at age six . . . a seductive energy that neither the weight of servitude nor work could diminish" (*Una gracia particular a las de su clase se advertía en ella a los seis años . . . una viveza seductora que nunca pudo amortiguar . . . el peso de la servidumbre y los trabajos*).[12] Such an automatic projection of sensuality onto Rosalía at this early age amounts to an almost sympathetic notion of the *mulata*'s sexual endowment as her inescapable curse, as an essential attribute and not a gratuitous construct.

Yet even while Tanco casts her in the sexual mould, Rosalía seems to represent something more. In her lies a vaguely intimated potential, somewhat like the national symbolism that Venezuela's Rómulo Gallegos envisaged in the half-breed Marisela in his 1929 novel *Doña Bárbara*. Even the language referring to them is similar. For Gallegos, this daughter of the white Creole Lorenzo and the *mestiza* Doña Bárbara is "the personification of the nation's soul, open like the land, to all ameliorating action" (*personificación del alma de la raza, abierta, como el paisaje, a toda acción mejoradora*).[13] Tanco envisages a comparable possibility in Rosalía:

> Everything in her was the work of nature, and if men laid their hands on her it was surely not to embellish and adorn, but to degrade and destroy her. A master's rough hands are not the hands of a teacher or mentor. [*Todo en ella era obra de la naturaleza, y si para algo puso el hombre su mano en esta obra no fue seguramente para embellecerla y perfeccionarla, sino para degradarla y destruirla; la mano rudo de un amo no es mano de un pedagogo o de un mentor.*][14]

Implicit in this statement is the belief in the mulatto as an emblem of potential for positive future development in Cuba – a potential vitiated by slavery.

Petrona's portrait, though a mere outline, reveals much upon close inspection. On the matter of her work experience as a house slave, as on the details of her sexual exploitation, the story is silent. Like his fellow writers at the time, Tanco presents us with a picture of slave work as serving a punitive rather than economic purpose. Petrona's suffering as a slave seems to begin only with her transfer to the sugar estate. Both the work routine and the physical ill-treatment there are barely glimpsed but still elicit feelings of horror. It is left to the reader to assume an easier existence as a house slave, given the slave woman's reaction to the punishment proceeding from her "fall from grace".

Though hardly any time is spent on the slave's perspective and world view, the story provides sporadic hints of the consciousness below the surface of her voicelessness. At first blush Petrona is the incarnation of sheer compliance and weakness. Referring to her variously as "poor" and "wretched", the narrator induces the reader to see her as a victim, devoid of agency. Fivel-Démoret laments the absence of any thought of escape on the part of either slave woman.[15] Such disappointment is justified by a passing glance at their normal posture and response. Not only do the female slaves express no direct verbal protest, but Petrona's habitual response to ill-treatment is to appeal for Don Antonio's intervention to mitigate his wife's gratuitous punishment. Slavery research has shown that while the majority of escaped slaves were male, female slaves resorted to acts of *petit marronage* that included self-administered poison and abortion. Tanco's fictional slaves, it is true, are not allowed this option. Fivel-Démoret's comment would benefit nevertheless from a reference to the historical fact that *marronage* was understandably more common among the more brutally treated field slaves than their domestic counterparts; it was also not unheard of but indeed less common among female than among male slaves. In addition, one should not minimize the importance of evidence pointing to the myriad accommodations that powerless slaves were forced to make, including controlled acts of protest. As Lewis reminds us, "not every slave was a Spartacus, or even potentially one".[16]

While open rebellion is not one of the options contemplated by either Petrona or Rosalía, Tanco imagines other strategies to which the slaves might have had recourse within the constraints of their bondage to signal their discontent or to influence their fate. Conscious of the meagre legal provisions that favour the slave, Petrona tries to negotiate her way out of her punishment by seeking a "paper" to allow her to find a new master. Tanco therefore construes her submission as a mode of action contingent upon her specific powerlessness rather than a natural response. Thus, it is implied, the absence of active protest or of an antislavery voice is not synonymous with lack of an antislavery consciousness and will. Petrona's response to her punishment amounts to limited resistance against the power of her owners. Moreover, her expectation that she will not be separated from her young daughter, we are told, is based on her pristine sense of justice: "Petrona imagined that she would also go with her daughter, which seemed natural and just *to her way of thinking*" (*se figuraba Petrona que ella también iría con su hija, como le parecía natural y justo* en su entender).[17]

What this understated reasoning highlights is less the naïvety of her expectation and more her sense of slavery as a contradiction of all natural norms. This in turn puts paid to the notion of the slave as a mindless victim, for the mind is by definition the centre of consciousness, thought, volition and feeling. Echoing a similar pattern used to discredit the slave owners' value system, here the phrase *en su entender* serves the opposite purpose of legitimizing the slave's outlook. Petrona is made seemingly to conform to the master's stereotype when she beseeches him in tones of utter deference and subservience. After all her imploring fails, however, her simple exasperated final exclamation, "Oh, what a man, dear God!" (*¡Ah! ¡qué hombre, Dios mío!*),[18] conveys eloquently the notion that, denied all opportunity of free and full self-expression, the slaves consciously deluded the master by masking their true feelings.

Through the slave's reaction the author also reveals the master's mentality. It is Petrona's understanding of the psychology of her owners that determines the strategy she uses in her attempt to influence her fate. Her appeals to Don Antonio, though fruitless, derive from her awareness of his compassionate disposition towards her. Conversely, it is her discernment of her mistress's temperament that determines a contrary strategy, since, as the narrator puts it, "she knew Doña Concepción's domineering and condescending character very well" (*conocía sobrado bien el carácter imperioso y poco condescendiente de doña Concepción*).[19] Studies of the covert psychological ploys used by slaves to ameliorate their treatment have exposed the ways in which they feigned subservience or used flattery to exploit their masters' weaknesses and ego-satisfaction needs. Petrona's failure to move Don Antonio (because of his sense of his own powerlessness) and Doña Concepción (because of her heartlessness) again reflects the author's will to avoid any equivocation in his antislavery stand, such as might be caused by the investment of any real power, however minimally, in the slave.

Varying the technique of the open polemic staged in the conversation between slave master and slave mistress at the beginning of the story, the author uses Don Antonio's self-reflexive voice to reveal the reality hidden behind the enslaver's ideological posture. Don Antonio observes that the father of Petrona's unborn child could be "any grocer or shop boy, any of the thousands of needy men among us, or any of the thousands of men with an affinity for blacks" (*cualquier bodeguero o mozo de tienda, cualesquiera de los mil menesterosos que hay entre nosotros, o de los mil aficionados al colorcito africano*).[20] In this single ironic stroke, he shatters the racist pretences of whites in colonial Cuba. As Barbara Bush reminds us, "although lower class [white] men became the moral scapegoats, in reality, men of all classes, married or unmarried, engaged in sexual liaisons with black women. Few [white] men . . . openly admitted their attractions for black women."[21] More important, this voice reveals Don Antonio's sense not only of what he is but also of what he is not. By including only lower-caste whites (represented by the shopkeeper types) in his reckoning of the "thousands" of white men with an affinity for non-white women, he tacitly constitutes himself as one of the elite. On the other hand, Don Antonio's comment signals both acknowledgement of the creolization process in its racial form and the beginning of colonial estrangement from the outmoded doctrine of racial puritanism inherited from Cuba's metropolitan Spanish forebears.

The interpretation of the thesis to which the author leads the reader is not the only available one. Tanco's comparison of the slaves with their white rulers is intended to favour the slaves. Interpreted in a sceptical light, however, his intention appears to be contaminated by class prejudice and discrimination. The white Creole elite can be regarded as an absent presence in this story; they constitute the authoritative social enclave that would seek to control all others by setting right standards to live by. What Tanco ultimately seems to be saying is not that slaves are superior to whites but that they are superior to *these* degenerate whites who are regarded as parvenus by the colonial Creole elite. In the final analysis, this protest against the slave experience serves as a weapon in the battle for social turf.

The author's ideological engagement with the story, be it subtle or explicit, is offset by the dispassionate and even ironic posture he assumes at times to suggest his detachment from the subject matter. Its unadorned style, the predominance of dialogue and the paucity of description befit

THE DEVIL IN THE DETAILS

the work's dramatic approach and the human interest that impels it. Its use of more economical discourse demands, for example, deft encapsulation of the horrors of slavery in small emblems, such as the sugar press, and terse allusions to the horrors of plantation life, such as the whippings the slaves received. In keeping with the exigencies of short story writing, the author engages other frugal means to telegraph his message. He forgoes diatribe in favour of swift epigrammatic commentary. Understatement makes his point powerfully in this passing observation in which voice and ideology collide:

> For a long time they did not speak again about the unimportant subject, that is, about the wretched Petrona living on the Santa Lucía estate, cutting cane and suffering hardship and misery with her mulatto daughter. [*Por mucho tiempo no se volvió a tratar más de la materia que era de suyo de ninguna importancia; es decir, de la infeliz negra Petrona que vivía en el ingenio Santa Lucía cortando caña y pasando trabajos y miserias con una hija mulata.*][22]

A similarly shocking effect is achieved through masterful juxtaposition of the horrific and the humdrum in the ironic note that follows the wanton cruelty of Petrona's sentencing in the opening pages of the novel: "The clock struck eleven and the couple rose from the table and in total contentment and satisfied with what had to be done with Petrona, they retired to their bedroom" (*Sieron las once de la noche y levantándose los dos esposos en sana paz, y conformes en lo que había de hacerse con Petrona, se recogieron en su aposento*).[23]

Stylistic economy also typifies this comment on racial attitudes in the narrator's account of Rosalía's birth: "Petrona gave birth to a baby girl; no, not a baby girl, but a little mulatto baby girl" (*Petrona dio a luz a una niña, una niña no, sino una mulatica*).[24] This gloss on the sociological reality brings to the foreground colonial Cuba's notorious obsession with race, race-mixing and racial purity. No less noteworthy than the sociological point being made is the narrative sleight of hand used to make it. With this thrifty technique the author/narrator has succeeded in separating himself from the dominant white society's denial of the humanity of nonwhites. Viewed more broadly, the dexterity of the narrator's self-correction points up the insidious penetration of negrophobic racism into the consciousness and language of the dominant sectors of nineteenth-century Cuban society.

That the sentiment in this work is antislavery is self-evident, but his oblique expression of his ideas is what distinguishes Tanco's story. By presenting the corruption, immorality and profligacy of the sugar-planter lifestyle, *Petrona y Rosalía* allows the ill-treatment of the slaves to be seen not as arbitrary or random but as a function of, and inextricably connected to, a broader social practice. Tanco's opportunistic denunciation of the *nouveau riche* planter is just one instance of the varied strains in Cuban antislavery ideology. His criticism of the sugarocracy is as much an antislavery statement as would be the celebration of *marronage*. His dispassionate approach enables Tanco to avoid the mawkish sentimentalism of other literary compositions that end with the slave's suicide, and allows him to leave the reader instead with a sense of horror and revulsion for the scourge of Cuban slave society.

# ·2·

# "PLUMBING THE MURKY DEPTHS"

*Anselmo Suárez y Romero's* Francisco

UNLIKE THE ICONIC *Sab* and *Cecilia Valdés,* which have received much individual critical attention from local and international scholars, Anselmo Suárez y Romero's *Francisco* is sometimes treated as a nondescript novel of dubious literary stock and suspect ideological pedigree. Nevertheless, this work occupies a special place in the gallery of antislavery narratives. It was one of the first responses to Richard Madden's request for compositions by young writers illustrating the Cuban view of slavery. As one of the first full-length literary pieces on the slavery theme, it began a cycle that was to last for half a century. Suárez, who was born in Havana in 1818, started writing the novel in 1838 and completed it in 1839, at the age of twenty-one. His youth qualified him for special mentoring by the more experienced members of del Monte's writers' club. *Francisco* is, in addition, the novel whose genealogy has been most fully documented. It was composed co-operatively, being in part the product of ongoing exchanges between the author and club members who contributed to its production by their commendations and criticisms. Whether to shed light or to cast their shadow on subsequent interpretations of the novel, the letters between members of the writers' circle during the course of its composition have been included in its various editions as indispensable extensions of the text.

The amended version of the manuscript, which was included in the album delivered to Madden, has not been published and seems to have been lost. According to the author, the unedited version was the one that finally appeared in print in New York after the abolition of slavery in Cuba. Neither version was subject, therefore, to the constraints of official censorship; the modified one was destined for Madden, not for public consumption in Cuba, while the original was published under a more liberal political regime. Carlos Alonso's apt characterization of these narratives as "texts whose depths are as murky as the genealogies [in] whose exploration and unveiling they obsessively persevere"[1] provides a useful premise for my reading of the unedited version of *Francisco*, which will broaden and deepen our understanding of the novel. My analysis will highlight the undercover subversion of the dominant proslavery ideology effected through various unobtrusive signs. By delving beneath the surface, such an analysis will help to balance existing perceptions of Suárez's composition.

At the centre of the novel is the clichéd Romantic fable of ill-fated love between Francisco and Dorotea, two favoured house slaves, which is thwarted by their widowed mistress, Dolores Mendizábal, and her son, Ricardo. Doña Dolores not only refuses their pleas for permission to marry but eventually forbids their relationship. The slaves continue their affair in secret, and this leads to Dorotea's pregnancy, a crime that earns them debarment from serving in the house. Francisco is stripped of his position as family coachman, banished to the sugar estate and sentenced to receive the most severe punishment, while Dorotea is demoted from handmaid to hired laundress. Although Doña Dolores has a change of heart subsequently and agrees to the slaves' marriage, Ricardo, whose sexual advances Dorotea has repeatedly rejected, contrives to prevent their union by falsely accusing Francisco of a host of misdeeds to justify his continued torture. In a desperate bid to save Francisco's life, Dorotea finally capitulates to Ricardo. His heart broken by the news, Francisco commits suicide and Dorotea dies shortly thereafter.

The complete work, or parts of it, met with general approval from writers such as Félix Tanco y Bosmeniel, who had composed *Petrona y Rosalía* a year earlier, the poet José Jacinto Milanés and Cirilo Villaverde, who at the time was writing his *Cecilia Valdés*. Based on his reading of the first chapter, Milanés concluded that Suárez was a literary sensation and was exuberant in predicting his outstanding potential as a writer. The work's verisimilitude and ethical significance caught the attention of other *tertulia* members and of Suárez's chief literary guide, José González del Valle, who applauded the novel's concern with social justice. Richard Madden himself was so convinced of its veracity that he was led to challenge the reliability of the historian José Antonio Saco's so-called factual version of Cuban slavery. Anthropologist Fernando Ortiz boosted its truth-bearing value by relying on and even quoting directly from *Francisco* in his ethnographic study *Los negros esclavos* (1916). Indeed, the historical validity of the perspective of the sugar plantation that Suárez offers has rarely been challenged. Nineteenth-century Cuban readers of the manuscript were likewise unanimous in their conviction of its subversive implications, and the novel has continued to benefit from a generally favourable reception by Cuban scholars, who have taken its objective to be the total abolition of slavery.

Critics outside of Cuba have been somewhat less approving in their interpretations of this and other antislavery works belonging to the same period, noting the tameness of the authors' privileging of the image of slave submission over that of slave rebellion. In promoting this idea of the novel's conservatism, much has been made of del Monte's recommendation that Suárez eliminate its subversive aspects. However, the letter in which González del Valle clarified the intention behind del Monte's comment suggests that it was directed less to ideological content and more to tone and expression. Protest against slavery, in del Monte's view, should emerge spontaneously from the events in the story rather than through overt statement or diatribe. Despite the influences and constraints that might have been faced by the author of *Francisco,* there is no conclusive evidence of writers being hobbled by a strictly enforced orthodoxy within the del Monte circle.

Though *Francisco* was written at Madden's bidding for use in his international campaign against the slave trade, Suárez was also drawn to the subject for personal reasons. One of his letters to del Monte reveals the enlightened self-interest in his wish to live in a society free from suffering and filled with peace and kindness. Positive self-presentation is also a significant motive in the process: his novel would be the voice of the minority of Cuban whites who genuinely sympathized with the slaves. Slavery for Suárez was both a social and a moral problem; writing the novel served as a form of personal catharsis. Buoyed by his self-perception as an authority on sugar-based plantation slavery, the young writer was confident and unapologetic about his aim of promoting moral reform in Cuban society. It is therefore no surprise that when he tried to have part of his novel published in Cuba in 1859, it was rejected by the censor, who no doubt understood the subversive potential of its denunciation of slavery and its indictment of the Creole slave-owning class. Even while he declares his enlightened self-interest, the novelist stakes out his nationalist position, proposing commitment to social improvement as a more meaningful measure of patriotism than uncritical love of country; in his words, "A patriot neither flatters nor fawns" (*El patriota no adula, ni lisonjea*).[2] His statement of motivation in these straightforward terms should not blind the reader, however, to the complexity of his depiction of slavery and the slave.

*Francisco* is the human story of nineteenth-century Cuban slavery, depicting the dynamics of both the house- and field-slave experiences. It provides both close-up and wide-ranging views of life on a sugar estate. The work regime and conditions, personnel and relationships all form part of this picture. Suárez dramatizes the extreme abuse that the system permitted because of the slave owner's control over the bodies of the slaves, both male and female. An almost monotonous litany of descriptions of physical brutality inflicted on the slave comprises the work's second and third chapters. More specifically, and as will be discussed in greater detail later, this novel foregrounds a major aspect of the gender politics of slavery: the emasculation of the male slave occasioned by the master's desire for the female slave. For it is his specific role as the black slave who symbolically defeats the white slave owner in the contest for the mulatto slave's favours that causes Francisco to be singled out for vengeful treatment.

His experience speaks mainly to these specific circumstances, and that must be taken into account in any assessment of his role.

Suárez's concern for the lot of the slave had its roots as much in his sentimental disposition as in his ideological principles. Francisco's individual experience of slave work as punitive is placed against the general background of this work as productive. The novelist provides detailed descriptions of the whole spectrum of occupations and tasks involved in the process of sugar production. His view is grounded in a quasi-Marxist awareness of the alienated nature of slave labour. Suárez conveyed his moral distress over this aspect of slavery in a letter to del Monte dated March 1839, in which he reported on his stay at the Surinam estate.[3] In his autobiographical reflections the author also cites his principled refusal of the fruits of unpaid slave labour as evidence of the consistency of his beliefs.[4]

Revisionist studies of slavery are wont to decry any representation that might compromise the unequivocal denunciation demanded by the system. That slavery in the master's house was less harsh or more tolerable than slavery on the master's sugar plantation is one such proposition that has been firmly repudiated. Suárez, in like fashion, shows the difference between the slave experience in the two locations as one of shade rather than of substance. The illustrious slave mistress's manipulation of the mind and her trifling with the emotions of the house slaves are only more sophisticated than the sadistic physical torture used to control the field slaves by her *mayoral*, the lowlier white overseer, and the *contramayoral*, his black slave driver. In the house that control functions at a less perceptible cultural level and includes the education of the slave, the imposition of "white" attire and the granting of certain social and economic privileges. Various travel writers who visited Havana during the nineteenth century were impressed by the apparent lack of distinction between the house slaves' children and the children of their masters. But Francisco's torment at the hands of Ricardo, his childhood playmate, shatters the myth of a less virulent practice of slavery in the Spanish colonies. Dorotea's connection to Ricardo has even deeper roots in the prevalent practice of compelling slave women to serve as wet nurses for white babies. Suárez evokes the resulting sibling-like relationship shared by the young Dorotea and Ricardo, but only to demystify it with the unfolding of the grown Ricardo's quasi-incestuous desire for his foster sister.

While the record of the correspondence between the author of *Francisco* and other members of the del Monte group has generated a discourse on the novel's ideological significance, the discourse of the novel itself has received only modest attention. Comments from the group reveal that their concerns centred not only on the work's moral and political imperatives but also on its expressive methods. In fact, favourable judgements of the novelist's vision and the validity of the work's content are normally accompanied by dismissive references to its style. Upon reading the manuscript, Madden judged its moral message and verisimilitude to be adequate compensation for its artistic limitations. In particular, González del Valle expressed his opinion (which he claimed was shared by Villaverde and del Monte) that the author's heavy-handedness left nothing for readers to infer or imagine.[5] Later commentators have made light of the novel's literary value and have helped to divert attention from its technical dimension.[6] Writing in 1976, Cuban author and critic César Leante discredited the novel on literary grounds.[7] Suárez himself, though confident about his work's moral merit, was far less sanguine about its literary calibre. In offering his preferred reading of the work, his unabashed defence of its compelling message is counterbalanced by his apologetic posture over what he perceived as its stylistic shortcomings. His repeated and earnest soliciting of advice from his more experienced fellow writers, as well as his deprecating comments about his writing style, also suggests that he felt he lacked the technical means to give his ideas appropriate literary expression.

Suárez's use of classical Spanish as the language of narration highlights the dilemma of the colonial writer wanting to capture the specificity of local reality but needing to appropriate the dominant imperial language to make it intelligible to an outside reader. Signs of an emergent linguistic nationalism appear in the incorporation of forms of the Cuban vernacular to give the work a distinctly Creole Spanish impress and to differentiate the colony from the imperial power. Members of the del Monte circle, who understood its anti-colonial and anti-Spanish import, lauded the speech of the white overseer with its many *cubanismos*. On the other hand, except for a few phrases of heavily accented Spanish standing in for the peculiarities of slave speech, which the author inserts into the second chapter, the unique voice of the slave is an eloquent absence. It reflects the limits of the Euro-Caribbean imagination in this early attempt to represent the Afro-Caribbean person, a deficiency to which the author tacitly confesses when he refers on one occasion to the slaves' language as "a lingo after their fashion, but unintelligible" (*un guirigay a su manera, ininteligible*).[8]

In his study of metaphorical portrayals of the Negro in the Western literary tradition, Lemuel Johnson notes the use of a similar "unintelligible" language in the burlesque (mis)representations of the Negro in early peninsular Spanish writing: "The Negro's phonetic and syntactic distortion through interference from his origins was used for linguistic caricature. Lexically meaningless Negroid percussions, *jitánforas,* became indispensable adjuncts in one-dimensional representations of the Negro."[9] The consciousness underlying the reference to the slaves' language in Suárez's novel implies no such mockery, for by qualifying *"guirigay"* with *"a su manera"* the author shows understanding of the communicative power of slave speech within the slave community. Moreover, by separating *"ininteligible"* orthographically from *"a su manera"* he tacitly acknowledges the exclusion of the white Creole writer from the world of the slaves. Suárez's attempt to present an authentic picture of slave life was hampered by his inability to give the slaves a unique language in which to think and to express themselves appropriately. That he lacked the resources to allow them to speak with their own voice does not detract from his demonstration of their personhood, however, as we shall see. Moreover, the absence of a slave voice mirrors the power politics of colonial society and the liberal white Creole makeup of the Cuban antislavery lobby group to which Suárez belonged.

Impelled by his desire to impress his reader with the horror of plantation slavery, Suárez orchestrates the action in the opening pages to create maximum shock effect. He plunges the reader unceremoniously into the surreal nightmare of the sugar plantation, where the young, bloodthirsty slave master and the sadistic overseer hold sway. Mikhail Bakhtin's theory of the novel as constituted by dialogues between different voices is useful for decoding the process by which Suárez communicates his message. In the opening episode the author converts the narrative into drama by allowing the narrator to remain behind the scenes, while the action unfolds through an extended dialogue between Ricardo and the overseer Antonio. In this strategically placed and unrestrained exchange, the author has distilled essential tenets of proslavery ideology and the cruder arguments used both to defend the system and to rationalize brutal treatment of the slaves.

The voice of Antonio has a mainly expository purpose. His gleeful description of the sadistic violence inflicted on the slave brings out, in a striking and economical fashion, both the psychopathology of slave oppression and the horror of plantation slavery as lived experience. His voice is complemented by that of Ricardo, who supplies the "philosophical" justification for slave abuse: "treat 'em mean to keep 'em keen". His version of the relationship of slave owner to slave, as one of kindness versus ingratitude, and his characterization of Francisco as recalcitrant are classic modes of proslavery rhetoric. The third voice in this chapter is that of the narrator, whom the reader is induced to regard as inseparable from the author. His intervention marks a shift from the dramatic mode used in the first seven pages. He takes control of the story, pretending to be the voice of objectivity and pledging implicitly to recount, without prejudice, the circumstances surrounding Francisco's "crime".

In the recounting, which occupies the bulk of the chapter, the narrator constructs images of the three remaining primary characters, Doña Dolores, Francisco and Dorotea. Of the three, it is the slave mistress and the peculiarity of her standpoint that most engage the author/narrator, who soon abandons the pretence of objectivity and assumes the role of judge. Thus Ricardo is allowed free rein to build up a philanthropic image of his mother. This view is immediately undermined by a challenge from the author/narrator, who puts her benevolence into correct perspective by revealing the crypto-racism that it masks. With such narrative manoeuvres, the novelist not only dismantles the view of the two villainous characters but also ensures that the only view to which his reader will acquiesce is the one that favours the slaves. Thus, although three different voices have entered the novel, only one – the author/narrator's – has been allowed, in Bakhtinian terms, to "flourish".[10]

Much of the existing discussion of Suárez's depiction of the slave has centred on the titular protagonist. The controversy to which the character gave rise in the del Monte *tertulia* can be illuminated by an appraisal of the strategies used in his portrayal. Francisco is first presented to the reader *in absentia*, as the topic of the opening conversation between Ricardo and Don Antonio. Conventionally, this strategy is used where the absent character plays a heroic role. The energy that the overseer has expended on brutalizing the slave leads the reader to expect to find in Francisco a rebel who has to be tamed, not the innocuous character we meet a few pages later. This narrative practice serves therefore to demonize the slave master and his surrogate rather than to build a heroic image of the protagonist.

On the surface, Francisco is a pathetic picture of passivity, bordering on caricature. His self-denying loyalty to his mistress appears incredible. He lacks the courage to pursue his freedom, striving instead for a meagre happiness within servitude through a love relationship with Dorotea. His role is to elicit pity, not admiration. His thoughts are typically lamentations and his characteristic actions and reactions are expressions of grief. William Luis has compared his portrayal as a compliant slave to the self-portrait in Juan Francisco Manzano's slave autobiography, which Suárez had read and edited.[11] With his innocence, natural good manners and intelligence, Suárez's protagonist also shows some affiliation to the idealized stereotype of the noble savage, a figure that had been standardized for the depiction of the Negro in Europe, and most notably in the metropolitan French literary tradition. His portrayal caused disquiet in del Monte, who viewed Francisco's meekness and tolerance with some impatience. In his response Suárez defended his strategy, establishing that his construction of the image was by design and not born of naivety or ignorance. While conceding that his meek reaction was not commensurate with the brutality inflicted upon the average slave, he designated Francisco an "outstanding exception". The author reveals further that self-projection figured prominently in the creation of his protagonist; he developed the slave's image out of his Christian belief in the spiritually ennobling power of adversity and as a reflection of his own long-suffering self.

In Suárez's Christian cosmology, stoicism and meekness in the face of a world filled with suffering confer greater moral prestige than rebellion. Francisco's character is mythologized by analogy with Christian martyrdom: "That sad tinge on his face that enthrals and enchants; that tinge used to represent martyrs for the faith" (*aquel tinte lúgubre de su rostro que cautivaba y seducía; aquel tinte con que son representados los mártires de la fe*).[12] This last comment highlights his primary status as an ideological construct rather than a literary facsimile of a real slave. He is the creature of Suárez's Christian ideals, used to strengthen his indictment of the architects of slave oppression.

Although his role as slave is inseparable from his role as Christian martyr, martyrdom was by no means a condition exclusive to Francisco. Indeed, the temperament of the protagonist of Suárez's first novel, *Carlota Valdés* (1838), is said to be in many ways Francisco's female equivalent. In the Latin American religious tradition too, many Catholic believers prefer to identify with the pathos of the suffering Christ of Good Friday rather than with the message of hope in the risen Christ of Easter. One need only recall the staging of elaborate rituals re-enacting the Passion of Christ to be reminded of this glorification of Christian suffering in Latin American societies. This, then, was the emphatic way Suárez chose both to reflect the condition of the slave and to reconstitute his image: through the use of a metaphor filled with powerful cultural meaning. Admittedly Francisco lacks the strength of a rebel, but he endures incredible physical torture. His endurance recalls the fortitude that allowed the Africans and their culture to survive displacement across the Atlantic and through the hell of slavery. Francisco dies only when his spirit dies, when Dorotea's capitulation to Ricardo's desires leads him to despair – a reminder that the most devastating and durable consequences of Caribbean slavery have been mental and psychological.

Although gender suggests itself as an important aspect of Suárez's version of the slave experience, critical interest in the protagonist has obscured the role of his lover, Dorotea. To some extent she is Francisco's female counterpart, compliant and virtuous. Despite not being named in its title, she plays a decisive role in the novel's action. Francisco is identified by his voiceless, tearful responses; he dares to verbalize his discontent only in secret, to his confidant, the old slave Taita Pedro. Dorotea, on the contrary, endowed with a more robust spirit and a firmer will than her pusillanimous lover, is articulate and confrontational in her rejection of Ricardo's advances. In one of the novel's most powerful rhetorical interludes, like a true heroine she respectfully but bravely defends her virtue against Ricardo's designs:

> I am your slave, master; I am a poor mulatto girl and your lordship is white and you are my master. Your lordship can order me to be put in the stocks, whipped and even killed, if you so desire; but your lordship can never take away my integrity. [*Yo soy su esclava, Niño, yo soy una pobre mulata, y su merced es blanco, y mi amo. Su Merced me puede mandar meter en el cepo, y que me den bocabajo, y hasta matarme, si le parece; pero su merced no podrá nunca quitarme la vergüenzai.*][13]

Francisco's fatalistic self-pity is a counterpoise to Dorotea's bold self-assertion. This investment of strength in Dorotea prefigures the revaluation of the Caribbean slave woman's historical and literary role that has formed part of the research agenda of feminist and other scholars since the 1970s.

Based on his belief that a precedent change in the consciousness of their enslavers would bring about a change in the condition of the slaves, Suárez set out to generate an alternative to the dominant strains of proslavery discourse. In the nineteenth century, fixing the ethnic and sexual identities of people of African origin was an almost universal white Creole obsession, born of the negrophobic desire to separate the non-white Other from the white Self. For example, Suárez refuses the customary negative aesthetic value ascribed to negroid racial features. He perceives the beauty of Francisco's jet-black skin shining in contrast to his pure white teeth and eyes, which reflect his soul's nobility and generosity. When he adds innate intelligence and proud bearing to this portrait, the image translates into a calculated contestation of the equally calculated racist portrait of black slaves painted by Ricardo in the novel's opening chapter. Dorotea's identity is constructed using a similar strategy. Many writers of the period sexualized their racial rhetoric through fetishization of the mulatto woman's body. Not fortuitously, Suárez avoids the essentialist cliché of the sensual *mulata* in his portrayal of Dorotea, suggesting his adherence to the demands of Romanticism and to the ascetic approach to sexuality in Christian doctrine. Viewed by Francisco through Romantic eyes, Dorotea is sexualized only in Ricardo's libidinous gaze, a compelling reminder that the non-white woman as erotic body was primarily a construct of the white imagination.

In creating an alternative discourse for the definition of his slave characters, the novelist accentuates in them the traits that define human beings – his way of retreating further from the racialized mythology of slavery. The author stresses their humanity almost to the point of redundancy. He misses no opportunity to put human faces on the two slave lovers. If one of the effects of proslavery discourse was to normalize the view of slaves as non-human, Suárez responded in his novel by naturalizing their humanity. Dorotea is cast in the mould of the generic woman, as mother and nurturer – a rare image of the *mulata*, and one that displaces her conventional association with non-reproductive sex. Suárez's portrait of the two slaves in these terms stands once more in diametric opposition to their initial representation by Ricardo. In attributing humanity to the slave, Suárez has made what amounts to an antislavery statement by demonstrating the idea of the slave's identity as constructed rather than given.

Another commonly held opinion in nineteenth-century Cuba was that slaves were intrinsically immoral. In an opposing view, this immorality was construed as a consequence of slavery, which brutalized body and soul. Suárez proposes an alternative to both beliefs. He reverses the "rigid hierarchy of difference"[14] by investing in the "savage" slaves the moral values that white civilization has ascribed to itself, and this despite the abuse to which the slaves are subjected. Again not fortuitously, Francisco is shown to possess the *capacity* to use violence against his mistress; his non-violence is taken to be a matter of conscious choice rather than a reflex response, and it becomes the measure of his moral superiority.

Suárez's depiction of his two main slave characters may be interpreted in the light of thinking about human agency and assumptions about subjectivity that are fundamental issues in postcolonial meditations on colonial discourse. These concepts provide a valuable medium for appraisal of the authors' presentation of the slaves. Postcolonial theorists have postulated that their powerlessness constrained the colonized to assume the subjectivity that was constructed for them by colonial discourse.[15] Judged from a Marxist theoretical perspective, the ideology of New World slavery created a false view of their identity, and the slaves were not agents endowed with the ability to act autonomously. Accordingly, both the action and inaction of the two slaves in Suárez's novel may be seen to be determined by the ways in which their identity has been constructed and by the politics of slave society.

A natural corollary of their feelings of powerlessness is their awareness of the slave owner's irresistible power. Their response and relationship to the white world are shown to be specific to the house-slave experience, the condition out of which their subjectivity has been formed. What Suárez seems to be highlighting is the alienating consequence of this experience. Doubly exiled – from their origins and from their local community – their capacity for radical rebellion is no doubt hampered by their location in the bosom of the slave owner's world, removed from "the social construction and political organization of resistance".[16] Other practitioners of postcolonial criticism, among them Frantz Fanon, believe that since the process of subject construction can be recognized, it can also be contested.[17] This latter perspective was not completely alien to Suárez's way of thinking, as demonstrated by the various nuancing strategies he uses to enrich the texture of his portraits of the slaves and their world.

As noted previously, one of this novel's limitations is the unavailability of a unique slave voice. Suárez nonetheless sought to compensate for this failure of language imaginatively, through acts of ventriloquy and a focus on the protagonist's mental state. R. Anthony Castagnaro, one of the early commentators on the novel, cites "the rudimentary character delineation of Francisco" as one of the few literary flaws of Suárez's work.[18] Careful examination of this aspect reveals that, though not fully developed, the protagonist's portrait delivers somewhat more than Castagnaro's comment implies. His kinship with the noble savage notwithstanding, Francisco does not conform completely to the simplistic pattern of the stereotype; his meek persona does not constitute his total personality. First, the author discloses the origins of his compliant attitude. Taken from the slave barracks at the age of ten, the malleable Francisco easily assumed the role of compliant slave in the sugar planter's house. But even this exposure of the roots of his temperament does not take full account of his image. As he turns the focus from the outer world of the slave's life to the inner universe of the slave's mind, Suárez reveals not only the despairing thoughts but also the hidden symptoms of psychological resistance and self-assertion that temper the slave's manifest docility.

Fivel-Démoret reads complicity in the silence of Suárez's slave characters: "The reader is struck by the comparative absence of rebellion or dissatisfaction with their status in the privacy of the slaves' thoughts or intimate conversations."[19] However, in postcolonial analyses of literary and other accounts of subaltern groups, important subversive meanings have been found to reside in such silence. Francisco's voicelessness, Suárez is careful to indicate, is not a reflection of total conformity. The author senses in the depths of the slave's soul the muffled noise of discontent that sabotages the surface appearance of accommodation. Francisco's perennially sad countenance speaks less to his weakness than to his sense of the misrepresentation of his identity under slavery, and to his enduring desire for the dignity of freedom. Moreover, in a rare show of mettle, the slave expresses his unequivocal dissatisfaction with his preferred-slave status in an insightful confession to the old slave watchman Taita Pedro.[20] Francisco is not blind to the subtle indices of his inferior station for which good treatment acts as a cover. In addition, his enjoyment of the relative comfort of a house slave's life does not prevent him from identifying mentally and emotionally with the suffering of his counterparts in the fields. Even though the author does not endow him with the ability to translate promise into action, attributing this feeling of solidarity to the slave is itself an antislavery gesture in a situation where division in the slave community was inimical to the process of resistance and conducive to the sustainability of slavery.

As in the case of Francisco, the inner workings of Dorotea's mind belie her outward behaviour. Her small acts of defiance – ranging from disobedience of her mistress's instructions to her sacrificial efforts to save her lover – are a modest counterweight to her demonstrations of subservience. The slave lovers do not surrender to their mistress's tyranny without first expressing their desire for freedom. They contemplate avenues of escape, and reject them through a process of prudent reasoning rather than through instinctive cowardice. In outlining the different categories of slave resistance, Gordon Lewis reminds us of such slaves: "Those who openly rebelled, after all, were always a minority, if only because the penalties for revolt – being broken on the wheel or literally roasted alive, as the many accounts of the judicial records of rebellions grimly testify – were in themselves sufficient to deter all but the most intransigent."[21]

In the novel, Antonio's account of the draconian measures used to hunt down and punish rebels further justifies the two slaves' reluctance to take the runaway path to freedom. In this way Suárez has pre-empted Fivel-Démoret's assertion that "never does he [Francisco] contemplate running away – an option that, together with outright revolt, was taken by many more slaves than was comfortable for many slave owners and the authorities of the day to admit".[22] Moreover, their secret defiance of their mistress's despotism signals the two slaves' ability to translate psychological resistance into small-scale rebellion, thus challenging the Marxist theory of the dominant ideology's stranglehold over the subordinate classes.

Despite the choice of a timid protagonist, Suárez does not labour under the illusion that Francisco's attitude is replicated in the general slave population. In fact, his claim that Francisco's attitude is "exceptional" is a tacit admission of the prevalence of slave resistance. For alternative values and responses in the slave community, one must look to the author's vision of the shadowy mass of slaves, the nameless and faceless *negrada*. Suárez demonstrates this historical awareness in various economical and understated ways. In the first chapter Don Antonio recalls an incident of retaliation by the slaves on the San Salvador sugar estate, who killed the overseer and buried him in the forest. Thus the author demonstrates that the actions of rebellious slaves did indeed give the planters reason to be fearful.

Suárez also uses the occasion to dispel the stereotypical notion that, like the *contramayoral* on the Mendizábal estate, black slave drivers were always collaborators with the slave owners: he acknowledges another *contramayoral*'s role as leader of the San Salvador revolt. The overseer's suspicion that the old slave watchman Taita Pedro is hiding a fugitive is, in addition, an oblique reference to a steady undercurrent of slave rebellion.

Although the author provides only fleeting glimpses of the experience of the other slaves on the estate, their presence and actions at various points in the story point significantly to the broader reality of slavery. Various episodes bespeak the solidarity and resistance that ultimately enabled the enslaved to maintain the integrity of their human spirit while appearing to conform or submit to the dominance of their white owners. A case in point is the reference to the work song of the slave cane-cutters, which forms a backdrop for one of the many episodes of Francisco's torture.[23] Suárez risks no possible interpretation of their singing as a sign of contentment, as might have been claimed by some of slavery's avid supporters. He demonstrates, on the contrary, that it is an expression of solidarity with their suffering brother, thus deflecting the focus from disunity within the slave community. In addition to this passive expression of fraternity, Francisco's fellow slaves surreptitiously sabotage the overseer's sadistic intentions by conspiring to alleviate the punishment.

While the house slaves function as individuals in isolation, community is shown to characterize slave life in the fields. When one adds the complicity of Taita Pedro in facilitating clandestine meetings between the slave couple, these responses constitute acts of resistance – less dramatic than open rebellion, but no less significant. Suárez's overall depiction of the slave workers on the plantation defies Gabriel Coulthard's description of them as "all good, simple people".[24] Not content with merely exposing their subversive acts, the novelist conjures up their secret vengeful thoughts.[25] The primary action of the novel does not include radical acts such as *marronage*, open rebellion, or even the less blatant *petit marronage*. Yet when account is taken of the controlled forms of resistance of which his slave characters avail themselves, Suárez may be seen to anticipate postcolonial thinking in his interpretation of the relative power of slave and slave owner.

He suggests that the conditioning to which the slave was subjected was neither complete nor fully successful. Rather than the absolute powerlessness of the slaves, he portrays the *limits* of their power.

In Suárez's fictional universe there is an implicit moral scale on which he measures his characters. Francisco and Dorotea are located at the highest extreme while the slave owner's son, Ricardo, the white overseer and the black slave driver occupy the lowest end. Between these two poles is Dolores Mendizábal, the slave mistress and the other main character in the drama. As the personification of moral ambivalence, Doña Dolores provides the novel with its most interesting character portrait. This portrait may be illuminated by Mikhail Bakhtin's concept of the dialectic of rapprochement and dissociation evident in a novelist's relationship to the novel's language, and by extension to its characters: "The language of the prose writer deploys itself according to degrees of greater or lesser proximity to the author: certain aspects of language directly and unmediatedly express . . . the semantic and expressive intentions of the author; others refract those intentions . . . . Therefore the stratification of language . . . that of particular world views, particular tendencies, particular individuals . . . upon entering the novel, establishes its own special order within it, and becomes a unique artistic system, which orchestrates the intentional theme of the author."[26] It is in the spirit of this Bakhtinian theory that Suárez as author-narrator may be seen to interact with Doña Dolores, displaying his intimate understanding of her disposition, motivations and anxieties. Her goodness, like Francisco's submissiveness, makes her "exceptional". In the words of the author/narrator, her compassionate treatment of her house slaves conforms to the practices of the minority group of "good" slave owners on the island.[27] It is the influence of her exemplary virtue, not only their own natural inclination, that determines the goodness of Francisco and Dorotea. Suárez punctuates the action of the novel with acts of generosity by which Doña Dolores strives to maintain her benevolent self-image.

González del Valle was apprehensive of the danger in what he considered to be the excessively benign portrait of Doña Dolores and urged Suárez to adopt a more subversive strategy.[28] On the other hand, R.

Anthony Castagnaro, writing in 1971, is seduced by the author's brighter vision of the character: "[Suárez's] strong indignation against slavery does not blind him to the moral virtues possessed by some slave owners, as he demonstrates in his depiction of the compassionate Doña Dolores Mendizábal."[29] Viewed from the Bakhtinian perspective, her image takes on a less transparent appearance; her character, like that of her son, serves to refract the author's antislavery intentions.

With a sharp eye for nuance and subtlety, Suárez engages various strategies to tarnish Doña Dolores's aura of benevolence. While Don Antonio and Ricardo articulate an undisguised antislave bigotry, Dolores's prejudice is played out in a more insidious manner. To illuminate her portrait we may turn to the postcolonial theory of the ambiguity of the colonized–colonizer relationship: "Ambivalence also characterizes the way in which colonial discourse relates to the colonized subject, for it may be both exploitative and nurturing, or present itself as nurturing at the same time."[30] In the overall portrayal of Doña Dolores, the author/narrator's perceptions collide at several points with the consciousness of the slave mistress. From her perspective, the young slave with his "humble character" is a blank slate on which she has inscribed the superior cultural ways that make him acceptable to the Euro-Creole elite. To pre-empt any interpretation of this acculturation as an unqualified benefit of slavery to the slave, the author dilutes its value by subtly evoking the deculturation involved in his forced uprooting from Africa. For Doña Dolores, slavery is inseparable from Francisco's identity. Her ultimate aim, therefore, is to make him "an excellent servant", to elevate him without changing his servile status. Although Francisco as an individual benefits from her benevolence, this does not conflict with the negrophobic stereotype she holds of people of African descent in general. This character's way of being alienates her from the author. In the final analysis she speaks the same proslavery language as her son and her overseer.

In a similar fashion, her self-perception and self-presentation diverge from the author's view. Doña Dolores sees and presents herself as the paternalistic mother, obliged to use a well-meant but rigorous discipline to limit the freedom of her slave-child. But Suárez's account of the benefits enjoyed by the house slave, such as learning to read and write, is simultaneously undercut because the total obedience she demands speaks to the threat of insubordination she fears in that very education. The author/narrator at no time allows appearance to obscure reality. Slaves – even favourite house slaves – are never allowed to forget their place. Dolores's desire for total control over the life of her most favoured slaves stands in sharp contrast to her ignorance and lack of interest in the condition of (field) slaves generally. The author uses understatement to place a cynical accent on her thoughtlessness, characterizing her visit to the sugar mill as "entertainment". Probing further beneath the façade of the slave mistress's goodness, Suárez reveals a deep-seated anti-black racism in her attitude to Ricardo's relations with women; though indulgent of his sexual escapades with white women, she is intolerant of any thought of a liaison with a black or mulatto slave.

Analysis of her complex psychology and the motives driving her actions reveals a tension in Doña Dolores. She struggles to reconcile the incompatible demands of her desire to be perceived as humane and the social and economic self-interest and negrophobia that require her to keep her slaves under strict control. Lewis's reference to the work of Caribbean historian Elsa Goveia sheds light on this inner conflict:

> The mental atmosphere of the white world was dominated by the ever-present fear of black servile revolt . . . It was only natural that the Caribbean ruling class . . . should construct, as one defence mechanism, a code of behaviour every member was required to observe . . . The behavioural code, then, demanded that the master not compromise his authority and thereby the collective prestige of the white race by behaviour that could call it into question . . . Planter public opinion was brought against especially newcomers who "spoiled" the blacks by inconsiderate kindness.[31]

This scenario, outlined in reference to the British Caribbean experience, is no less applicable as an explanation of the affront that the slaves' autonomous desires signify for Suárez's fictional slave mistress. Neither whimsical nor merely perverse, Doña Dolores's anxious efforts to crush the slightest act of disobedience or insubordination stem from her desperate need to maintain her grip on power. With this the author has brought to the forefront the precariousness of the planters' hold over the slaves and, in its most neurotic manifestation, the fear of granting them even the slightest freedom.

At the same time, part of Suárez's plan also appears to be to reconcile the image of the slave mistress's philanthropy with her complicity in the wanton brutality visited upon the slave. First, he seems to amend his denunciation by exposing the socio-genetic roots of her mentality and her inescapable conditioning by the environment. He also creates a divide between mother and son, making the latter into the real villain. She is referred to repeatedly as "innocent" and as "naive", and it is her excessive love for her son that blinds her to the atrocities he commits. However, any goodness the reader may be inclined to perceive in Doña Dolores is rendered null and void by the malevolence that her overindulgence breeds in her son. Suárez does not entertain the thought of any significant oasis in the wilderness of slavery. Bearing in mind the widespread concern expressed in Cuba at this time about the demoralizing consequences of the sugar planters' parental incompetence, Suárez, like Tanco, uses the family situation in his novel to intimate that it is the overindulgence of white children, not black slaves, that constituted the bigger social menace.

Relations between slave owner and slave are a major theme in *Francisco*. Writing about the novel in 1962, Gabriel Coulthard remarked on the oppositional aspect of these dealings, labelling it as "the confrontation of two worlds, that of the masters and that of the slaves".[32] Homi Bhabha's theory of ambivalence as a defining feature of colonial discourse permits a more complex view of Suárez's depiction of the dynamics of this exchange: "The relationship between colonizer and colonized is ambivalent because the colonized subject is never simply and completely opposed to the colonizer. Rather than assuming that some colonized subjects are 'complicit' and some 'resistant', ambivalence suggests that complicity and resistance exist in a fluctuating relation within the colonial subject."[33] Such ambiguity lies at the heart of Suárez's understanding of the slaves' response to their owners. Time and again he points up the discrepancy between their true mental state and their consciously assumed stance. Outward compliance is a mere masking of resistance, and disclosing this ambivalence is one of the most subversive aspects of the novel. It undermines the slave mistress's belief in her unassailable power at the same time that it renders less tenable the notion of a polarity between total submission and total rebellion in slave responses.

As a house slave, Francisco's reaction attests to the complexity of the ties that bound slave to slave owner. He is motivated to heed his mistress's advice to forego his love for Dorotea because of his incredible self-denying fear of disturbing "the tranquillity of the house".[34] Indeed, by creating this anxiety in the slave, Suárez seems to point to his surrender to the slave owner's interests and to indicate the extent to which his thinking has been shaped by the expectations of his oppressor. But this collusion is not sustained. Whereas the imposition of European trappings and the granting of special privileges are expected to bring about the house slave's happy accommodation to his owners' culture, Francisco experiences his preferred-slave status as a form of both physical dispossession and psychological isolation. Suárez refuses the rationalization of slavery as a means of bringing the savage African into civilization, making Francisco instead an example of the tragic effects of cultural alienation. His education separates him from other slaves, hindering his participation in their acts of solidarity. In addition, his relegation from the house to the sugar estate highlights the transience of his acculturation, for it is accompanied by removal of the signifiers of Euro-Creole culture, including a change in his mode of dress and the cutting of his hair.

An important part of this combination of submission and subversion is the slaves' deluding of the slave owner as a survival strategy. Far from being mindless, Suárez's slave characters psychoanalyse their mistress and pander to her egocentrism, mitigate their suffering, and claim some control over their lives. By adopting a submissive posture, Francisco plays deliberately to "ole massa", feigning humility to appeal to what Orlando Patterson calls the slave owner's "see-what-I-mean" mentality.[35] Unlike the plantation arena, where the novel affords the reader a view of the master–slave divide as unambiguous, the house is depicted as a territory of negotiation between slave owner and slave. The author emphasizes the transactional nature of the slaves' relationship with their owner when Francisco advises Dorotea to don the meek mask to satisfy her mistress's need to see humility in her slaves.

While Francisco is inclined to see himself as a victim overwhelmed by his fate, Dorotea responds to her misfortune by engaging in elaborate bargaining with her mistress. Acting upon the awareness that submission is rewarded and recalcitrance punished, she employs sophisticated subterfuge to bring about a change of heart in Doña Dolores. She plans carefully to time her request for permission to marry Francisco to coincide with the New Year festivities, at which many visitors will be present. The slave is here shown to exploit her understanding of her mistress's psychic need for positive self-presentation, a need that is alluded to repeatedly in the latter's musings and conversations. The vocabulary used to describe Dorotea's negotiation is tellingly ironic. She succeeds in disarming her mistress through her sad tone and melancholy demeanour. Such metaphorical weapons are the only ones available to the slave, but she uses them to her advantage. Similarly, Francisco is not only cast in the role of a Christian martyr by the author, but he also wilfully adopts martyrdom as a pragmatic posture, a conscious strategy of self-protection. Ascribing such strategic thinking and action to his slave characters allows the author to pre-empt the charges of critics such as Fivel-Démoret, who would later accuse him of not ascribing agency to the slaves.[36]

Postcolonial theory of colonial discourse has foregrounded the reciprocal nature of colonizer–colonized relations: "The self-identity of the colonizing subject, indeed the identity of the imperial culture, is inextricable from the alterity of colonized others."[37] This syndrome is addressed in Suárez's tale through the paradoxical ties that bind slave and slave mistress. As the slaves' performance constitutes a conscious living up to the master's expectations, so too is the owner's response tantamount to involuntary fulfilment of the slaves' predictions. With the latter's frequently assumed prostrate position in her presence and their many demonstrations of devotion, the slave mistress's ascendancy seems assured. But her dependence on the slave for sustaining the image of her own goodness is seen graphically in Doña Dolores's elated response to Dorotea's respectful compliance:

She was filled with unspeakable joy when she heard her promise to forget him . . . and she felt even more satisfied with the mulatto's obedience because she believed that her humility was only the result of her desire to please her. [*Llenóse de indecible gusto al oírle que le prometía no acordarse más de él . . . y tanto más de satisfacción experimentó con la obediencia de la mulata cuanto que le pareció que su humildad nacía de sólo el deseo de complacerla.*][38]

Through this bifurcation of the view of the wise author/narrator (who is privy to the hypocrisy in the slave's expression of allegiance) and the belief of the gullible slave owner (who is blind to the slave's insincerity), the wished-for integrity of master's dominance over slave has once again been undermined.

Interracial sex and the attendant issues of power constitute what is perhaps the most pervasive theme of antislavery narrative. It ranks high on Suárez's agenda since it plays a large part in the oppression of both slaves. The house-slave privileges that Dorotea is allowed to enjoy come with a price: the sexual persecution she must endure. Central to the expression of this theme is the young slave master, Ricardo, a character whose role has not been fully evaluated. His pursuit of Dorotea not only bears witness to the destabilization of the separatist principle on which race relations were constructed but also underscores one of Tanco's themes: the divergence in outlook between the white Creole slave master, who was generally not averse to sexual liaisons with non-white women, and the white Creole slave mistress, who interpreted these liaisons as a grave threat.

In the world created by Suárez, sex is another area of negotiation in master–slave relations. Here one sees an erosion of white privilege, as it is the master who must bargain with the slave woman. Ricardo does not resort to vulgar sexual abuse, as was the custom of many slave masters. He seeks instead the more psychologically gratifying alternative of engaging the slave in a consensual sexual alliance. Dorotea, however, feels no desire for her white master, his social and racial privilege notwithstanding. The depth of the desperation that leads Ricardo to prostrate himself before her is equalled only by the contempt with which she rejects him. Moreover, the author/narrator's use of the term "bastard desires" [*bastardos deseos*][39] to describe Ricardo's feelings for Dorotea is an invitation to rethink the notion of illegitimacy as a feature of the social dynamic of colonial Cuba. Most frequently associated with the mulatto offspring of white slave owner and black slave woman, the condition of bastardy is here shifted to Ricardo, the legitimate Mendizábal son and heir. The creation of this dissonance between (illegitimate) desire and (legitimate) legal status is nothing less than a backhanded allusion to the unnaturalness of the master's power over the slave.

His awareness of the enslaved woman's elusive power is the cause of Ricardo's anguish. The contempt with which she rejects him in favour of the slave coachman wounds his pride and causes his power to falter. Thus the inviolability of Dorotea's free will marks equally the frontiers of the slave's bondage and the limits of the master's supremacy. In Ricardo's perplexed mind, the significance of the "wretched slave's" resistance lies in its patent incongruity with her social and racial status: the woman "overpowering" him is coloured and a slave.[40] Secretly encoded in this response is the ever-present Euro-Creole alarm over the threat to their dominance posed by the demographically superior African-descended Cuban slaves. In commenting on the coexistence of sex and slavery, Lewis asserts that "slave master met slave woman on unequal terms leading to her sexual exploitation".[41] However, Dorotea's capitulation to Ricardo's aggression is given a more ambivalent meaning. As a counterpoint to her victim persona, Suárez stresses the agency in her action. She *chooses* to sacrifice her honour and her happiness in the (futile) hope of saving her lover, a choice reminiscent of a similar self-sacrificial spirit in the acts of *petit marronage*, such as self-administered poison, abortion, self-inflicted illness and suicide, for which female slaves were famous.

Entangled in this web of sex and power is the white master's subliminal envy of the male slave's virility. It is this that explains Ricardo's insatiable cruelty towards Francisco, for not only is he preferred by Dorotea, but Francisco's masculine potency is made manifest through the act of procreation. Ricardo's symbolic emasculation of Francisco is therefore intended not only to bend Dorotea's will but also to allay his own sexual anxiety. Though Francisco is not presented in overtly sexual terms, the initial discreet reference to his proud bearing – he walked always with head held high – subsequently acquires sexual resonance. In the fourth chapter, after his body has been mangled by repeated whippings, this aspect of his demeanour is the only remnant that enables Dorotea to recognize him. The image is evoked tacitly again at the end of the story, in his suicide, where his hanging head symbolizes his ultimate castration.

Suárez's claim of humanity for the slaves does not cause him to minimize their cultural difference. Offsetting the account of the urban house slaves' proximity to the dominant white Creole culture is his recording of unique African cultural retentions in the everyday life of the field slaves. Under the antislavery rubric, Lewis includes the ideology immanent in these survivals that fuelled different types of resistance in the minds and actions of the slaves. Suárez mediates his Romantic idealization of the two protagonists and his naturalistic rendition of slave life on the plantation with *costumbrista* insertions that counterbalance the stereotype of the slave as subhuman and the misperception of slave culture as barbaric. His intense observation of slave music and dance prefigures the nationalistic interest that these cultural forms were to inspire in later writers, especially the poets of the 1920s *negrista* movement.

Suárez's description of the dance is remarkable in the rich resonance of its dramatic details.[42] He describes the performance using a neutral and transparent vocabulary, without the hyperbole and sensationalism of the grotesquely exaggerated imagery preferred by his *negrista* successors. The emphasis in his lengthy anthropological sketch is on making the unfamiliar intelligible to the uninitiated outsider. The account does not reflect the racism of the *negrista* writers, who invested animal sensuality in the black bodies they described. At first glance, Suarez's view of the scene appears to anticipate the voyeurism for which these writers would become known, but where the later *negrista* spectacle would fixate on the dancers to the exclusion of all others, Suárez's account captures the audience's active participation with the performers. Given the anti-African tenor of the dominant proslavery world view at this time in Cuba's history, the absence of any trace of white ethnocentrism in Suárez's comparison of African folk forms to those of Euro-Creole culture is remarkable. His enlightened vision is a far cry from the jaundiced perspective of the Havana sugar planters who in 1790 reported to the Spanish king that their barbaric African dances were the slaves' favourite form of entertainment.[43] One discerns an approving tone in the language of Suárez's account, suggesting openness to the slaves' cultural difference and a will to understand it in Negro terms.

Suárez displays more than a momentary interest in such activities of the slave community. His detailed exposition of the varied uses of song also bears witness to two of the processes that slavery entailed: resistance and accommodation. Whereas the emphatic tone with which the author calls attention to the resilience of this cultural practice translates metaphorically into the slaves' defiance of their bondage, the allusion to cultural interchange between African and Creole slaves attests to a con-current adaptation to the alien environment.[44] Such recognition of the validity and vibrancy of a distinct Negro counterculture may be interpreted as attribution of a self-constructed cultural identity to the slaves. Its dura-bility forms a contrast to Francisco's previously noted ephemeral accul-turation. By his own admission, this slave subculture provided Suárez with something to relieve the bleakness of the picture of oppression and suf-fering that confronted him during his stay at the Surinam estate. His fas-cination with African-derived song and dance makes unavoidable a comparison with the cultural void in the Euro-Creole world he creates in the novel.

Africa is also evoked in a more direct way, through the slave's autobio-graphical memory. In the first chapter Francisco recalls his idyllic African past, a strategy by which the author seeks to counteract the dominant view of African savagery. Here he promotes the minority Romantic view found (though not exclusively) in European literature. The theme of the African homeland makes a strategic reappearance at the end of the novel, in the slave's final thoughts before his death: "Without father, without mother, without brothers, without family, without friends, in Cuba, the land of the whites; a slave, a son of Africa and black" (*Sin padre, ni madre, ni her-manos, ni otro pariente alguno; sin amigos; en Cuba, tierra de blancos; esclavo, hijo de Africa y negro*).[45] Here Suárez uses punctuation to good effect: the staccato rhythm of the short phrases gives sensory expression to the slave's dispossession. His self-identification in the final phrase involves both separation from his imposed New World (slave) identity and reconnection with his African racial and national roots ("son of Africa and black"). Of greater significance than the obvious mythologizing of the African home is the author's imaginative interpretation of the meaning of slavery to the slave. Understood in a longer view, these details signal early recognition of the slave's connection to a vital African past of freedom and personal dignity. This perspective was to become a major theme in postcolonial accounts of slavery. That Suárez in his time lacked the knowledge and language to write about the real Africa does not diminish the importance of his thinking.

In *Francisco* Suárez has created a multifaceted picture of Cuban slavery in the first three decades of the nineteenth century. He turns the spotlight equally on slave and slave owner. Because of its potential for compromising the required unequivocal denunciation of slavery, his portrayal of the great divide between them does not obscure the ambiguities and hidden dimensions of their relationship. The ambivalence in his perspective of the slave experience might be disturbing for some readers. Some may even doubt the earnestness of his antislavery stance because of his disruption of the notion of unremitting enmity between the slaves and their enslavers and his suggestion that not all slaves were heroes or forthright in their resistance. Suárez's Christian humanitarianism collides with the radical political position of black nationalism, which is by definition humanist after the manner of René Descartes and Frantz Fanon, thinkers who invest the oppressed not only with the ability to recognize their subjugation but also with the power to end it.

In sketching his characters on both sides of the socio-economic and racial divide, the author displays his understanding of "the discrepancies between people's thoughts and their actions" and "the diversity of their wishful impulses", to use Sigmund Freud's expression.[46] Far from compromising the novel's overarching antislavery purpose, highlighting the ambivalence of the characters and the paradoxes of their relationships is one more way of undermining the established order of slave society, premised as it was on belief in the separation of an all-powerful and superior master class and a powerless and inferior slave body.

Suárez makes no pretence of objectivity, for his dissociation from the slave owners and their economic interests matches his identification with the slaves. Like his contemporaries, he vocalized his antislavery sentiments in a tacit dialogue with proslavery ideology. If one speculates only about the subversive elements that might have been excised from the novel, one is prone to miss the subversion it does offer. Netchinsky's observation that "there remains little in the speeches and dialogues of Suárez y Romero's characters that appears subversive in the slightest"[47] is difficult to defend, for *Francisco* is subversive in its entirety, even if not radically so.

To use the attitude and behaviour of the slave protagonist to prove otherwise is to ignore the many streams in Suárez's antislavery thought. These range from the significance of references to African cultural retentions to the various dimensions of his protagonist's character and the diverse oblique challenges to the notion of the superiority of Cuban planters and their European-derived culture. Francisco's egregious meekness and apparent mental enslavement may be viewed as counterproductive to the antislavery principle. Yet his consciousness of and discontent with his status and his enduring desire for freedom together constitute the difference between total submission at one extreme of the slave continuum and radical rebellion at the other. In lamenting the absence of a distinctive racial personality in Suárez's slave characters, Gabriel Coulthard concludes that the novelist was "too intent on presenting a revolting picture of the master-slave relationship to notice such things".[48] Even more damning is the judgement of Sharon Fivel-Démoret, who believes that *Francisco* is a novel that "actually confirms white dominance".[49] The preceding pages have sought to dispel such views by directing attention to the complexity of Suárez's vision and the additional meanings that emerge from the big picture of the novel when one plumbs the "murky depths" of its creative and ideological currents.

# ·3·

## CROSSED IDEOLOGICAL LINES

### *Gertrudis Gómez de Avellaneda's* Sab

ALTHOUGH GERTRUDIS GÓMEZ DE AVELLANEDA'S novel *Sab* was first published in Spain in 1841 (three years after her relocation to that country), its genesis, setting and subject matter have earned it a place in Cuba's literary canon. Cuban-born of Spanish descent, Avellaneda spent the first twenty-two years of her life in Puerto Príncipe (Camagüey), which is where most of the novel takes place. Its difference from *Petrona y Rosalía* and *Francisco* is attributable in part to the author's gender and her distance from the centre of agitation against slavery, the del Monte literary circle. With its many thematic threads, *Sab* presents multiple possibilities for interpretation. Since the nineteenth century this novel has been the subject of extensive critical coverage. Following its publication it received general approval in Spain but was perceived as threatening by Cuba's colonial administration. Its entry into Cuba was banned in 1844, which did much to boost its reputation as a subversive text. Subsequent opinion has been divided, and its various interpretations have at times been regarded as mutually exclusive.

Some commentators have referred *Sab* to the literary conventions of its day; Catherine Davies's inscription of the work within the sentimental novel tradition is a recent example.[1] An incisive formalist reading has been proposed by Jill Netchinsky, who gives a lucid demonstration of its structural balance and of the author's mastery of rhetorical strategies. Davies, writing in a similar vein, has discovered new significance in the author's use of gift-giving as a literary trope that evinces the connection between domestic and political economies.[2] Many reviewers take their cue from the author's position as the lone female among the antislavery authors, and by exploring its feminist underpinnings, recent scholarship has extended the work's revolutionary reach. Featured in other critical programmes are ancillary themes emerging from the work, such as the politics of race. Its connection to the literature of the broader region of the Americas and to US and British traditions has inspired another recent trend in the study of this work.[3] Moralistic meditations on subjects such as the nature of love, jealousy and desire, its adaptation of European Romantic conventions to a New World reality, and its *costumbrista* interludes, which link it to the early Latin American narrative tradition, are also noteworthy features of this multilayered novel.

Its ideological significance has been the most vigorously contested aspect of this novel. Some scholars have characterized *Sab* as categorically abolitionist, unlike contemporary male-authored narratives, which are normally referred to more reluctantly as "reformist". Others have questioned its relevance to the struggle against slavery. Sharon Fivel-Démoret's claim that it "attacks the institution of slavery with greater forthrightness" than other novels[4] and Stacey Schlau's reference to the novel as "clearly and irrevocably abolitionist"[5] appear to compete with William Luis's description of its denunciation of slavery as marginal.[6] Writing in 1997, Brígida Pastor minimized its Romantic features and antislavery significance to promote her view that expression of the author's feminist ideology is the novel's "prime and sole message".[7] For reasons that will become clear, some of the views expressed in studies of the novel are not inevitably incompatible. Interpreting it through a postmodern optic can mediate the conflict between the various critical readings.

In elaborating on the link between culture and imperialism, postcolonial literary theorist Edward Said has appropriated the musical concept of counterpoint and applied it to analysis of narrative discourse. The contrapuntal reading technique gives primacy to the reader's role in the meaning-production process. It can revitalize literary texts by reading against the grain of their manifest meanings or their authors' intentions.[8] As an instance of postmodern thought, this general interpretive strategy has been adopted in many postcolonial appraisals of colonial writing. The present reading of *Sab* will dismantle the text that Avellaneda has constructed to reveal how its subliminal subscription to mainstream ideology sabotages its oppositional discourse and, conversely, how antislavery meaning may be seen to underlie its ostensibly transparent content.

Lorna Williams and Jerome Branche have taken an appropriately sceptical line of interpretation of the novel. The former uncovers the conservative assumptions and implications of the feminization of Sab's character, and her analysis leads her to conclude that this strategy simultaneously ennobles the slave and confirms the slaveholder's sense of her own importance.[9] Branche, in like fashion, has read political meaning into important areas of silence in the novel, which causes him to challenge its abolitionist classification.[10] To complement these findings, in this chapter I will examine the text's heteroglossia (to borrow a Bakhtinian term), that is, its orchestration of competing and complementary voices,[11] with particular attention to the content, context and motivation of utterances by different characters. Rather than seeking to locate the novel in a discrete ideological category, the analysis will shed light on the peculiar strategies of its ambivalent and often tacit participation in the slavery debate.

The novel tells a Romantic story of the secret, all-consuming love of Sab, a mulatto slave, for Carlota, the daughter of his white master, Don Carlos de B. Sab is the illegitimate son of his master's deceased brother, Luis, and as such he is given a privileged place within the family as well as the nominal position of overseer, a job usually reserved for whites. In a society with no tolerance for sexual unions between white females and non-white males, Sab's love is doomed to be unrequited. Oblivious to the slave's feelings, Carlota gives her heart to Enrique Otway, the opportunistic son of a rapacious British merchant. Having lived only for Carlota, Sab dies as she marries Otway, a marriage that he has facilitated by anonymously donating his winning lottery ticket for the bride's dowry. Also playing a critical role, as confidante to both Sab and Carlota, is Teresa,

Carlota's impoverished cousin, who renounces her own secret love for Otway and retires to a convent, where she achieves peace of mind. Meanwhile Carlota's dreams of happiness are shattered by the bitter reality of marriage.

*Sab* continues the tradition of transmitting antislavery messages through individual voices in dialogue with each other. Here, however, its similarity with other contemporary narratives ends. To begin with, in the latter, proslavery ideology is planted but not allowed to flourish, for it is frequently eroded by a dominant oppositional discourse. *Sab* reverses this paradigm, as the illusion of radical opposition to slavery evaporates in the light of a conservative subtext and the use of counterproductive narrative strategies. Avellaneda's attack on slavery is most clearly expressed through her characters' propagandistic rhetoric. Their utterances, designed to conform to the author's aspirations to positive self-presentation, are almost religiously fraught with contradictions and inconsistencies. In the two narratives studied so far, the prevailing voices, whether of the characters or the author/narrators, serve as consistent purveyors of the ideology the author would promote. Avellaneda, on the other hand, is somewhat more promiscuous than her predecessors in assigning roles to her characters, putting antislavery language or words with potential antislavery meaning into their mouths without regard for their race or social status. White characters are as likely as (and sometimes more likely than) the mulatto slave protagonist to make assertions or suggestions opposing slavery.

The tone is set in the very first chapter, in the meeting between Sab and Enrique Otway. Acting as an informant for the outsider, the slave compresses into a thumbnail sketch a complete picture of the plantation-slave experience that amounts to a robust assault on slavery as a system of forced labour.[12] In chilling detail he paints for Otway a picture of the brutality, degradation and hopelessness experienced by the slave. Simultaneously, certain aspects of the exchange between the two characters render this statement less than convincing. In the first place, Sab's criticism is not spontaneous; it is extracted, as it were, by Otway's prior allusion to the slaves' harsh existence. Furthermore, as the immediate supervisor of the field slaves, Sab would be expected to play a large role in implementation of the oppressive work regime he describes. Yet his words imply denial of his own agency. In fact, prior to the description referenced above, Sab's first words on the subject of slavery (a dispassionate comment on the economy of sugar production on the Bellavista estate) assume a planter perspective. His neglect of slave labour as the basis of that economy, and of slavery as a social ill, does not escape the reader's notice. Such a consciousness is instead invested in Otway, who insinuates that the slaves' death from ill-treatment is responsible for the decline of the estate. Contrary to expectation, Sab quickly dispels the implied criticism by attributing the decline to the sale of slaves and land. Not only has this explanation diminished the potentially subversive impact of his earlier account of the slaves' lot, but it also translates into pandering to the Cuban sugarocracy, to which the transplanted Avellaneda presumably still felt loyalty and attachment.

Moreover, Sab's synopsis of the horrors of the slaves' lived reality is quarantined within the episode to avoid contamination of the work's Romantic aura. There is hardly any difference in tone between the stylized language he uses to describe the brutality of slavery and the narrator's lighter descriptions of the exemplary good looks of the two men and the remarkable beauty of the landscape. Sab's characterization of slavery as "a cruel spectacle" aptly reflects his posture of detached voyeurism. Although the author has staged the scene in order for the slave to provide an insider's view of slavery, it is Otway the outsider – the literal "tourist voyeur" – who has effectively supplanted him to make the more meaningful critique of slavery.

Carlota's expression of sorrow for the slaves is intended to fulfil a similarly subversive purpose and fits into an equally ambivalent rhetorical pattern.[13] Her words strip away the façade of good treatment to reveal the dehumanization at the heart of their bondage. Yet various anomalies inhere in this lament. Not content with merely investing awareness of the evils of slavery in this member of the slave-owning class, Avellaneda allows her to go further, by denying such awareness to the slaves. Also telling is the placement of Carlota's utterance. It follows closely on the heels of a preemptive statement whose purpose is to establish the goodness of this slave-owning family. In response to her charming kindness towards them, the slaves shower a tearful Carlota with their blessings and extol the benevolence of Don Carlos, their master, and Sab, their overseer. With such an expression of gratitude, the previously noted anomaly of Sab's overseer role dissipates as the slaves are explicitly co-opted to block any notion of his cruel exercise of this function.

What this illusion of humane and individualized treatment of slaves further disguises is the contingency of slave owner benevolence upon slave demonstrations of subservience. Carlota, despite her protestations, is gratified by this display. Her words also relieve the slave owner of responsibility for their bondage. Carlota's tears bear no relation to the experience of the Bellavista slaves; far from being miserable, they endure their servitude with gracious contentment. Rebellion can have no place in such a scenario. Carlota's subsequent failure to fulfil her pledge to free all her slaves after her marriage to Otway also detracts from the sincerity of her lament. Her pronouncement against slavery is therefore discredited as a puerile promise associated with the rashness and idealism of youth.

As noted in the case of *Francisco*, the linguistic divide separating Euro-Creole authors from their slave subjects was an impediment to the emergence of a true slave voice in this narrative tradition. Avellaneda circumvents this hurdle by creating Sab as a slave educated according to Euro-Creole norms and by giving him a language with which to speak. It is a language that, after the manner of the subaltern Caliban in Shakespeare's *The Tempest*, he uses to inveigh against the slavery establishment. To Sab is given the task of delivering what Jill Netchinsky refers to as "the most daring antislavery speeches".[14] The speeches bring to mind the type of propagandistic utterances in Suárez's work that del Monte described critically as "preaching".[15] A close look will help to put their radical content into perspective.

In his extended conversation with Teresa that opens the second part of the novel, Sab demonstrates his understanding of the social and political origins of discrimination against the slave person. Despite the profundity of his insight, the studied modulations of the slave's voice give a purely rhetorical sound to this speech. Sab himself makes light of its implications when he hastens to allay Teresa's fears of an impending slave revolt. Like Carlota before him, he assumes the slaves' absolute and mindless victimhood. It seems, furthermore, that for Avellaneda it is not enough to make Sab default in his reasonably expected duty to his suffering fellow slaves; he must also explicitly renounce the rebel-leader role, thereby implicitly betraying his allegiance to his owners. It is also not insignificant that what triggers the slave's indignation is his personal dilemma created by Carlota's inaccessibility, and that his contemplation of vengeful revolt against his enslavers is similarly informed by individualistic motives.

In his posthumously released letter to Teresa, Sab fires a virtual barrage against the ideology of slavery, challenging the racist bigotry in its logic, attacking the Church for its role in maintaining the status quo, and contesting the social construction of his identity. Like the voice modulations in his earlier speech to Teresa, the proliferation of rhetorical questions in the letter invites a reading of this utterance as a staged dramatic performance. Though rhetorically powerful and boldly militant, these expressions leave much to be desired in the way of conviction and sincerity. Although Sab speaks with the tongue of a rebel, his protest is uttered in a contextual vacuum, having little basis in either his lived experience or that of his fellow Bellavista slaves. Slavery as denounced through this rhetoric is practised elsewhere, for the Bellavista slaves' situation is one of ignorant bliss. They are no more than a phantom presence in the novel, putting in only momentary appearances to shore up their owners' liberal image and to deflect the focus from their status as exploited labourers producing wealth for their owners' consumption. Thus the novel's condemnation of slavery and the support for abolition it implies come across in real terms as only half-hearted, for in each of the foregoing instances the author has contrived to undermine the rhetoric of slavery's chief critic. Sab pays lip service to the dissident cause, but little if any credibility can be ascribed to the words of one suspected of complicity with his enslavers. Richard Jackson's comment on this aspect of the novel is even more damning: he characterizes Sab's pronouncements as camouflage for Avellaneda's "natural repulsion towards the black".[16]

Sab's flamboyant oratory conveys a conscious and direct critique of slavery. His theatrical utterances are complemented by other, subliminal and oblique expressions of the message. In the opening episode, for example, Otway assumes from his almost-white appearance that Sab is a slave owner. Through Sab's response the author studiously dispels the illusion: "I am not an estate owner, esteemed stranger, and though the heart that I feel beating in my chest may always be ready to sacrifice itself for Don Carlos, I cannot call myself his friend" (*No soy propietario, señor forastero, y aunque sienta latir en mi pecho un corazón pronto siempre a sacrificarse por don Carlos, no puedo llamarme amigo suyo*).[17]

Sab's identification of Otway as a foreigner brings to mind the travel writers who visited Cuba during the period, and the fine distinctions in the race and power relations of slave society that escaped their untrained eyes. Thus Sab gives the lie to the myth of Cuba and the other Iberian colonies as less racist than other New World slave societies, a myth recruited as part of the slavery apologetic. This discrepancy between appearance and reality is highlighted with similarly subversive effect in the psychological and emotional spheres of Sab's experience.

Using the North American one-drop-of-black-blood criterion of racism, some reviews of the novel refer to Sab as a black slave. This is the premise on which Richard Jackson, for example, makes his case for the antislavery/anti-black paradox he discerns in the novel: "some of the nineteenth-century writers were reluctant to accept blackness as being aesthetically pleasing. This reluctance . . . led some authors to depict 'black' protagonists with white features that clearly distinguish them from other black Africans, and is especially acute in Gertrudis Gómez de Avellaneda's *Sab*."[18] Catherine Davies surmises, somewhat more generously, that Avellaneda's choice of a mulatto slave protagonist is a function of the sentimental novel imperative, since black signified revulsion and white readers would not have empathized with a black slave protagonist.[19] Sab's dilemma is fully understood not in the light of the insufficiency of his blackness or the expediency of his near-whiteness, but from the perspective of his specific mulatto (that is, hybrid) identity.

Having shunned the classic image of physical brutality visited upon the body of the ostracized black slave, the novelist turns to the less visible but equally painful injury to the psyche of the co-opted mulatto slave. His psychopathology is the measure of Sab's individuality, and it translates into the author's fundamental objection to this form of slavery. Attention is drawn to Sab's emotional torment through his forbidden thoughts. His privileged position and appearance are at odds with his mental state, and outward complicity with his servitude masks deeper feelings of discontent. Attributing this subjectivity to the slave is in itself an ideological challenge to shallow perceptions of the mulatto as a "felicitous human type produced by ethnic fusion of Iberian and Negro", as Castagnaro has put it.[20]

Analyses that use the ideal-slave model to measure Sab's character portrait have tended to advertise its shortcomings, which arguably function to buttress the ideological foundations of slavery. Any suggestion of the need for resistance or revolt is blocked by his benign slave experience and his proximity to the slave-owning class. His manifest docility and his refusal of the offer of manumission and of the rebel-leader role also aggravate the charge of ideological conservatism. Yet one may discern an underlying layer of antislavery meaning in this very syndrome, for Sab's story is an ironic commentary on the damaging psychological consequences of the mulatto slave's assimilation into the master's world.

The essence of Sab's socially constructed identity is his difference from the common slaves, from whom he is separated both physically and psychologically. Otway remarks on his "refined and noble air" that distinguishes him from other, "coarse and servile" slaves. Writing in the 1960s, Frantz Fanon notes a similar condition for acceptance of coloured students in France. "Society refuses to consider them genuine Negroes. The Negro is a savage, whereas the student is civilized."[21] At the same time, Carlota's assertion that Sab has not been confused with the other slaves begs the ironic inference that, though not to be confused objectively with the common slaves, in his own mind Sab is a confused man, the incarnation of a paralysing psychic ambivalence. In a society that promotes racial division and holds white as the ideal and black as its inferior polar opposite, Sab's racial in-betweenness leads to his confusion. Caught between two poles, he finds himself trapped in limbo.

The psychoanalytical insights derived from Fanon's reflections on the effects of colonialism on the psyche of the colonized are pertinent to our understanding of the mulatto slave protagonist. In elaborating his thesis of the family as the environment that engenders psychological health or sickness, Fanon cites Joachim Marcus: "The family structure is internalized in the superego . . . and projected into political [though I would say *social*] behaviour."[22] Unlike Rosalía's ostracism in Tanco's story, Sab's blood connection with the de B family is given tacit acknowledgement. On the surface, his position within the family is an instance of what is often cited defensively as an indicator of the greater fortune of slaves in the Iberian colonies. David Turnbull, for example, reporting on his travels to Cuba in the first half of the nineteenth century, noted in the planter household "a little colony of slaves of every variety of complexion from ebony to alabaster". He continues:

> Most of them have been born in the house, have grown with the growth of the family and are perhaps foster brothers or foster sisters of the master or his children. In such circumstances, it would be surprising if an uncivilized barbarian were to treat them harshly; and for a Spanish, and much more for a Creole, master to do so, imbued as he is with all the warmth of the social affections, is totally out of the question.[23]

This impression has been largely erased in the nineteenth-century fictions and early post-independence historical accounts that emphasize the universal brutality of slavery. Postcolonial theory of colonial discourse, however, has sought to understand master–slave relations neutrally – in terms of different modes of coexistence – rather than exclusively – in terms of either absolute antagonism or perfect harmony. Though it merely alludes to the existence of a hostile form of master–slave relations, *Sab* has laid bare the forgotten frictions of an apparently conflict-free mode of coexistence. Her slave protagonist's psychological profile is the main basis for Avellaneda's cynical view of the "benign" practice of slavery.

The author traces the roots of Sab's personality and temperament, as well as his sense of his own identity, back to his socialization as an elite slave, and more specifically to the false sense of equality and the dissimilation that it fostered. Despite his outward and constant self-deprecation,

Sab's collusion with the ideology of slavery is not total; his behaviour also contains an element of role-playing and self-restraint in the presence of his owners. To enable the emergence of another persona from behind his mask, the author recruits Teresa, to whom Sab bares his soul in their meeting on the riverbank. Here it emerges that he has misread Carlota's sisterly love as erotic. His misperception is confirmed economically in the sole instance of physical contact between the two characters. Emboldened by Carlota's (innocent) embrace, Sab kisses her hand. The shocked discomfort in Carlota's response to his unwanted overture and her expression of mystification as she recoils from this passionate gesture admit no suggestion of reciprocity on her part.[24]

Teresa diagnoses Sab's malady when she points to the dysfunctional effect of a family upbringing that exposed him to the danger of sexual attraction to Carlota. Similarly, Otway's earlier questioning of the usefulness of education to an enslaved man has a double edge. Though intended as an endorsement of the slave's presumed inferiority, it serves as an indictment of the paradox of this allegedly benign practice of slavery: the "(mis)education" for which Sab is held up as superior is also shown to be the root cause of his psychological misfortune. Inspired by fictions about mixed-race love, Sab aspires to win Carlota's affection. Hence, what is being criticized is the (self-)delusion of the co-opted mulatto slave who has been led to believe in an illusory equality.

Sab's tragedy is not only the futility of his quixotic desire for Carlota but also his deterministic perception of his identity. By representing himself as trapped in the quandary of natural potential arrested and repressed by slave society's racist ideology, Sab seeks to exonerate himself and to lay the blame for his inaction and passivity on the social order. While he denies or is denied social and political agency, he, paradoxically enough, can claim for himself only the autonomy of a "career" slave, one who has *chosen* to play different slave roles. His tragedy also lies in his false consciousness, his inability to mediate or reconcile the two poles of his ethnic makeup or to compensate for his exclusion from the dominant Euro-derived group by connecting with his African heritage.

In contrast with the epidermal transformation of Suárez's Francisco,

Sab's acculturation extends to the far reaches of his psyche. His rootlessness and alienation result from his entrapment in a binary and hierarchical mode of thought. His cursory rhetorical identification with the black slaves pales in comparison with his persistence in the futile hope of full assimilation into the ranks of the white Creole elite. The historical grounds of this desire have been established in Martínez-Alier's study of marriage practices and racial and sexual attitudes in nineteenth-century Cuba, where it is noted that increasing dissolution of the demarcating colour lines was attended by strong aspirations among the mulatto population to improve their racially determined inferior social status.[25] When he recalls his mother's royal pedigree in the first chapter, Sab is merely expressing a typical subaltern psychological need: to prove self-worth in a society where lineage is a critical variable in determining status.

If Sab understands that a love relationship with Carlota is socially taboo, no less inconceivable to him is a relationship with a non-white woman. Though he laments his lack of a woman's love, in his imagination the category *woman* includes only white women. Mulatto slave characters in similar narratives, though not the beneficiaries of comparable privileges, are shown to enjoy greater psychological health. Despite her preferential treatment, in Tanco's *noveleta* Rosalía identifies with her black mother, and in the case of Suárez's Dorotea, her mulatto identity does not prevent her from loving the black slave Francisco. Sab, on the other hand, implicitly and almost totally identifies with and desires full integration into the family of his white father. His tragedy is both his social marginalization and, more specifically, the warped mentality it creates. A Freudian reading of a line in his letter in which he speaks of the burden of his thoughts is a signpost that points to the enslavement of Sab's mind.[26] Such references to his psychological bondage pervade the novel; their abundance is indicative of the importance the novelist attaches to this theme in her critique of slavery. Given his psychic disposition, Sab's repeated refusal of offers of freedom is natural. His physical freedom is a contingency of his mental freedom. His Euro-Creole education aids his intellectual opposition to slavery while hindering his capacity for political action. In the final analysis, therefore, the more critical perspective of the educational "benefit" of the mild form of slavery is the one that prevails. Sab's education has effectively converted him into a wordsmith – rational and articulate, but ineffective. Criticism of this (dys)function of colonial education would become one of the main themes in post-independence Caribbean writing.

It is a commonly held view that Sab, the slave, is a figure of the author. Nara Araujo, for example, has theorized that he is Avellaneda's alter ego.[27] Yet Avellaneda can be identified neither consistently nor exclusively with her protagonist; his voice is not always hers. On the contrary, there are moments when the novelist seems deliberately to distance herself from him by allowing other characters to critique his postures and to point the way to "right" thinking and action. Through Otway's judgement of Sab's psychological complicity in his own enslavement, the author may even be seen to implicitly anticipate Fanon's prescription of "nothing short of the liberation of the man of colour from himself" as a treatment for the inferiority complex sown in the minds of the slaves and their descendants.[28] Fanon's injunction to the black man to "wage war on both levels [subjective and objective] since any unilateral liberation is incomplete" is also applicable to Sab's malaise.[29]

In this regard, Teresa plays an important role as the voice that tries to sensitize Sab to the shared nature of his slave experience. In like fashion, the injunction of his surrogate mother, the old Indian rebel Martina – "lift up your head, son of a slave woman" (*levanta tu frente, hijo de la esclava*)[30] – seeks to egg him on to assertive action. Yet Sab remains trapped by his ego and blinded by his single-minded obsession with thwarting Otway's union with Carlota. In this show of authorial detachment, Avellaneda has thus chosen the situation of the slave residing in the bosom of the slave-owning family and treated it with no less critical an eye or subversive an intent than her contemporaries, who preferred to focus on the slave in the remote location of the sugar estate. In the final analysis, the portrayal of Sab's character signals not so much the author's promotion of a docile slave stereotype as her demystification of the elite-slave fable.

Sab is more a figure of the historical mulatto than one might think from merely looking at his Romantic profile. Similarly, Carlota's elevation to celestial status (by Sab and the narrator) is not merely a convention for depicting the Romantic heroine but was based on lived sociological reality. Barbara Bush's observations about the British colonies no doubt have Caribbean-wide relevance. A consequence of the consolidation of sugar monoculture, Bush notes, was the artificial elevation of the leisured white woman as the embodiment of virtue and gentility, and the equally artificial debasement of the black woman as "scarlet wench or passive workhorse".[31] "White women's superiority and sexual untouchability", she continues, "were emphasized in order to reinforce the cultural and racial distinctions necessary for the preservation of slavery".[32] Avellaneda writes the false images of black wench and mulatto prostitute out of the text but promotes the false image of white female virtue. She expresses this supremacy structurally by making Carlota, the Romantic idol and object of Sab's obsessive love, the subject of much of the novel, despite the title's implication to the contrary.

The pervasiveness of the theme of cross-racial sex in the narratives and history of slavery reflects its importance to the politics of colonial society, the hallmarks of which were prohibition of interracial sex and promotion of endogamy. While shared love between a mulatto slave and a woman of the white slave-owning elite was both literary and real anathema in colonial Cuba, Sab's adoration of Carlota poses no threat to the dominant ideology. It does double duty as a Romantic trope and as a manifestation of the real relations of power. It does this and it does more: it represents (and is represented as) a supreme act of transgression by the slave. The desire Sab feels for Carlota lies outside the pale of his owners' racist imagination, and therefore beyond their power to foresee, prevent or control. Only fulfilment of the slave's desire can be proscribed by his owners; desire itself knows no bounds. More risqué still is the carnality of the slave's perception of and desire for Carlota, which erupts into the discourse of Romantic love. Carlota is both the angel of Sab's dreams and the woman who ignites the fiery passion of his waking hours. The ultimate revolutionary statement in this interracial drama would have been, of course, to make Carlota reciprocate Sab's love, even secretly. But envisaging the slave's desire for his white mistress marks the limits of Avellaneda's transgression of the dominant racial ideology.

Teresa's offering of herself to Sab as a surrogate for Carlota has often been cited as a symptom of Avellaneda's liberal attitude towards this version of interracial sex. This offer, however, is a token gesture, inspired by pity for the slave, who interprets it as such, and which therefore does not qualify as meaningful transgression. Carlota, on the other hand, betrays in both word and deed her acceptance of the social and racial barriers to interracial love. Moreover, fully steeped in her society's racial and sexual mythology, she responds with horror to the idea of Teresa, a white woman, loving Sab, a slave: "Love him! Love him! . . . Love him! . . . Oh, that's not possible! . . . Love him! . . . him, a slave! . . . Love is for tender and passionate hearts . . . like yours and mine" (*¡Amarle! ¡amarle! . . . ¡amarle!. . . . ¡oh, no es posible! . . . ¡Amarle! . . . ¡a él, a un esclavo! . . . el amor es para los corazones tiernos, apasionados . . . como el tuyo, como el mío*).[33] Once again the novelist distances herself from Carlota's prejudiced view, through Otway's corrective voice reminding her that love can abide in any heart. This comment, though intended to defend Teresa's humanity, is by inference a vindication of the humanity of the slave.

Somewhat greater revolutionary significance may be claimed for the author's allusion to a relationship of mutual love between black slave woman and white master. The converse of formal prohibition of exogamous liaisons was tacit acceptance in some quarters of the widespread sexual exploitation of enslaved women by their masters. This model of interracial sexual relations, a commonplace of antislavery fiction, is the one that led most frequently to the destabilizing of slave society's racial divide. Thus it is that much has been made of the revolutionary significance of Avellaneda's reversal of the interracial model through Sab's love for Carlota. Relatively less attention has been paid to the sexual liaison between Sab's black slave mother and his white slave-master father. Avellaneda's representation of this experience also bears her trademark ambiguity. As an initial indictment of slavery, Sab's evocation of his mother's life story accentuates briefly the suffering of her violent uprooting from Africa.[34] But the novelist soon makes short shrift of this vision of suffering, replacing it with a message of adaptation.

Like her son after her, Sab's mother falls in love with her white owner.

This love magically renews her "African spirit" and compensates for her displacement and bondage. But her love, unlike Sab's love for Carlota, is reciprocated. In addition, she maintains secrecy about the identity of her son's father, further suggesting collusion with her enslaver. This is echoed by the father's secret acceptance of paternity and his ensuring Sab's well-being by entrusting him to his brother's care before he dies. This privileging of consensual interracial sex, coupled with failure to portray the slave woman in the classic role of victim of sexual abuse, is susceptible to interpretation as a defence of one of the most iniquitous aspects of slavery. However, filtered through a postcolonial lens, this episode acquires another meaning. It is now well-established and generally accepted that the story of interracial sex in slave society was a story of rape in some cases (the vast majority) and romance in others. Sab's mother escapes the agent/victim binary: she is not a victim or an agent, but a victim *and* an agent.

In Avellaneda's favour, it might even be said that her (consensual) romance version of cross-racial sex deals as severe a blow to slavery's ideology of racial separatism as the more prevalent and violent rape version. Likewise, given the sexual threat that white slave mistresses perceived in black slave women, conceiving the mother's agency as initiator of the sexual liaison has more subtly subversive implications. Her representation as a sexual agent is no less heretical than the standard representation of female slaves as sexual victims. Such a view is a reminder that if, as is being increasingly recognized, the slave community and their responses were not monolithic, narratives whose object was to criticize slavery did not constitute a homogeneous corpus. The value of Avellaneda's contribution to this diversity must not be underestimated. Through Sab's experience the novel obliquely attacks the double standard governing interracial sex. It foregrounds the impossibility of union between male slave and white female, which makes Carlota's romantic interest in Sab unthinkable, but it also calls attention to the society's tacit acceptance of the union of white male and female slave.

It is not difficult to concur with Mary Cruz's characterization of the world of the novel as illusory.[35] Sab is an "elite" slave and an exceptional overseer on an exceptional sugar estate. As an invention of a Romantic imagination, the novel might indeed lead the reader to overlook its ambiguous participation in the politics of slave society. *Sab* was not intended as total fantasy – witness the documentary details of the natural landscape and the sprinkling of references to historical reality. Besides this, it carries within it the seeds of its own deconstruction. Invisibly present is a subtextual layer of meaning that has as much to do with Avellaneda's ideological location as a Euro-Creole woman from a slave-owning family as with her adaptation of the European Romantic model to a New World context.

The exigencies of the novel's Romantic mode may account for the disproportion in Avellaneda's representation of the slave experience, which gives precedence to the emotional variant of the standard motif of the suffering slave. Nonetheless, various recalcitrant emblems of slavery in the historical world resist erasure by the discourse of Romanticism and elicit an antislavery reaction. One instance is the location of Sab's midnight meeting with Teresa on the riverbank behind the cane fields. The author transforms the cane fields into a mere backdrop for the scene and turns the spotlight on Sab's self-indulgent confession of the emotional pain of unrequited love. The venue of the meeting nonetheless calls attention to itself for another reason. In juxtaposition with Sab's individual suffering, the shadowy fields loom large as the historical site of untold physical abuse of the vast masses of the slave population. Yet another instance of such ironic, though implicit, juxtapositioning is the recasting of the sugar estate, a hell-world of unspeakable torment, as the paradise of Carlota's childhood memories.[36] Even more paradoxically evocative of slavery's horror is the lovelorn Sab's conversion of this sugar estate – a place from which real slaves risked their lives to escape – into a place of voluntary exile and refuge.[37] When Sab claims to be sacrificing himself on the altar of pain,[38] the emotional agony of his self-immolation on the altar of love has the contrary (albeit unintentional) effect of bringing to mind the physical torture of slaves sacrificed on the altar of the sugar plantation.

To impugn enslavers, both male and female, for slavery's atrocities is one purpose of works such as *Petrona y Rosalía* and *Francisco*. Criticism of the Creole slave-owning elite, another pervasive theme, takes on a special nuance in *Sab*. In the first place, the de B family members are criticized not as perpetrators of the wrongs of slavery but for their sins of omission: their failure to safeguard their power and Cuba's patrimony (represented by Carlota) from the inroads of the foreign interloper (represented by the Otways). Standing as Cuban Euro-Creole models are Don Carlos, who, like his counterpart in *Petrona y Rosalía*, is ineffective, and his deceased brother Luis, whose concern for the well-being of his illegitimate mulatto son, Sab, places him above reproach. As a foil for the Otways, Don Carlos is neither greedy nor materialistic. His ostensible liberal-mindedness does not admit the stereotypical class consciousness of the Euro-Creole elite and the crass materialism of the foreign merchants. Though accustomed to the pleasures of plenty, he is, in the words of the narrator, unconcerned about status, power or wealth. Read in a contrapuntal light, this attempt to vindicate Don Carlos is ironically undermined: the non-materialistic sugar planter enjoys his wealth without appreciating the human price paid by the slaves who generate it.

A landmark occasion in the story is Sab's reporting of Martina's seditious prediction of bloodshed by the Negro slaves to avenge their Amerindian predecessors.[39] Unlike other incidents of his protest against slavery, Sab repeats this grim forecast in the presence of the de B family. Testimony to his understanding of its radical import is the assertive persona assumed by Don Carlos, hitherto the epitome of weakness and apathy. He silences Sab with a sharp rebuke, which the narrator attributes to negrophobia inspired in the Cuban planters by the Haitian slave revolt. It is a response that implicitly undermines the notion of the enslaver's unassailable dominance. Don Carlos betrays his anxiety in two ways: by his derision of Martina, whom he subsequently describes as a lunatic, and by his suppression of Sab's voice. Don Carlos's assertion of his authority as the father who places a gag on the slave son brings to mind Fanon's theory of the "repressed [African] spirit in the consciousness of the slave by the authority symbol representing the Master".[40] The slave master/father's approval is once again a reward for good behaviour only, pointing in effect to the malignancy of the "benign" practice of slavery. Don Carlos is innocuous only until he feels threatened by the slave.

Sab's words might incline us to conclude, as does Netchinsky, that he has more in common with the black slave rebels of the Haitian Revolution than with his exoticized Romantic equivalent in the European literary tradition.[41] But any concession to his affiliation with such resistance must be tempered by the proviso that it is entirely verbal. Keen scrutiny of the details surrounding the statement, and the manner in which it is spoken, will reveal a surreptitious attenuation of the message. To begin with, in the same way that Sab is created as a non-functioning overseer, the shaping of this utterance as an act of ventriloquy – a mouthing of words originally spoken by the Amerindian-descended Martina – again denies the slave's engagement with the discourse of rebellion. He assumes instead his distinctive oratorical role as a channel for Martina's subversive thoughts. Thus another opportunity for genuine protest by an actual slave is squandered. Moreover, his editorial mediations of Martina's words further dilute the radical message. Sab's description of Martina's manner in terms that bespeak derangement also takes away credibility from the utterance.

This incident is often cited as a defining antislavery moment in the novel. However, it loses much of its vigour when taken in conjunction with the belittling references by the narrator and Don Carlos to Martina's "superlatively ugly face" (*semblante superlativamente feo*) and her "ridiculously majestic air" (*aire ridículamente majestuoso*)[42] – this in a novel in which the subaltern figures are generally romanticized. Sab pre-empts the assault on slavery inherent in Martina's frightful prophecy with this largely rhetorical strategy to placate the anxieties of his slave-owning audience. His loyalty to his owners must therefore supersede concern about slavery and its discontents. And so the radical voice of resistance has been twice muzzled – by the emasculated slave and by the negrophobic slave owner.

Despite this restraint, Martina's pronouncement is important because it expands the scope of the antislavery theme. By projecting the struggle against slavery as a continuation of Amerindian resistance against the Spanish *conquistadores*, this declaration anticipates Cuban political discourse of more than a century later, when the Castro-led Revolution came to be represented as the latest episode in a long liberation struggle of which nineteenth-century slave revolts were an early manifestation. Neither is the reference to the past to be regarded as fortuitous; there are insistent, though ambiguous, references to the Amerindian origins claimed by Martina and reluctantly conceded by the narrator in this episode. These references hark back to the narrator's earlier attempt to construct Sab's racial identity. The Amerindian legacy, albeit by means of a discourse of absence, is placed on an equal footing with Cuba's white and black ethnic heritage: "He neither looked like a white Creole, nor was he black or to be taken for a descendant of one of the first inhabitants of the Antilles" (*No parecía un criollo blanco, tampoco era negro ni podía creérsele descendiente de los primeros habitadores de las Antillas*).[43]

In addition, although Martina's militant Amerindian voice has been silenced on this occasion, it is recalled in Sab's posthumous letter. In contrast to the emasculating effects of his implied identification with his white heritage, Martina invokes Sab's black slave origins explicitly to inspire him to resist his bondage. These are the signs of the author's more inclusive view of Cuba's colonial history, in which the European and African interaction has been the dominant focus. Caribbean cultural historian Nigel Bolland has recently argued for a revaluation of the Amerindian role in the region's history and culture. He points to the specific need to consider what he refers to as "the third side of the triangle", that is, the political and cultural interchange between African slaves and the indigenous Amerindian population. Bolland notes that in the early period of colonization, escaped African slaves were known to have made common cause with the Amerindians in attacking the Spanish colonists. Avellaneda's uniting of "black and copper-coloured men"[44] in the struggle against oppression stands, therefore, as incipient acknowledgement of the Afro-Amerindian side of the colonial triangle. Unlike Martina's words, which forge a link between the Amerindian resistance of Spanish colonization and the African slaves' struggle for freedom, Carlota's tearful, horrified response is limited to the past atrocity of the Spanish conquest, and thus divorced from the present brutality of slavery.

Yet one question remains: Why did Avellaneda go to such lengths to take the edge off her protagonist's rebellion and the novel's antislavery discourse? Why did she choose to write about this "mild" form of slavery?

Composition of the novel coincided with her departure from Cuba and it was published in Spain, which released her from the rigid censorship faced by her male counterparts in Cuba. The answer lies in the connection between antislavery intent and the novelist's gender interest, which has most endeared her to feminist critics.

In readings of *Sab*, feminism is regarded as the most noteworthy inference of the antislavery theme. Commentators who favour a feminist interpretation have stressed the autobiographical influence in the novel and aligned Avellaneda with feminist abolitionists of the period, especially those in the U.S.A. Conclusions about the conflation of feminist and antislavery protest have been drawn in the main from Sab's letter to Teresa, with further grounding in references to *Dos mujeres*, another of Avellaneda's novels,[45] and her advocacy of women's rights in her other writings.[46] In such readings the (feminized) slave protagonist becomes a transmogrified figure of the author. In the same way that the critical voice of Otway, the English outsider, is the one that prevails in the first chapter, in the final chapter the mulatto slave, through his letter, becomes the feminist mouthpiece speaking for women like Carlota and, by extension, Avellaneda. The following lines of the letter resonate with feminist meaning:

> Oh women! . . . Like the slaves, they drag their chains patiently and bow their heads under the yoke of human laws. With nothing to guide them but their ignorant and gullible hearts, they choose an owner for their whole life. The slave may at least change masters; he can hope that by putting money together he will buy his freedom some day. But as for the woman, whenever she raises her weakened arms and abused head to beg for freedom, she hears the monstrous and deathly voice shouting from the tomb . . . Obedience, humility, resignation . . . [¡*Oh, las mujeres!* . . . *Como los esclavos, ellas arrastran pacientemente su cadena y bajan la cabeza bajo el yugo de las leyes humanas. Sin otra guía que su corazón ignorante y crédulo eligen un dueño para toda la vida. El esclavo, al menos, puede cambiar de amo, puede esperar que juntando oro comprará algún día su libertad: pero la mujer, cuando levanta sus manos enflaquecidas y su frente ultrajada, para pedir libertad, oye al monstruo de voz sepulcral que le grita en la tumba . . . Obediencia, humildad, resignación* . . .][47]

The idea of the slave experience as a rough analogue for the situation of women, though uttered by a slave, may reasonably be said to reflect a white Creole feminist consciousness. The signs of this sensibility resound in Avellaneda's personal life. At fifteen she defied her family and broke off her engagement to a distant relative. This was a traumatic experience, and together with her cousin's suffering as a victim of her husband's tyranny, it fuelled her abhorrence of arranged marriages and patriarchal authority and her conviction that married women were in law and in practice hardly better off than slaves.[48] But while the parallel may give no pause to the sceptical reader, the same cannot be said for the plausible but specious notion of the slave's advantage over these women. To arrive at another understanding of the relationship between the novel's feminist and anti-slavery concerns, one must take into account not only the content but also the circumstances surrounding this utterance, its relation to the rest of the letter and to the novel's themes.

The letter is primarily a rambling exposé of Sab's many discontents, and the correlation between antislavery and feminist ideas forms but a small part of the whole. These feminist ideas are also engaged as part of the pattern of retraction and deflection, obstruction and dilution that, as we have seen, aborts the birth of a robust antislavery expression. After allowing Sab to deliver a searing assault on the racist value system by which slave society has determined his subordinate status, Avellaneda's message takes an unexpected feminist turn, consigning the issue of slavery to a lower place on the novel's ideological agenda. Yet this feminist message is delivered by a slave whose credibility as a voice of subversion is dubious. As an attempt to secure the ascendancy of a feminist cause at the expense of the antislavery theme, it fails, not least because the reference to female oppression appears so belatedly. Moreover, as in the lived reality of slavery that undermines Sab's rhetoric, there is no firm basis in the novel's depiction of the total lived experience of the white female Creole to sustain meaningful comparison with slavery. In the same way that we hear about but do not witness cruel treatment of the slaves, Carlota's situation does not evince victimization, domination or exploitation. The novel attests to white female *privilege*, not oppression.

A more sceptical view of this feminist protest becomes available when it is placed in the context of the change in lifestyle that accompanies Carlota's marriage to Otway, a situation on which Avellaneda's autobiographical writings shed much light. As a member of Cuba's slave-owning elite, the novelist enjoyed a privileged life of leisure, the loss of which, as reported in her *Diario*, she felt acutely upon her relocation to Spain. Carlota's unhappiness presents initially as a result of the clash of her sensitive and naïve spirit with the gross materialism of the Otway family. A close reading of the narrator's account of her new life reveals a more fundamental cause of her distress:

> Poor, delicate flower! You were born to adorn gardens, your pure beauty shyly caressed by heaven's gentle breezes! As a spinster, Carlota had enjoyed the advantages of wealth without knowing its cost. She knew nothing of the work it cost to acquire it. As a married woman she learned . . . how wealth is achieved. *Carlota lacked nothing, however. Comforts, recreation and even luxury, she had it all.* [*¡Pobre y delicada flor! tú habías nacido para embalsamar los jardines, bella inútil y acariciada tímidamente por las auras del cielo! Mientras fue soltera, Carlota había gozado las ventajas de las riquezas sin conocer su precio: ignoraba el trabajo que costaba el adquirirlas. Casada, aprendía . . . como se llega a la opulencia.* Sin embargo, de nada carecía Carlota, comodidades, recreaciones y aun lujo, todo lo tenía.][49]

These words suggest that the other side of her conscious identification with Sab's feminist voice is the novelist's subconscious affinity with Carlota.

Carlota is a figure of the transplanted Avellaneda, a woman of the leisured class, accustomed to planter privileges in colonial Cuba before becoming a misfit in metropolitan Spain. Like her father, of whom it is said (almost verbatim) that he enjoyed the fruits of slave labour without counting the cost, Carlota has been fed a Romantic illusion, enjoying her family's sugar wealth but shielded from the brutal reality of the forced and unpaid slave labour that produced it. Her marriage to Otway brings her face to face with the distasteful reality of the means of wealth production. Carlota rues her marriage and sees herself as a victim because she has lost the privileges she enjoyed as a planter's pampered daughter. It is this loss, as much as the loss of personal freedom or the weight of the marriage yoke, that appears to be the impetus behind the novel's much vaunted feminist protest. Nor is Sab's pronouncement on gender relations allowed to go unchallenged. Teresa, who becomes increasingly a bearer of the novel's truth, being far less trenchant and a good deal more conciliatory in her advice to Carlota, mitigates the horror of the picture of married women's lives painted by Sab: "Do not despise your husband, Carlota; he is what most men are; and how many of them are worse! . . . Men are imperfect, Carlota, but you should not hate them" (*No desprecies a tu marido, Carlota; él es lo que son la mayor parte de los hombres, ¡y cuántos existirán peores! . . . Los hombres son malos, Carlota, pero no debes aborrecerlos*).[50]

What might seem, then, like a bizarre suggestion – that the forced bondage of slaves is somehow preferable to a marriage bond freely entered into – finally becomes intelligible as the manifestation of a logically orchestrated process. Avellaneda has created an image of her protagonist and of slavery as the leg on which her association of female bondage with slavery can stand. The gift of freedom, incredibly refused by Sab, serves the author as proof of the slave's advantage over the married woman; Avellaneda's "happy" slaves are happier than the married Carlota. Furthermore, a comparison between Sab's slave mother's romance with his slave-master father and Carlota's dismal marriage to Otway drives home the preposterous point about the relatively more miserable lot of white Creole women. Based on such a skewed view, the linking of the two conditions amounts to a trivialization of slavery. In addition, humane treatment of the slaves and the possibility of their purchasing their freedom or changing masters refer to legal provisions rather than actual practice, which puts paid to this attempt to correlate slavery and marriage. The feminist protest is found even more profoundly wanting in what it excludes. The women on whose behalf it is expressed are white women; no thought is spared for the condition of the female slave, who had no power to choose and, in most cases, no control over her own body.

This focus on Carlota's dilemma, albeit belated, further separates Avellaneda from male authors of the time; they do not speak to the specific problems of the white wives and daughters of the Creole sugar planters. Barbara Bush sheds light on the subject with an analysis of the role of white women and the complexities of sex, class and race in slave society. Among the dissatisfactions white Creole wives experienced in their marriages, which were "cemented by property rather than affection", Bush highlights their lack of emotional and sexual fulfilment and of opportunities for intellectual development. Above all, these women had to suffer the indignity of their husbands' sexual proclivity for black and mulatto women. Creole husbands, as reported by Bush, "were gross bores [sic], who ate like cormorants and drank like porpoises . . . materialistic philistines, solicitous to make money without appreciation of the finer sensibilities of human existence".[51] Although Carlota's experience speaks only partially to this syndrome, the criticism of male supremacy and female subordination has been made without prejudice to white Creole husbands because her husband is a foreigner.

But Bush also cites advantages enjoyed by white women of the planter class: "Black female slaves made it possible for white women to [live] a leisured pampered life . . . Black women served, white women consumed."[52] Thus it becomes clear that the truly invisible slave woman who has been written out of the novel's feminist discourse is not the protagonist's mother, who as we have seen helps to create a history for Sab, but Belén, Carlota's handmaid, who serves her faithfully to the end and receives no more than a few passing mentions. In the final analysis, Avellaneda's defence of white Creole women works to the detriment of the antislavery message.

A nationalist strain also lies embedded in the novel's antislavery discourse. This thread, unlike the belated feminist suggestions in Sab's letter, is sustained throughout the novel. Even while she may be seen to be ensuring the supremacy of the planter class to which she belonged, Avellaneda, in much the same way as did Suárez, simultaneously makes an antislavery gesture by shaping an alternative to the negative stereotypes associated with the slave person. Part of this subversive proposition is investment of a fledgling nationalist feeling in the slave protagonist. Sab's reference to Otway as a foreigner, which is merely descriptive in the first chapter, acquires a persistent xenophobic complexion later in the story as more is revealed of the Otways' opportunistic motives. The slave's perception is shared by the narrator and, it may be inferred, by the novelist, who has constructed the Otways' identity as non-Cuban and non-Catholic (they are of British Jewish origin) to separate the native Self from a foreign Other. Reminiscent of the *nouveaux riches* in Tanco's story (the elder Otway is a common peddler turned merchant), these materialistic foreigners are represented as the social antithesis of the spiritually oriented bluebloods of the Bellavista estate. Their foreign status is inseparable from their incarnation of the mercantilist ethos and its accompanying ills.

For Catherine Davies, the story of Sab, Carlota and Otway can be read as a kind of national allegory, with the mulatto slave representing the Cuban spirit or soul.[53] Stretching this interpretation further, Sab may be viewed as the native defender of Cuba/Carlota – "that naive and trusting soul"[54] – against the threatening aliens, represented by the Otways. The Euro-Creoles, Carlota and Don Carlos, are naïve; they welcome the foreign exploiters with open arms. Sab, a nationalist ahead of his time, and Avellaneda (implicitly) resist them. Such an antagonistic reaction evokes the strong anti-British sentiment in Cuba at the time and the adversarial relationship between the traditional planter class and foreign itinerant merchants and traders. The repeated contemptuous references to Otway Otway as "that Englishman" and "that foreigner" express a thinly veiled fear of the British threat posed to Cuba at this time. Britain had already spearheaded an international campaign to abolish the slave trade, but Cuba continued and enlarged the trade well beyond the legally required cessation date.[55]

In his conversation with Teresa, Sab threatens violence against Otway in defence of Carlota.[56] While it can be argued that he makes the threat in the context of a personal contest against his rival in a love triangle, not in a liberation struggle, this gesture could nonetheless be constituted as an expression of a spirited nationalism. Thus a nationalist discourse has enabled Avellaneda to rewrite the script, to direct liberationist energy away from internal slave oppression towards the external threat embodied by foreign forces. Originating from Sab, it implies revaluation of his stereo-typical debasement as a slave.

The badge of Cuban nationality is reserved for Carlota, the "beautiful Creole";[57] Cuba is her birthright. Sab, on the other hand, repeatedly self-identified as a mulatto and a slave, represents the dispossessed:

> I am all alone in the world. No one will mourn my death. Nor do I have a country to defend, because the duties of a slave are the duties of a beast of burden, trudging along while it can and falling to the ground when it can go no further. [*Soy solo en el mundo: nadie llorará mi muerte. No tengo tampoco una patria que defender, porque los esclavos no tienen patria que defender, porque los deberes del esclavo son los deberes de la bestia de carga, que anda mientras puede y se echa en tierra cuando ya no puede más.*][58]

With this distinction Avellaneda seems to imply the disjuncture between slave contributions to colonial Cuban society and the lack of recognition of these contributions. Claiming a nationalist role for the mulatto slave places the novel ahead of its time, as it prefigures perception of the mulatto as the true Creole icon of national identity – a prominent theme in Cuban and Caribbean post-independence literature.

While allowing that Avellaneda's use of a mulatto rather than a black slave protagonist might have arisen out of a felt need to make Sab's story palatable to the taste of readers of sentimental fiction, the choice of a whitened slave also speaks to the racial politics of slave society. On the one hand, Sab's hybridity makes him the best choice for this nationalist role. On the other, the choice is a reminder of the pigmentocratic distinc-tions by which mulatto slaves were elevated above their negroid peers, characterized (according to Otway) by their "servility and coarseness".[59]

A retrospective reading of the foreword to the novel, titled "Dos pal-abras al lector" (A Few Words to the Reader), is now in order. Avellaneda uses this publishing convention to constitute her writing of the novel as an act of whimsy, of innocent, youthful self-indulgence, "to amuse herself in times of leisure and melancholy".[60] The allusion to leisure evokes the privilege of white women of the slave-owning class, the loss of which, as we have seen, is a major contributor to Carlota's discontent. This opening gesture seems designed to stave off interpretations of the novel that would refer it to current political and ideological issues. After declaring her initial reluctance to publish, the author disavows any conscious design for the work while affirming its authenticity: "Whether it be due to laziness or to our aversion to altering what we have written out of genuine (albeit wavering) conviction, the author has not made any change to the first draft" (*Sea por pereza, sea por la repugnancia que sentimos en alterar lo que hemos escrito con una verdadera convicción [aun cuando ésta llegue a vacilar], la autora no ha hecho ninguna mudanza en sus borradores primitivos*).[61] Apparently minimized by its placement, the parenthetical phrase epitomizes the enigma that the novel represents.

Though it precedes the age of Said, Fanon and Bakhtin by more than a century, *Sab* yields new insights when framed by their ideas. The novel defies discrete ideological classification. Avellaneda is at one and the same time a maverick and a conformist. She is a maverick among her peers in the antislavery field, based on her vision of the slaves' struggle as a continuation of the anti-colonial struggle of Cuba's indigenous population and her staking out of a national(ist) claim for the Afro-Cuban slave. However, she is a conformist in her inability or unwillingness to conceive of slave rebellion and in her subliminal defence of slave-owner privilege. In true Bakhtinian fashion, insidious endorsement of the system of slavery is seen to coexist with antislavery ideas in an unresolved tension. Or like Sab, who sits (uneasily) astride two races, the novelist may be said to straddle the divide separating the opponents and the apostles of slavery. Avellaneda understood the evil that was slavery, and this consciousness finds its most flagrant and eloquent expression in her slave protagonist. She invests him with a subversive voice, but to protect her class interests she stops short of making him an outright rebel. The novel's ideological instability, its movement back and forth across boundaries, defies the exclusivist interpretations of binary thought systems and enables it to fit more comfortably within the open and flexible parameters of the postmodern world view.

# ·4·

## ANTISLAVERY NARRATIVE WITH A *COSTUMBRISTA* TWIST

### *Francisco Calcagno's* Romualdo, uno de tantos

FRANCISCO CALCAGNO WROTE *Romualdo, uno de tantos* in 1869, in the midst of the political turmoil of the first Cuban War of Independence, which had started the previous year. The slave trade had come to a belated end, and gradual abolition had been turned into a collateral issue of the war. Final emancipation (already a reality in other areas of the Americas) was two decades away on the horizon. On the literary side of liberal activity, the del Monte group had disintegrated and state-sponsored censorship continued to be sensitive to expressions of opposition to slavery, however veiled, which explains why *Romualdo* was not released until 1891. The author's name does not feature on the list of famous contributors to anti-slavery fiction. His claim to fame rests more on his work as a biographer and historian and on his compilation of the first collection of Afro-Cuban poetry, published in 1878, than on his output in what is normally regarded as creative writing. A member of the Creole elite, this son of an Italian doctor was a founding member of and active participant in the del Monte *tertulias*. The liberal values espoused by the group are, not surprisingly, those that he seeks to promote in this literary effort.

Like *Petrona y Rosalía*, Calcagno's composition belongs to the subsidiary group of short narratives that have attracted only modest critical interest because of the dominance of the full-fledged novels. Yet it offers a unique though not fully acknowledged perspective. The importation and sale of Africans was not the complete story of Cuba's illegal slave trade. Kidnapping and selling of free blacks and mulattoes into slavery, a phenomenon known as *plagio*, was also rampant in Cuba during the nineteenth century, though it does not feature as a prominent theme in historical or literary accounts. Calcagno makes this underground activity, together with slave *marronage* (also conspicuously absent in this narrative tradition), the focal points of his story.

At age six, Romualdo, a free mulatto, is kidnapped and sold by the slave trader Jacobo Vendialma to the owner of the Esperanza sugar estate, Don Juan Castaneiro. For thirty years Romualdo endures this bondage in which he is pitted against the white overseer, his sexual rival for the black slave woman Dorotea, who bears Romualdo's daughter, Felicia. After Dorotea's death Romualdo escapes from the estate with his daughter to save her from increasing physical abuse. Felicia dies and Romualdo subsequently joins a band of maroons, but his spirit has been crushed beyond repair by his daughter's death. Thereafter the plot shifts its focus to the activities of a group of maroons led by the fearsome Juan Bemba, himself a one-time victim of *plagio*. At the end the fugitives are betrayed and massacred, but not before they kill the slave trader and Don Robustiano, the overseer. In a final twist to the plot, through the intervention of the village priest, it is revealed just before his death that Romualdo is Castaneiro's illegitimate son.

As his basic narrative resource Calcagno chose the *costumbrista* sketch, in which the (stereo)typical rather than the unique is emphasized, individual human interest is minimized and documentary description holds sway over creative invention. He put together a literary potpourri by adding historical ingredients to a collection of vignettes and binding them with a slender fictional thread. The thinness of the storyline is possibly what has discouraged detailed commentary on this work. According to Roberta Day Corbitt, one of the first Cuban examples of the *costumbrista* sketch was written by Ventura Pascual Ferrer, who published a series of eight letters in a Spanish newspaper in 1798 "to correct some erroneous statements respecting his country made by the editor of the paper".[1] In a similar spirit, Calcagno sought with his sketches to fill some of the gaps in the works written during and about the 1830s.

All antislavery narratives are historical to a greater or lesser extent, but few are more manifestly so than *Romualdo*. It is this historical consciousness that no doubt influenced the writer to choose the *costumbrista* approach, because of its ready association with empirical truth. The work's full title, *Romualdo, uno de tantos*, signals the heavy weighting given to fact over fiction. Romualdo is not the one-of-a-kind protagonist of the fables created by Suárez and Avellaneda; he is merely one of many actual cases of free blacks and mulattoes sold illegally as slaves. To add a historical accent to the narrative, the author introduces what he claims to be facsimiles of two authentic documents: a list of the slaves (including Romualdo) sold to Castaneiro in 1806, and a copy of an agreement for sale of a female slave in a slave market. Both documents purport to confirm the veracity of his account.

The author's obsession with historical precision manifests further in the phrase "*Estamos en 1836*" (This is 1836), repeated throughout like a refrain to keep the time of the story's action constantly in the reader's mind. But even as he presents a snapshot from a bygone era, the author is careful to include allusions to the present to create an optimistic sense of Cuba's history as progressive. The exposure and denunciation of malpractice carry in their wake assurance that the sins belong to the past. Things and times have changed and are changing (for the better), the author states or implies, and will continue to do so in the future.

*Romualdo* invites comparison with Avellaneda's *Sab*. Though written nearly three decades apart, these two works share a common historical and geographical setting. *Sab* treats events of the 1830s from a contemporary perspective, while *Romualdo* is a late-1860s re-creation of the state of affairs in 1836. However, there is little resemblance between their fictional worlds. In many ways *Romualdo* serves as a counterpoint to *Sab*. For her part, Avellaneda divorced slavery from the real world in which it was practised, painting a bright picture of peaceful coexistence between enslaved and enslaver. While this representation may bear some relation to the pre-sugar-boom period of Cuban slavery, it does not completely reflect the situation in the 1830s, when Cuban sugar production was at its highest and exploitation and abuse of slaves and their labour at its most brutal. In fact, by some accounts the slave experience in the Puerto Príncipe area, the location of both narratives, was one of Cuba's harshest. This is a reality to which Calcagno's story appears to be far more attentive. While it does not make for complex character development, the *costumbrista* method allows the author to capture the complexity of slavery and its grim manifestations in the human, social and economic spheres of the life of the period.

Calcagno has woven a storyline into what is essentially a documentary account of slavery. Documentary art, in its film or written version, typically provides information, often about a little-known or hidden subject. It is of course not unusual for a political purpose to coexist with this educational intent. The documentary impulse in *Romualdo* manifests itself at various intervals in objective descriptions of the operations of the plantation system. Calcagno also carefully fosters the impression that the atrocities he is bringing to light are only the tip of a scandalous iceberg. Snapshots of the more infamous horrors of the slave experience are sprinkled throughout the story to remind the reader of the pervasiveness of slave oppression and abuse. Explanations of estate jargon and descriptions of *realia* are included for the benefit of the presumably ignorant reader. Far from being neutral, the explanations are designed to demystify the language and discourse used to put a civilized gloss on savage practices. The author has left us with a perspective of slavery as engendering and sustaining a web of industries and occupations – whip manufacturers, slave hunters, slave traders – in addition to manual labourers on the estates. Instruments of torture are displayed as products of industry and described in terms of their manufacture and abstract use. But the writer's interest goes beyond documentation of their inert properties to describe what these instruments signify in the painful life experience of the individual slave.

Though it avoids maudlin narration, the story of *Romualdo* is not told through lifeless sociological discourse. The author adds emotive ingredients and puts a human touch to his protest, but sparingly, through brief digressions from the more dispassionate narrative of *costumbrista* realism. The tragedy of slavery as lived experience presents most dramatically in the compassionate depiction of Romualdo's nerve-racking flight from the estate, his frantic efforts to save his daughter's life and the grief brought on by her death. Here the author shows that the slaves, in the words of Rebecca Scott, could be treated worse than beasts yet not become beasts.[2] At the same time, his general sympathy for the slaves does not blind him to the existence of conflict in their relations. The threat perceived in Romualdo's status as a mulatto and a *habanero* places him between the rock of the overseer's hatred and the hard place of resentment from his negroid companions on the plantation.

Despite the resemblance between his opposition to slavery and the posture assumed by Suárez in *Francisco*, Calcagno's message manifests differently: he compels the reader to view the institution primarily through a socio-economic lens. In his way of seeing, one cannot and should not criticize slavery and its practitioners without condemning the society that breeds and feeds them. Slavery as a practice, though reprehensible, is engendered by social and cultural norms from which it can hardly be divorced. This message, alluded to in *Sab* and *Francisco*, becomes a dominant theme of *Romualdo*. The author returns to it again and again, with almost evangelical insistence.

Calcagno's concern with the problem of slavery centres equally on the detriment to the slave person and the damage to society's moral character. As did Suárez in *Francisco*, Calcagno repeatedly imbues his judgements with a Christian humanist sense of slavery as a contravention of the teaching that all men are equal in the sight of God. As he sees it, violence against the slave is normalized in a society that has become inured to cruelty, and, he observes wryly, the human capacity for adaptation is inexhaustible: "*a todo se habitúa la máquina humana*".[3] Through skilful *double entendre* he shows how material interests become the new gauge of morality in a slave society. Goodness loses its moral meaning in the sugar plantation system; the overseer's worth is measured only by his ability to use violence to increase production. Economic ends justify brutal means.

But while condemning the illegal practices of slavery, Calcagno accepts the premise on which slave society is built. The crime, he posits confidently, is not owning slaves but abusing them.[4] Such support for the benign form of slavery is not unexpected; after all, Mosaic Law in the Judaeo-Christian tradition permitted slavery.[5] The author instead vents his distaste on the ill-treatment of slaves and the corrupt practice of *plagio*. His comment contains clear echoes of the gradualist approach to abolition embraced by some slave owners and many members of the Cuban intelligentsia of the period, as well as by the revolutionary leaders of the Ten Years' War.[6] Taken to its logical conclusion the argument recognizes, albeit half-heartedly, the need for and inevitability of eventual abolition. Change is in the air, the author seems to say, and slave owners too will (have to) change, but in their time.

Cuban Creole support for gradual abolition reflected what Rebecca Scott refers to as "a strategic acceptance of an eventual transition to free labour and a tactic to delay that transition".[7] This ambivalence was displayed by Cuban reformers in an 1866 meeting of delegates from the colonies and the Spanish government, as Scott reports: "In theory, they believed in the eventual extinction of slavery, and in theory they also believed in the superiority of free labor. But they insisted that, for the moment, slavery had to be sustained to prevent the collapse of the sugar industry. On slavery itself, the furthest they could go was to support a very 'gradual' emancipation."[8] Calcagno voices this white Creole interest. Slavery is legal, not criminal; the need for reform is more urgent in the (illegal) practice of slave trading than in the (legal) practice of slave owning. Such uneven criticism points, nevertheless, to a nagging sense of slavery as a fundamentally immoral practice for which humanitarian treatment does not quite compensate. Therefore what is needed in the meantime, Calcagno intimates, is a reconditioning of the minds of slave owners in conjunction with good treatment of the slave to maintain some measure of social peace.

*Romualdo* is built on a firm historical foundation, but what the author has created is not a historical document. This work tells us as much about the author as it does about his subject. What he omits or implies generates as much interest as what he expresses. In true *costumbrista* fashion, an element of self-portrait is inseparable from his portrait of Cuban slave society. *Francisco* and *Sab* make use of a preface for the author's self-reflection. This strategy creates the illusion of an arm's-length separation of the author from the work. Calcagno makes no such pretence of self-effacement; everything in the story points to a conflation of author and narrator. Not only does he intrude, unmasked, to deliver editorial asides and clarifications, but he does so self-reflexively, identifying himself as a slave owner through first-person-plural narration. And indeed, though the writer's family might not have been plantation owners, they, like most of the Cuban Creole elite at the time, would have owned slaves.

Apart from his conscious self-identification, the author also unconsciously frames his own persona while constructing the identity of his characters. This self-portrait serves as a means of positive self-presentation, in the interest of which he repeatedly puts an ironic distance between his enlightened perspective and the dominant perspective of the boorish slave trader and practitioners of a vulgar form of slavery. His lack of self-righteousness, coupled with the candour of his criticism and self-criticism, beguiles the unsuspecting reader.

As urgent as his denunciation of the overt practices of slavery is the author's demonstration of a deeper and wider understanding of the nature and meaning of slave-owning power. Power in slave society, Calcagno seems to say, resides in language: the "civilized" holders of power use language to shape reality and to construct identities in a manner that ensures their supremacy over the "savages" they have subordinated. A power advantage permits, for example, corrupt use of language to vary the definition of a crime to suit the race and social position of the victim. Euphemisms in the plantation vernacular, which renders the rape of a slave woman as *"un desliz reproductor"* (a reproductive mishap) and a shipload of slaves as a *"cargamento de ebano"* (load of ebony),[9] are exposed for what they are: insidious naturalizing of horrific practices and flagrant whitewashing of vile abuse.

The author magnifies to the point of parody the master's awesome power over the slave, deriding it through brilliant mimicry of the Old Testament God of the Ten Commandments: "The master commands like a father, he commands like a mother, he commands like a judge, he commands like a supreme being. All these commandments are summed up in two words: absolute lord" (*El amo manda como padre, manda como madre, manda como juez, manda como ser supremo. Todos estos mandamientos se reúnen en dos palabras: señor absoluto*).[10] It is an omnipotence that the author demonstrates practically by pointing to the owners' exercise of control over the slaves' most elementary acts of will, such as their reproductive rights or the freedom to choose their own names.

By invoking these realities, Calcagno displays his profound grasp of the psychopathology of slave subjugation in the plantation regime. The savage treatment of Romualdo, the proud slave who refuses to be humiliated, is shown to be logically justified by the system of power relations. With the succinct comment that "sugar is not made with dignity and pride" (*con dignidad y vergüenza no se hace azúcar*),[11] the author interprets the constant mortification of the enslaved not as acts of gratuitous physical cruelty but as a psychological ploy to reduce them to sugar-producing automatons. Pointing to such a neurotic obsession with psychological control betrays the shaky foundations sustaining slave-owner power. At the same time, the irony of these (under)statements serves to further the author's desire to put a safe distance between his own liberal thinking and the dominant proslavery ideology.

According to one school of thought, the greater its empirical basis, the less a text's effectiveness as literature. By putting a premium on fictional elements, this normative view tends to inhibit consideration of the strategic design of works such as *Romualdo* that do not live up to classical expectations. But the documentary mode has come to be associated not only with notions of accuracy and veracity but also with ideas about artistry. Calcagno has carefully crafted his story to achieve his ideological purposes, using various means. The very first sentence gives a hint of his narrative method: "Let's begin by taking the reader to the old Guanabacoa quarter, because it is there on Los Cocos Street that we can find the fellow I am going to describe" (*Empezaremos por conducir al lector a la vieja villa de Guanabacoa, que allí en la calle de los Cocos, es donde podemos encontrar el tipo que aquí me propongo describir*).[12] In addition to serving as a *costumbrista* flag, the *double entendre* of the Spanish word *tipo* – which, neutrally speaking, means "type" but also has the derogatory meaning of "fellow" – foreshadows the basic satirical strategy to which the author will have recourse in his portrayal of the slave trader. Also noteworthy in this opening is the fixing of the reader's position in relation to the author. The latter presents himself as both mediator and guide, leading the reader into unknown territory and in the process controlling the response to what is revealed. Reader and author will retain these relative positions throughout the story.

Rather than rely on lurid descriptions that appeal to the emotions, Calcagno adopts the standardized language of commerce to provide a graphic understanding of the total dehumanization of the slaves. In fact, the signature of his narrative voice is its dispassionate tone. The matter-of-factness of the subdued voice recounting slave abuse intensifies the sense of horror because of the muted suggestion that such horrors were normalized and taken for granted. Deadpan humour, satire and biting irony serve to savage and stigmatize the objects of the author's disfavour. It is with mild amusement that he mocks, for example, the habit of referring to grey-haired slave masters as *niños*.[13] Understatement quietly conveys revulsion when the narrator explains the absence of any difference between the master's ownership of his slave's offspring and his ownership of a colt borne by his mare.[14]

While distancing himself from this way of thinking, the author under-lines the impregnable logic of the belief system that rationalizes commod-ification of the slaves: "the will of one who is sold is of no consequence. An object has no will" (*La voluntad del vendido no cuenta para nada. No hay voluntad en lo que es cosa*).[15] Through irony he conveys an understand-ing of the unimaginable inhumanity of the traffic in slaves by invoking, for example, mundane comparison – selling a slave is like selling a horse. Abundant newspaper advertisements from the period attest to this lack of distinction between dumb animal and black slave. Donkeys and slaves were put up for sale as a single package, and the exchange of a slave for an animal was not an unusual offer. And the criticism inherent in Calcagno's use of such simplifying analogies is all the more powerful because of the deadpan manner in which it is uttered. Far from minimizing the atrocity, the coolness of the voice in such instances has the effect of magnifying it.

Yet another strategy the author uses to drive home his perception of Cuba and other New World slave societies as modern anomalies is comparison of their corrupt culture with the civilized mores of which European countries were held to be benchmarks. He cites the vicar of Wakefield, the emblematic priest in English literature, as the standard from which Cuban priests deviate. He invokes the difference between the conventional European use of the term *plagio* to mean plagiarism – the more "innocuous" theft of ideas – and Cuba's application of the term to the theft of people. In short, the practice of slavery makes colony inferior to imperial centre.

In contrast to *Francisco* and *Sab*, which were written primarily for non-Cuban readers, *Romualdo* is a depiction of Cuba for Cuban consumption. Writing more than two decades later than his forebears, Calcagno has a sense of a wider Cuban readership, to whom he speaks directly and with an air of cosy familiarity. In the interest of effective persuasion, he inscribes the reader into the text of his narrative, using a conversational tone to establish the desired rapport. He anticipates questions, answers them and guides the reader away from the points of view he wishes to discredit and towards those that he favours.

Though he writes with Cuban readers in mind, Calcagno still assumes their ignorance of or, even worse, their wilful blindness to slavery as lived experience. Unwilling to leave it to the vagaries of the individual imagination, he spares no gruesome detail in his account of the physical and mental torture visited upon the slaves. But he vacillates between this feigned assumption of ignorance and appealing to a reader who is no stranger to what is being described. He even dares to imagine that his work will reach the people against whom it is written. By drawing the reader's attention so bluntly to the hidden face of slavery, Calcagno leaves the impression of one who has assumed the duty of shaking his society out of its complacent acceptance of the nefarious practices of this institution.

Forever mindful of the socio-genetic nature of the problem of slavery, Calcagno implies a need for change in world view as much as in laws and institutions. Nonetheless, his admission of the social origins of the problem of slavery does not lead him to deny all individual responsibility. Rather, he also seems to lean towards Fanon's postcolonial view that, though formidable, the power of the system can be defied. These twin faces of his vision manifest in his characters. Although the drama of slavery offered a variety of actors, the constraints of short fiction forced Calcagno to be selective. His choices and omissions are instructive.

Jacobo, the man behind the illegal trade in slaves, is the author's prime target. Appropriately demonized, and in a turnabout of the African slave stereotype, he is referred to disparagingly as "that creature", not fit to be labelled human. The author is relentless in his satirical portrait of Jacobo. Adopting Tanco's tongue-in-cheek strategy, he sows the seeds of derision by investing the man, who, figuratively speaking, has sold his soul to the devil, with the pretentious title *"el señor don Jacobo Vendialma"*. And as if the discrepancy between the pompous-sounding title and the character's ignominious occupation were not enough, he further diminishes his target with a humorous taunt: Don Jacobo is as short in stature as he is mean in spirit.[16] The indignation of which this character is repeatedly the object surpasses in intensity any sympathy that the story elicits for the slaves who are his victims.

The author's antipathy towards Jacobo is inseparable from the virulence of his opposition to slave trafficking. High on the list of the slave trader's sins is his appalling lack of compunction, which makes him totally irredeemable. Even though he is acknowledged to be a creature – a "blind instrument" – of the system, Jacobo is only partially exonerated, for he has refused a decent occupation befitting his social status, such as bricklaying or carpentry. And if Jacobo is being condemned, even more so is the society of which he is a product and which accepts his immorality. Time and again the author creates an impression of the illogical, topsy-turvy value system of a society that, for example, sees no conflict between religious observance and practice of an inhumane form of slavery, or that bases social exclusion on religious and ethnic identity rather than on ethical conduct.

Individual character traits are hardly the focus of *costumbrista* literature;

its characters are typical rather than unique. Calcagno adheres to this practice selectively. While he conveys the impression that the villainous slave trader and overseer are typical examples, in portraying the priest and slave owner he resorts to indirection, illustrating only obliquely the norms from which they deviate. His portrayal of the estate owner Don Juan Castaneiro is yet another example of the author's manipulation of the story to control what he considers important for the reader to know and to think. In his portrait of this character he employs both candour and subterfuge, a strategy that takes on added significance when compared with the depiction of the slave trader. Calcagno makes a tacit distinction between Castaneiro, whose role as a master of slaves is his birthright, and Jacobo, whose ignoble profession, as seen before, is a matter of choice. Indictment of Jacobo's selling of his fellow human beings for profit makes very glaring the exception made for this and other slave owners, who buy and use them for a similar purpose.

Rebecca Scott explains the hidden motives in this ambivalence: "Cuban reformers did support . . . repression of the slave trade, for the contraband trade appeared to them as a weapon of Spanish merchants against Cuban planters, and the influx of Africans seemed a threat to the racial balance of the island."[17] Like Avellaneda before him, who relegated the more brutal reality of slavery to the margins of her story of unrequited love, Calcagno surreptitiously leads the reader away from a direct view of the slave master. This approach brings to mind a similar manoeuvre in Tanco's disparaging of upstart Spanish slave owners to avoid pointing the finger at the Cuban Creole elite. In his lack of interest in the slave master, Calcagno is more forthright. To justify his summarily painted portrait, the author declares that Castaneiro is of only secondary importance to the story, and thus expendable. By anticipating and pre-empting a potential charge of bias, Calcagno has effectively disarmed the reader. Talked about impersonally as a distant figure, Castaneiro is shielded from the direct glare of *costumbrista* scrutiny. Furthermore, when he finally puts in an appearance, he bears little resemblance to the godlike slave master with boundless power described previously. Every attempt is made to mitigate any condemnation that he might appear to deserve.

Citing psychosocial reasons becomes part of this author's need to exonerate individual owners. Castaneiro's shortcomings, in Calcagno's view, are not idiosyncratic; they are defects of the institution of slavery, and common in the majority of planters. He sums up the entire syndrome in a classic declaration: "There was more crime in his era than in his character" (*Había más crimen en su época que en su carácter*).[18] Any misdeed of which Castaneiro is guilty belongs to his rakish past, and his spontaneous reformation after his father's death prepares the way for his full exoneration in the end. To give the appearance of even-handed treatment, he is created with some imperfections – excessive pride, authoritarianism, irritability, unrelenting demand for subservience – but the author seems to beat a hasty retreat from any outright condemnation that these faults might imply.

As another manifestation of his will to deflect blame from the master, the author makes his truly evil white characters of lowly rank. He associates sexual exploitation of the enslaved woman, for instance, only with the estate overseer. The thesis that the evils of slavery are socially determined does not apply universally; it serves as an alibi for the slave master but cannot completely wash away the sins of the slave trader. The possession of a moral conscience by Castaneiro, this "man of good faith", also stands in contrast to Jacobo with his "heart made of mud". In a manner reminiscent of Sab's benevolent slave-owner father, Romualdo's father wants to assume paternal responsibility for his mulatto son when he discovers his identity. Compared with the energy he expends on excoriating the slave trader, Calcagno has given no more than a perfunctory slap on the wrist to the slave owner.

His obvious favouritism notwithstanding, Calcagno cannot be accused of being an uncritical defender of slave owners. Shared class identity does not amount to unqualified identification with his kind. One of his aims seems to be corrective – to create a different consciousness in his peers and to caution against their mistaken assumptions about slaves and about the error of some of the practices of slavery, such as separation of mothers from their children. In a rare impassioned moment, he emphatically defends the slaves against their white detractors, albeit with a trace of Eurocentrism:

We whites believe that blacks do not love and so we easily separate daughters from their mothers. Wrong! Blacks do love, albeit in a primitive way . . . They love their wives sometimes, and their children always. [*Los blancos nos figuramos que los negros no aman, y separamos fácilmente la hija de la madre. ¡Error! Los negros sí aman, tal vez más salvajemente . . . aman a su mujer, a veces; a su hijo, siempre.*][19]

He appears to lash out against those members of his group who by their inhumane treatment of slaves bring slavery as an institution into disrepute. Calcagno wishes to give the impression that he is liberal-minded without being self-righteous. He criticizes the institution without alienating his fellow slave owners, a stance that all but converges with the proslavery apologetic.

It is true to say that whether their sentiment is firm or feeble, none of the authors concerned with the antislavery project pretends that the slaves were universally happy with their condition. All take some account of their resistance, most frequently that of the covert kind. But the image of controlled confrontation that recurs in these fictional works obscures the radical spirit of open rebellion displayed historically by many slaves from the very moment of their enslavement. Few narratives of the period capture this spirit as dutifully as does *Romualdo*. With the shift in emphasis from victimhood to dramatic resistance in this story, the classic themes of other narratives are displaced. Rivalry for the female slave between male slave and white overlord, for example, is relegated to the sidelines of the story. Similarly, the author's imagination refuses the ineffective and futile submissive slave response and admits only the varied expressions of resistance. The conditions of oppression and exploitation, Calcagno is at pains to show, breed defiance, not deference. Thus he translates Francisco's psychological recalcitrance and Sab's verbal resistance into action, through slave characters he conceives of primarily as agents with not only the ability to recognize their subjugation but, more important, with the will to actively resist it. The enslaver's power over the enslaved, though awesome, is not absolute.

Calcagno's representation of slaves' acts of self-assertion counteracts the prevailing view of slaves as mindless chattel. At every turn the author pictures resistance as the slaves' instinctive and unequivocal reply to abuse, from the woman who silently curses her rapist to the coachman who reacts with anger to a whipping. Romualdo is a figure of the rebel slave inside the plantation. Though he is not given a voice or psychological depth, his rebellious attitude is perennial. In fact, his dignified and unflinching response to ill-treatment is recognized for the defiance it signifies and earns him the hatred of both overseer and slave master. Romualdo's silently rebellious temper is not subdued by thirty years of enslavement; rather, it matures into open action when he escapes from the plantation.

Moreover, slave suicide in Calcagno's story is an instinctive exercise of autonomy rather than the Romantic solution to despair it represents in the case of the broken-hearted Sab and Francisco. At the same time, although he displays an intellectual understanding of the religious significance of such suicide and accords it legitimacy as a politically motivated act of resistance, the author cannot stretch his imagination to take seriously the efficacy of African spirituality. He appears oblivious to the slaves' perception of suicide as an escape through death from the hell of slavery into the paradise of freedom. But while he does not conceive of their religion as a possible source of liberation, neither does he – unlike Suárez before him – endorse an attitude of Christian martyrdom on the part of the slaves.

In the search for fictional slave rebels, *Romualdo* has been largely overlooked in favour of Miguel Barnet's more recent biography of the runaway slave Esteban Montejo. Yet Calcagno could hardly have avoided taking *marronage* into serious account, given its pervasiveness in rural Cuba at the time he wrote. Two famous slave-hunter perspectives of *marronage* have been provided by Pedro Morillas's *El ranchador* and Francisco Estévez's *Diario del rancheador*. *Romualdo* complements them by adding a slave owner's perspective. Romualdo is our first introduction to a maroon. Fierce-looking and with eyes filled with hate, he is nevertheless not the typical fugitive; his fighting spirit dies with the death of his daughter. It is to the members of the original maroon community, therefore, that

Calcagno turns for a more drastic form of slave resistance. This is also the realm in which the tension between the author's conflicting ideological impulses is most striking. The *costumbrista*-sketch format gives the work an appearance of structural fragmentation rather than cohesion; each sketch can virtually stand on its own. A similar lack of coherence is discernible in the structure of the author's ideas. His resolve to display a consistent attitude is repeatedly threatened, and sometimes thwarted, by contradictory urges as he seeks to represent the slaves and their response to their bondage.

*Romualdo* and *Sab* present opposite ends of the spectrum of slave responses. In Avellaneda's novel, the mulatto slave protagonist's desire for acceptance by Euro-Creole society assumes pre-eminence. The maroons in *Romualdo*, on the other hand, are shown as examples of the slaves' outright rejection of coexistence with their enslavers. The free will that is violated or denied the commodified slave is powerfully expressed through the actions of Calcagno's maroons, who flee the plantation, establish their own community and fight their oppressors to the death. Adopting a posture akin to ethnographic surveillance, the author observes keenly the nuances in the human and social dimensions of the maroon scene. Surveillance, as theorized in postcolonial studies, is one strategy of imperial dominance, for it implies a viewer with an elevated vantage point from which to project a particular understanding of what is seen and to fix the identity of the viewed (colonized subject) in relation to the surveyor (colonizer).[20] In one sense, Calcagno's observation of the maroons and their lifestyle originates from such a position of superiority.

As his liberal will struggles with an obstinate negrophobia that clouds his perception of maroon identity, the author cannot contain the revulsion evoked in him by these "hellish monsters", who are indistinguishable from an equally monstrous nature.[21] The alliterative force of the language that describes the maroon leader distills the author's disgust: "His heart was as cold and fierce as his features were ugly and repugnant" (*Era tan friamente feroz su alma como feas y repugnantes todas sus facciones*).[22] Josefa Lucumi, the female maroon, fares no better; she is identified as "a horrible specimen of the African woman".[23] These descriptions show no trace of the authorial distance noted elsewhere in Calcagno's exposition of proslavery ideology. Rather, they rival and surpass the most grotesque of the images of black people commonly found in the early artistic tradition of Spain and other European countries.

Calcagno resorts to deliberate negative stereotyping in his physical description of the maroons' leader, whose given name, Juan Bemba, recalls the *negro bembón* (blubber-lipped Negro) image associated with an earlier Iberian burlesque tradition. Close-ups of individual maroons create the most hideous effects. The author's eye picks out their leader for sharp focus:

> Like a monstrous reptile, a huge negro with reddish hair was seen crawling along . . . Juan Bemba was a suitable leader for those monsters of the mountain . . . Braided locks surrounding a savage face in which signs of intelligence were eclipsed by the signs of brute force gave a truly diabolic appearance to that head. [*Como si fuera reptil monstruoso, se vio arrastrarse . . . a un coloso negro de pelo rojizo . . . Juan Bemba era un digno jefe para aquellos monstruos de la montaña . . . Mechones trenzados que rodeando una cara salvaje, en que los signos de la inteligencia se humillaban ante los de la fuerza bruta, daban a aquella cabeza un aspecto verdaderamente diabólico.*][24]

Though deceptively neutral at times (flat nose, thick lips, small forehead, short neck, shining white teeth), the adjectives used to describe him also convey aesthetic prejudice with parodic malice: "Juan Bemba was a beautiful model of his race, that is, he was ugly when compared with Caucasians" (*Juan Bemba era un bello modelo de su raza; por lo tanto feo, si comparado con la circasiana*).[25] The portrayal of these blacks as fearsome is an unmistakable projection of the morbid dread of a mythical "African barbarity" felt and propagated by colonial white society. Calcagno's perception of the maroons' African-derived culture mixes awe with contempt. He recognizes its uniqueness but is hard-pressed to hide his disdain for the difference that it represents, implying in the process his subscription to the idea of civilizing benefits accruing to African slaves from their bondage. Thus his unconscious Eurocentric inclination has succeeded in sabotaging his conscious wish to present an enlightened self-image.

But there is much more than racist prejudice in Calcagno's portrait, for his description of the runaways in their world seeks to correct the pernicious myths that demonized them. He constructs a different identity for the maroons, showing them to be bound by common adversity despite national and ethnic differences, and challenging and reversing their official depiction as predators and as threats to the social order. In positing an image of the group as harmless, beleaguered "savages" escaping from the "civilized", doing what they must to survive and defending their right to freedom, the author succeeds in making the white *negrero*, the slave hunter (*rancheador*) and the bandit into types who by comparison represent a social menace. The revulsion the author feels for their physical appearance and the Eurocentric prejudice that colours his perception of their culture are not sufficient to render null and void his expression of admiration for the maroons' courage. His celebration of their recalcitrant spirit is as potent a protest as his more direct denunciation of the slave trader and the overseer.

What Calcagno has captured in his group of fugitives is the characteristic maroon spirit: defiant, freedom-loving, self-reliant and preferring death over a life of bondage. Where the slave in other narratives has recourse to submission and accommodation or sees freedom as a gift, Juan Bemba and his band fight to maintain their autonomy. Ultimately, therefore, their indwelling spirit of defiance and their heroic struggle assume more positive significance as a statement against slavery than the pessimism that might be conveyed by their eventual defeat. "Disgust" describes the author's vision of both maroon leader and slave trader, but while the moral revulsion aroused by the latter is implacable, his frank admiration for the maroons' bravery takes some of the burlesque edge off his aversion to their physical appearance and cultural expressions.

Calcagno's awareness of the signifying power of the language of representation also manifests itself in the author's naming of the maroons. He refrains from designating them as slaves, conferring on them instead the more politically appropriate status implied in names such as "African", "maroon villager", "negro" and "runaway slave". In this context, even the more controversial label of "savages", with its connotation of wild or untamed and uncivilized, translates into affirmation of their intransigent struggle for autonomy. Comparison of the author's unequivocal condemnation of the white Juan Rivero's banditry, on the one hand, with his apparent support for the guerrilla-type maroon freedom fighters, on the other, further strengthens the work's antislavery function.

The close-ups used for individual portraits are combined with longer views of the maroons in the environment they have created for themselves. Carefully avoiding the temptation to collapse them into a single (stereo) type, the author describes the mixed motivations of the maroon villagers. In the author's eyes, these maroons, hunted mercilessly as criminals, constitute a society of families with distinct customs and cultural expressions. A community of diverse national constituencies removed from the divisiveness of the plantation-slavery dynamic, maroon society fosters a counterculture of collaboration. Romualdo, who is hated by the black slaves on the plantation because of his colour and his presumed affiliation with the white world, is at first received reticently and coldly by the maroons, but is later treated with compassion and integrated into the group. As a community and in their consciousness, these maroons are the answer to their lone-wolf counterpart Esteban Montejo, memorialized in Miguel Barnet's *Biografía de un cimarrón*.

Calcagno's maroons are not rebels without a political cause. Their uncompromising demand for autonomy summarizes the conscious grounding of their stance in an ideology of resistance:

> They wanted no more *funche*,[26] no more administrator, no more beatings no more slavery. They preferred to die there rather than return to the estate; they wanted to be left alone in the mountains and to be given the empty land next to the plain to live and grow their food without bothering anyone. [*Que no querían más funche, ni más mayoral, ni más cuero, ni más esclavitud: que querían morir allí antes que volver al ingenio; que los dejaran quietos en las sierras; y que se les diera la erial llanura inmediata, donde vivirían sembrando viandas y sin meterse con nadie.*][27]

On the other hand, in anticipation of Afro-Cuban nationalism, Isidoro, the creolized maroon, loves Cuba but hates the humiliation of slavery.

Focusing on the maroons affords the author an alternative mode of expression of his subversive views. Whereas he previously relied on denunciation for his portrayal of the slave trader, affirmation becomes the dominant idiom in the maroon episode. When, for example, the narrator characterizes their attempt to defend themselves as an act of "madness", he intends it not as a negative judgement but as a remark on the incredible courage of these rebels, even in defiance of the dictates of prudence. Further eroding the ideological foundations of slavery, Calcagno links the maroons to a pre-slavery past. He pictures the *palenque* (maroon commune) as a kind of "little Africa", an emblem of resistance and a site for preservation of an African identity. His depiction also provides a first glimpse of the process of cultural interchange that Cuban ethnographer Fernando Ortiz would latter define as transculturation. In the maroon settlement Calcagno perceives the African influence on the process of creating a Cuban cultural identity. By casting the maroons in the role of agents of cultural transformation, Calcagno has provided an alternative to their image as inert objects of Eurocentric acculturation – the civilizing of the savage – which was one of the main arguments used to justify slavery. That it is a white Creole author of the dominant class who is already, in the nineteenth century, imputing this cultural agency to slaves is not insignificant.

In *Romualdo* the maroon centre represents the main but not the only site of resistance against slavery. Calcagno is mindful of white participation in the struggle against enslavement of Africans and their descendants. Priests, like slave traders, are rarely featured in the narrative of this period, perhaps because of what Franklin Knight and others recognize as the Church's ineffectiveness and loss of influence during Cuba's sugar boom. For his portrait of the priest, Calcagno uses an economical approach, conceiving him in reverse *costumbrista* fashion as the exception that proves the rule. Though the author alludes to the norm of clerical complicity in the abuses of slavery, this village priest represents the minority of whites who put good Christian principles into practice. Not only does the priest denounce abuse of the slaves but he acts in pursuit of justice for the enslaved. Testimony to his subversive role is the fact that he is regarded as a threat by the proponents of slavery. The chief and most outspoken defender of slaves among the characters, he is endowed with insight into the mechanisms of slave oppression. Moreover, he is recruited by the author to help heap ridicule on slave society's racist prejudices and to bring about the slave master's eventual conversion. The priest's success in this regard is one sign of the author's optimistic projection of hope, even as the novella puts to rest the myth that the Catholic Church's influence made slavery in the Spanish empire less harsh.

Although the author's voice is dominant, the story is not entirely narrated as a monologue. Towards the end the voices of the slave trader and the priest come to the fore. Each articulates an antislavery message, but with differing intent and consequence. The subversive rhetoric of Jacobo, who poses as a champion of the maroons, comes across as specious and hollow. It is an oblique indictment of the hypocritical voices raised against slavery in the real world, recalling the treachery of Jacobo's biblical namesake, who stole his brother Esau's blessing by deceiving his father, Isaac. In like fashion, Jacobo the imposter brings about the maroons' demise by betraying them to the slave hunters at the end of the story.

As the author's alter ego, on the other hand, the priest plays an oratorical role similar to Sab's in Avellaneda's novel. Slave masters, he believes, are guilty of dereliction of duty in not giving the slaves a Christian education, thereby (it may be inferred) denying them a source of strength to bear their condition. His choice for this role is not fortuitous, for religious faith is one of the author's prescriptions for the slaves' travails. By giving this instrumental role to the priest as mediator between enslaved and enslaver, the author signals his belief in the efficacy of moral suasion rather than force as an instrument of change. The successful revolution he envisages will come not from slave rebellion but from the goodwill of white society, in this case the enlightened priest and the reformed slave owner. Even though Romualdo dies at the end, what is important is that his father recognizes him as his son. In the redemption and reformation of the slave owner, Calcagno implies, lies the path to willing acceptance of the slave-descended person as part of the Cuban family.

To do justice to *Romualdo*, our understanding must take equal account of its positive achievements and its contradictions. An allegorical reading of the story's denouement is tempting. In spite of the author's earlier insistence on the relative unimportance of the role of the slave master, his survival at the end of the story proves the contrary. Castaneiro survives because of his perceived innate capacity for moral reform, already demonstrated by his renouncing the evil ways of his youth. The slave trader, however, is eligible for no such redemption. He dies at the hands of the rebel slave – as well he should, it is implied, because he represents that incurable malignancy that must be excised from the body politic. After all, the author/narrator has already willed his elimination at the start of his tale. Don Jacobo Vendialma has served his purpose as scapegoat for the sins of the slave-owning elite. In the case of the slave master, although his repentance guarantees his survival, he must still pay the penalty demanded by poetic justice. Romualdo's death frustrates his father's desire to make amends. Castaneiro must suffer the anguish of knowing that he has been complicit in the ill-treatment and ultimate death of his own son. And Romualdo's death serves as a veiled warning: he is, in the words of the priest, the endangered symbol of a possible rapprochement between whites and blacks.[28]

Calcagno's account poses an interesting paradox, for it is both anathema in its negrophobia and a monument to the heroism of African slaves who fought against their oppressors. The story takes on a dramatically charged tempo in the final episode, rising to a near-epic climax in the showdown between the maroons and their white adversaries. In his heroic last stand, Juan Bemba comes to represent fearlessness rather than fearsome savagery. In contrast to Romualdo's death, there is no pathos in the death of the other maroons. Like the warrior protagonists of epic literature, they sacrifice their lives in a fight for freedom. So this story does not end with the feelings of tragedy and despair that one gets at the end of earlier narratives – the maroons are not honourably outdone but cravenly betrayed. Their demise might be a concession to the awesome power of their oppressors, but their heroism mitigates the tragic potential of their deaths. The author acknowledges slave resistance as warranted and worthy of admiration, even when it is futile.

The author's ambivalence may be usefully understood in the light of the Bakhtinian tension between centripetal and centrifugal impulses. The confluence of aversion and admiration in the author's attitude, his wavering between empathetic involvement and detached voyeurism, is evidence of this syndrome. If this work is outstanding for its anti-black fearmongering, it is paradoxically just as remarkable for the antislavery resonance of its defence of *marronage*. The one cannot be acknowledged without the other.

Calcagno's vision of slave resistance is arguably the most significant aspect of the antislavery purpose of *Romualdo*, and a reflection of a liberalism that was not alien to his class during this period. As Caribbean historian Gordon Lewis reminds us, in their struggle for independence the emergent Cuban bourgeoisie embraced the liberal philosophies of their European counterparts, adding racist prejudice to their class-based bias.[29] The racism that compromises Calcagno's antislavery efforts might appear to be no different from the racism of the advocates of slavery. What the preceding analysis has shown, however, are the inflections in his representation that stand in the way of a complete equation of the two. It is possible to decry Calcagno's Eurocentric leaning while recognizing the value, however minimal or unwitting, in his critical perspective. Writing more than a century after him, Lewis places Cuba's antislavery novel and its "morally inspired social analysis critical of the slavery institution"[30] in the same politically subversive category as *marronage*, which posed a challenge to the sovereignty of the emerging European nation-state. That Calcagno's view from the centre of the colonial scene coincides with Lewis's postcolonial perspective is telling. For if he is attentive to the power of language as an instrument of slavery, the author of *Romualdo* is no less conscious of the subversive power of the language available to him as a writer – the power to speak out against social iniquity. Hence he includes among the doers of evil not only those who commit atrocities but also those who do not condemn them. "Silence," the author concludes, "is also criminal" – "*El silencio también es crimen.*"[31]

# ·5·

## "WITH ALL DUE RESPECT"

### Postmodern Parody, Drama and Antislavery Politics in Antonio Zambrana's El negro Francisco

ANTONIO ZAMBRANA'S *El negro Francisco* first appeared in manuscript form in Chile in 1875, a few years before the end of the decade-long war for independence (1868–1878) that sounded the death knell of Cuban slavery. Written at the urging of Doña Ascensión Rodríguez de Necochea, Zambrana's hostess on his visit to Chile in 1873, the novel served ostensibly to satisfy her curiosity about Cuban customs. However, this external remit converged with the author's own purpose, for as he observes in his introduction, denunciation of slavery was an inescapable theme of Cuban *costumbrismo*. Coming three decades after the dismantling of the del Monte literary circle, the Zambrana story is nevertheless both a beneficiary and a by-product of its activities. No discussion of this novel can ignore its antecedent *Francisco*. The relationship between the two is a near mandate for the comparative assessment to which both works have been routinely submitted.

*El negro Francisco* uses the same basic ingredients as *Francisco*: a slave-owning duo of widowed mistress and young master, two star-crossed slave lovers and action that shifts from urban household to rural sugar estate. While the second story substantially repeats the plot of the first, it also departs from it significantly with the addition of an epilogue telling of the young master's repentance and conversion to the antislavery cause. Commentaries on the two novels have been attentive to both their similarities and their differences. In his analysis, William Luis is careful to balance both without judgement;[1] however, some critical readings represent the similarities as imitation, while others have pronounced the second novel an improved version of the first. Although she concentrates on the differences that separate them, Jill Netchinsky calls *El negro Francisco* "a tardy echo" of *Francisco*.[2] Lorna Williams claims greater militancy and authenticity for Zambrana's "updated" version of Suárez's novel,[3] but notes that the second novel "retells the story of impotent, self-destructive slaves that Suárez and Avellaneda had already told".[4] Similarly, Pedro Barreda sees Zambrana as re-elaborating Suárez's story and reusing his theme while infusing it with "a militant and authentic abolitionism".[5]

Without minimizing the validity of these earlier interpretations, I propose the concept of parody as another way of understanding the convergence and divergence in the intertextual relationship between the two novels. Parody, in its postmodern interpretation, is a concept that eliminates the need to stress either correspondence or variance and that enables a reading of the second story as complementing rather than superseding the first. It is with this parodic understanding of the novel that this chapter will seek to illuminate the author's dramatization of the slave experience and his articulation of his antislavery views.

Although the nature and meaning of parody have changed over time, it is regarded conventionally as the act of invoking an earlier work with a view to ridiculing it. But in her study of modern artistic practices, Linda Hutcheon argues that ridicule is not a *sine qua non* of parody. Instead, she identifies "repetition that includes difference" as its common denominator.[6] This understanding of parody, as Hutcheon has shown, sits well with postmodern thinking insofar as it eschews the notion of polarity (mimicry *or* distancing), embracing instead the concept of hybridity (mimicry *and* distancing). Without minimizing the difference between a text and its antecedent by which parody is defined, Hutcheon notes that parody does not inevitably either target the parodied work for attack or endorse the parodic version, causing it to flourish at the expense of the original. To clarify her point she cites the distinction between parody and satire: "Both

parody and satire," she notes, "imply critical distancing and value judgements, but satire uses that distance to make a negative statement (to dis-
tort, belittle or wound), while the ironic contrasting of texts in parodic art
suggests no such negative judgement." She counters the traditional devalu-
ing of the parodied text by reclassifying it: "In parody another text stands
as the background against which the new creation can be both measured
and understood."[7] Parody, then, in this broader definition, is incorporation
of a pre-existing art form into a new work in a spirit ranging from destruc-
tive ridicule at one end of a spectrum to deferential homage at the other.
Such a flexible definition is a useful mechanism for viewing the connection between Zambrana's novel and Suárez's *Francisco*.

Though clearly mindful of the Suárez fable in writing his story, Zambrana is unlikely to have conceived of his work as having an active parodic
purpose as understood in postmodern terms. In practice, however, the
novel relates to the story that inspired it in a manner that suggests the
current understanding of parody. Applying late-twentieth-century ideas
retroactively to nineteenth-century texts, as proposed here, is an anachro-
nistic undertaking only in appearance. Hutcheon, for example, finds a
trace of the current postmodern formulation of the concept in Samuel
Johnson's eighteenth-century definition of parody as "a kind of writing in
which an author's words or thoughts are taken and by a slight change
adapted to some new purpose".[8] From a non-mechanistic postmodern
vantage point, *El negro Francisco* yields new meanings when read as a
respectfully parodic adaptation of *Francisco*. Sometimes, as Hutcheon
points out, "the work parodied is one that begs deflating; but more often
it is very successful works that inspire parodies".[9]

In composing *Francisco*, Suárez benefited from the culture of cooper-
ation fostered among the members of the del Monte writers' circle. Zambrana's adaptation of the older story is another expression of this collective
spirit. Hutcheon identifies this collaborative ethos as part of the significance of parody when she observes that "appropriation or borrowing of
the property of others questions art's status as individualized commodity".[10]
At the same time she is careful to note that "parody, whatever its form, is
never a mode of parasitic symbiosis, but a paradoxical structure of con-

trasting synthesis, a kind of differential dependence of one text upon another".[11] There is no need, she argues, to highlight only or mainly similarity or difference.[12] Many modern parodists do not mock the backgrounded texts but use them as standards by which to place the contemporary under scrutiny.[13] Viewed in this light, *Francisco* relates to *El negro Francisco* as a point of departure for the representation of late-nineteenth-century Cuban reality in terms of both correspondence and difference.

When Suárez wrote *Francisco* as a protest against slavery in the 1830s, the boom in Cuban sugar production was being achieved through the most heartless exploitation of slave labour. During this period the number of slaves grew dramatically, despite Anglo-Spanish agreement on an 1820 deadline for ending the African trade. The increasing heavy-handedness of Spain's political control of the island forced all dissent underground and into forums such as the del Monte circle, which provided a clandestine outlet for promotion of the antislavery cause. Suárez's novel reflects the literary temper of his time, for although Romanticism was the order of the day, realism also became a strategic imperative, given the urgent need to uncover the horrors of slavery.

The variance in the second novelist's perspective is attributable to the political climate in which he wrote. By 1875 the prevalence of slave rebellions, changes in economic interests and modes of sugar production, and the formal ending of the slave trade, coupled with a rising tide of anti-colonialism among the Creole elite, were some of the issues that conspired to undermine the viability of a slave-based society. Although slave emancipation was an early item on the agenda of the Ten Years' War, various factors delayed its immediate implementation, not least among them the fear of changes it would bring about in the existing social order. This explains the rebel leaders' initial cautiousness about sudden transition of the slaves from slavery to freedom. Three years would have to pass before abolition was fully embraced as part of the anti-colonial enterprise. Zambrana's alteration of the Suárez story is intelligible in the light of his intimate involvement in a changing *independentista* politics.

Two preliminary documents – the author's letter to his Chilean hostess that accompanies the manuscript and his *ex post facto* introduction to the published work – provide a helpful guide to comparison of the two stories. Zambrana's indirect referencing of *Francisco* invests the earlier novel with authority at the same time that it lends weight to his own story. Moreover, because parody depends for its effect on the reader's prior knowledge of the parodied text, this reference may be said to point the way to an intertextual reading of *El negro Francisco*. The double genesis of the novel is the focus of its modest but ideologically tendentious introduction. In it the signs of validation of Suárez's achievements are inescapable. In affirming the value of the earlier story, Zambrana describes it as both sad and true. Using an impersonal voice, the author admits to having been deeply moved by reading *Francisco* in 1862, when he was a mere sixteen-year-old. The experience, he recalls, marked the birth of his antislavery consciousness and his decision to devote his life and soul to the cause of abolition.[14] This confession of the impact of the Suárez story constitutes Zambrana's greatest tribute to his predecessor. With the advance display of his credentials, he also, wittingly or not, forestalls any questioning of his ideological and practical commitment to abolition to which the novel itself might give rise. He may, in fact, be seen to be claiming for his work the same truth value that he ascribed to Suárez's novel.

Zambrana was more of a political activist than a writer. In the independence movement he found the means to fulfil his youthful promise to translate his revolutionary ideas into action, for he was not only a participant on the rebel side of the conflict but one of the architects of the 1869 Guáimaro Constitution, which, among other things, declared freedom for all slaves. That he composed the novel virtually in the heat of a battle in which he was intimately involved (he was in Chile as an emissary of the revolutionary government) makes it not surprising that the work should show traces of his political activism at the time.

Zambrana seeks neither to discredit the value of *Francisco* nor to claim originality for his own work. Rather, his self-diminution – yet another sign of respect – implicitly reinforces his aggrandizement of his precursor, whom he describes elsewhere in the introduction as "one of the most important members of the literary circle".[15] In a further tribute to Suárez, he ascribes any success achieved by his version of the story to the merits of the original, reserving for himself the blame for any of his novel's flaws. But if the introduction is noteworthy for displaying Zambrana's reverence for Suárez, it is no less so for its signalling of some distance between them. Underlying his acknowledgement of *Francisco* is his concern with avoiding charges of slavish imitation of his source. This is succinctly expressed in the author's self-identification as *"el nuevo historiador"* (the new story-teller), but only after having accorded Suárez priority as *"el primer narrador"* (the first narrator).[16] Zambrana's representation of the relationship of his work to *Francisco* may even suggest a subliminal parodic connection between them when he describes his project as an undertaking for which he cannot claim originality. With this defensive statement, Zambrana has renounced any claim to innovation in his composition that suggesting the inadequacy of the original model would have implied. Here the novelist may be said to exhibit classic symptoms of the "anxiety of influence", a term that Harold Bloom has used to describe the tension between imitation and originality that dogs the process of poetic creation.

The title chosen for the later novel, which contains as well as modifies the title of the earlier work, points to a parodic interplay of deference and distance. Whereas the qualification *"negro"*, as has been noted by other commentators, accords with the author's investment of a more robust African consciousness in his protagonist, his retention of the name Francisco may be read as another homage-inspired gesture; with it Zambrana contributes to memorializing the male slave as a literary figure in the Cuban tradition. The adoption of the same name brings to mind the postmodern notion of unity in diversity. Thus the two Franciscos stand together with the famed autobiographical slave subject Juan Francisco Manzano as similar but separate figures in the gallery of male slave protagonists. Together the three make up a composite picture. Though united by their house-slave condition, they are distinguished by their responses to their situations. Juan Francisco is the assimilated mulatto Creole slave, while Suarez's Francisco is the almost totally emasculated African-born slave. Zambrana, meanwhile, makes his Francisco into the personification of slave defiance.

More with a view to explaining – but without judgement – the difference in their motivations, Zambrana states that Suárez wrote *Francisco* not as poetry but as protest.[17] This comment does double duty in warding off charges of aesthetic deficiency levelled at the first novel and in intimating the parodic slant of the second. His refusal to pass aesthetic judgement on Suárez's novel, pleading his then youthful inexperience, is even more suggestive of underlying respect. At the same time, the poetry/protest divide, coupled with an oblique promise to avoid propagandizing and tendentious editorializing, heralds a strategic difference in Zambrana's novel. His intention is to document rather than to denounce.

The tension observable in *El negro Francisco* comes from, on the one hand, the author's awareness that he cannot have recourse to an innocuous brand of *costumbrismo* that ignores or erases the horrible stains of slavery on the face of Cuba, and on the other, his desire to paint a complete and balanced picture of the country for his Chilean hostess. The view of plantation slavery offered by the novel has only vague outlines; the main interest is in following the misfortunes of the two transplanted urban slaves. In the process the author sets up a dichotomy between both sites of bondage, a separation that he not only creates with the bipartite division of the novel but also underlines anxiously. His ghettoization of the sugar estate as "a kingdom apart" tacitly privileges the urban slave experience and adds a mitigating nuance to his antislavery position. He acknowledges, in like fashion but summarily, humane exceptions to the virulent norm for the operations of the sugar mill. Zambrana will not bring his country's name into complete disrepute. Not willing, however, to dilute the strength of his antislavery statement, he paints the sugar estate as an absurd, topsy-turvy world in which the sound of slaves working the sugar mill "lulls" the supervisor to sleep, while their inactivity awakens him.[18] Like Suárez, Zambrana shows the enslavers themselves as slaves, living in a hell of their own making and seeking through violence to secure elusive peace of mind.

Zambrana's judgement of the sugar plantation makes no concession to economic necessity or historical contingency. His antislavery crusade is informed by a complex ideological mix. On one hand, it is partially coloured by a Marxist sense of plantation slavery as the classic incarnation of alienated labour.[19] A similar ideological principle guides his predecessor's indictment of slavery as enabling sugar planters to live off the fruits of their slaves' unpaid labour.[20] Zambrana's crusade is even more intricately bound up with anti-industrial Romantic ideals. Appropriately titled "El campo de batalla" (The Battlefield), the second chapter of part 2 casts the plantation as the site of a double struggle: the exploiter visits violence upon the exploited as the natural environment falls prey to the ravages of industrial technology and the disruptive and invasive modes of sugar production.[21]

Although the two slave protagonists and their love story occupy the centre of his novel, Zambrana is not oblivious to their kinship with their peers. Hence he is careful to portray the slaves as members of a community in which differences are inconsequential, contrasting with the divisive prejudice against the African-born Francisco implied in the xenophobic slave mistress's preference for Creole slaves. The passing mention of the slave who helps Francisco with his escape plans, for example, provides an intimation of the underlying slave solidarity so feared by the enslavers.[22] Moreover, the Cuban-born slaves not only accept Francisco but also accord him respect as a link to their African origins. As the converse of the master–slave conflict, this vision of unity culminates in the *rapprochement* between Francisco, "strange creature of the jungle", and Camila, "delicate product of civilization".[23] Both characters are portrayed in a manner that enriches their image and deepens the antislavery theme. Using their love liaison as a pretext, the author subordinates his novel's documentary impulse to its dramatic purpose. "The drama", as he states self-reflexively at the outset, "is what interests us and what we will try to use to hold the interest of others" (*El drama es lo que nos interesa y lo que procuraremos que interese a los demás*).[24]

Like Sergio Giral's 1975 film *El otro Francisco*, *El negro Francisco* has been adjudged a corrective for Suárez's depiction of his slave protagonist: Zambrana is deemed to have questioned implicitly the authenticity of the original model's meek nature. However, an absolute remedial intent hardly seems to inform Zambrana's portrait. There is no attempt to dislodge or discredit Suárez's portrait completely; each author, though in different measure, invests his protagonist's body with dignity, the differences in their temperaments and life stories notwithstanding. Upon his first entrance, Zambrana's Francisco, head held proudly, responds without subservience to the power of his superiors' accusatory gaze. This harks back to references to a similar demeanour which Suárez's protagonist maintains despite brutal beatings inflicted on his body.[25]

In view of the expectation that slavery would have destroyed the soul of the enslaved, centring this spiritual resilience lends credence to current postcolonial emphasis on the myriad (surreptitious) ways in which the enslaved subverted the designs of their enslavers. In like fashion, the slave's perceived endurance is made to transcend physical mystique to encompass mental and emotional fortitude. Zambrana avoids the reductive labour value that the economic self-interest of slave owners (even the more lenient of them) placed on the African slave's physical strength. His Francisco combines a warrior's strength with strength of character, "muscles of steel and a heart made of granite".[26] Zambrana, like Suárez, imagines a more personal benefit of this strength to the slaves themselves, making the point specifically when he attributes Francisco's survival of physical brutality to his strong constitution.[27] Thus the personal overlaps with the political, for though it is a despairing act motivated primarily by frustration of his love for Camila, Francisco's suicide at the end of the story also figures as an act of volition as he thinks of willing his own death.[28]

Zambrana's longer view of slavery includes what he imagines to be the slaves' relationship to Africa. Like his namesake protagonist in Suárez's novel, this Francisco remains consciously connected to his pre-slavery past. But the first Francisco's Romantic nostalgia contrasts with a radical African consciousness in his successor. As a sign of the importance given to his ethnic identity, the second Francisco is not characterized as a *bozal* (a derogatory label assigned to slaves from Africa) but is referred to more fittingly as "*negro de nación*" (African-born black), an embodiment of the spirit of African nationalism. Using his narrator privilege, the novelist underlines Francisco's persistent patriotism in order to legitimize the slaves' Africa-centred world view. He celebrates Francisco's memory of ancestral African religious rites as one means of preserving original identity under slavery. All this he does, however, without falling into the trap of over-idealizing the pre-slavery past.

Suárez's Francisco belongs to that primary group of Africans who, in the scheme of transatlantic slavery, were forcibly uprooted and transplanted to the Americas. That author's brief allusions to this experience emphasize its traumatic effect on his protagonist. With such a view, he implies that the burden of blame falls on the foreign predators. Zambrana's Francisco represents another group of Africans: those who were captured by their compatriots in warfare and sold into slavery. His "legitimate" enslavement stands not in opposition but as a complement to Suárez's version of Francisco's enslavement as a gratuitous act. Zambrana neither decries African complicity in these circumstances nor uses it as an apology for slavery. Stoicism is attributed to both Franciscos. It is expressed in the first instance as the victimhood of the Christian martyr. Zambrana, on the other hand, construes the second Francisco's stoicism as a soldier's courageous acceptance of his bondage as part of the game of war.

The second Francisco's character is not unproblematic. He experiences some anxiety when he realizes that he is a powerless black slave in an unequal contest with his all-powerful white master. Lorna Williams claims that, like its model, *El negro Francisco* is founded on a belief in the secondariness of blacks, and she cites in support the slave's self-deprecation when he envies his young master Carlos's physical and social advantage. What Williams describes as his "desire to be what he can never become" does indeed appear to be confirmation of slave-owner omnipotence.[29] Context, however, is everything. Not only does Francisco's perception not seem to be endorsed by the author/narrator (the novel's voice of authority), but his envy is far from absolute. Neither should one take it any more seriously than the parallel but reversed situation in Suárez's story, where Ricardo, the young slave master driven to desperation by the mulatto slave Dorotea's indifference, declares to her his wish to be black.

The feelings of both men arise from their belief that an ethnic makeover would improve their chances of winning the love contest. However, in a prompt move to neutralize the slave's self-deprecation and to ensure the integrity of his novel's antislavery message, the author exposes the second Francisco's thoughts as he chafes at the hegemony of white "civilization" and yearns for the life he would have lived in Africa. The episode therefore acquires no greater significance than that of a temporary psychological lapse on the part of the slave, a manifestation of a pervasive Bakhtinian tension rather than a pathological inferiority complex. Furthermore, race and language, as well as social and economic standing, are in Francisco's eyes the measures of Carlos's ascendancy. But after being exposed to the two rivals, the reader knows that the moral advantage – a far more important measure of worth – lies with Francisco. The author has therefore, in the spirit of irony, highlighted the absurd racist value system on which slavery was built, and its damaging consequence: black self-hatred.

The second Francisco's African consciousness, though the most frequently noted difference from his predecessor, is not the only one. Zambrana endows his character with a complexity not attributed to his forebear. A development in the plot that deepens this portrait is the ambivalence of his attraction to Camila. Francisco falls in love with her despite his initial antipathy towards her for betraying her black ancestry. His attraction, however, does not derive from an imagined inferiority complex. On the contrary, their relationship weaves another antislavery thread into the fabric of the novel's Romantic drama. Having dismantled the Eurocentric construction of her identity, the author paves the way for construction of a more Africa-centred Camila as a fitting complement for Francisco's African nationalism. Francisco assumes the roles of raconteur and missionary in order to cement their union; by chronicling the events and life of the pre-slavery past, he instils in his Creole slave lover a consciousness of her ancestral connections as a potent antidote for her alienation from Africa. With this endorsement of the Africanization of the Creole slave, the author has subtextually expressed a repudiation of the white European supremacy that slavery assumed.

Camila is Zambrana's adaptation of Suárez's Dorotea. At first she personifies the mulatto's assimilation into Euro-Creole culture. Indistinguishable in all but the slightest details from her owners and blinded to her true status, Camila naïvely confuses her identity with theirs. Her ostensible privilege instances the co-optation strategy that often camouflaged the mulatto's secondary social placement. Where the first author only casually acknowledges the beauty in Dorotea, Zambrana's insistence on this aspect of Camila destabilizes the Eurocentric notion of beauty as pure white. Her beauty is measured and validated by contrast with the white woman: Carlos feels repelled by his intended, the white Creole Rosalía, whom he describes as unremittingly ugly. To drive home his radically subversive point, Zambrana makes another white woman, Juana de Dios, uglier still.

His portrayal of Camila is nonetheless ambiguous. As the contradictory embodiment of virgin and siren, she cannot be contained by the period's monolithic Romantic norm. Focused on Francisco and Carlos respectively, the third and fourth chapters of part 1 of the novel are paired to draw attention to the instability of Camila's identity. In chapter 3, "El amor de un negro" (A Negro's Love), she is unsexed in the eyes of Francisco, the noble black savage, who sees only her inner beauty. In contrast, in the fourth chapter, "El amor de un blanco" (A White Man's Love), Camila, like Dorotea before her but to a more emphatic degree, becomes a carnal creature in the eyes of Carlos, the white male beholder. Not only in the popular imagination but also for the author/narrator, this "angel" embodies a forbidden but disturbingly irresistible sexuality. Compared with his aversion to the prospect of marriage to Rosalía, the relish with which Carlos fantasizes about a liaison with Camila is, from a nineteenth-century Cuban perspective, a blatant instance of what Fivel-Démoret in another context has designated "race treachery".[30]

As if to avoid dilution of the novel's antislavery message, to which this view of the mulatto might lead, the author uncovers other sides of Camila as mythic aesthetic icon and irresistible sex object. He offsets the Romantic view of the miscegenation she represents with a reminder of the sexual violence against slave women of which mulattoes were often the products. To this he adds their suffering, which begins in the womb and later turns into the anguish of orphanhood: the emotional deprivation and lack of a sense of identity that attends the anonymity of their white fathers, coupled with separation from their slave mothers. This deprivation leads to even deeper psychological damage, as seen in Camila's unwarranted hatred of her mother for her presumed alliance with the slave master. Only after introducing this disquieting element does Zambrana turn to a celebration of Camila's sensual beauty. His celebration is nevertheless disrupted because the preceding moral outrage inspired by the violence of cross-racial sex tarnishes the stereotypical image of the female mulatto fetish.

Zambrana clearly saw in the mulatto slave the shape of things to come. In his reference to her as an unsung heroine and symbol of the country,[31] he displays his prescience of the iconic role that this descendant of slaves would play in twentieth-century Cuban nationalist discourse. Through her he also dramatizes the psychological dilemma of the biracial and bicultural Creole slave. Having painted the Romantic surface (her beauty), the author delves into the tragic depths of her psyche. *Mulatez,* in Zambrana's reckoning, is a painful racial condition, and because of the gendered mediation of the relationship between enslaved and enslaver, even more so for the female mulatto than for her male equivalent. With his encomium to the *mulata* the author might appear to essentialize Camila's sexuality, constructing it as the dangerous appeal of the *femme fatale.* What he achieves, however, is not reinforcement of ontological fact but deconstruction of a popular myth.

In the picture that emerges out of her self-awareness, Camila is stripped of the sexual mystique. She experiences her fabled sexual appeal not as an asset to be exploited but as a curse, an unwanted invention of the white mind. This revelation amounts to a disassembling of the beautiful *mulata* stereotype built up in the first chapters of the novel, where Camila becomes the involuntary temptress, purported to be responsible for leading the white man astray. One can scarcely miss the antislavery subtext in this scenario; the metaphorical torture of the white male's unfulfilled sexual desire pales in comparison with the real psychological torture of the mulatto slave who must suffer the tyranny of an imposed sexual identity. Zambrana juxtaposes and counters the Eurocentric eroticization of Camila with Francisco's resentment of her denial of her black heritage, an anti-white stance that effectively turns the enslaver's anti-black racism on its head. In the critical distancing achieved by this interplay of different perspectives, the author has acknowledged the painful instability of the mulatto slave's identity.

By repeating the fate of Dorotea in Suárez's story, Camila's experience is a little-needed reminder of the persistence of sexual exploitation of female slaves. It also reaffirms what previous authors revealed: the gender-inflected divergence between the white slave master's participation in interracial sex and the white slave mistress's disapproval of the practice. Carlos's hostility towards Camila stems from her rejection of his advances. Doña Josefa's response is, unconsciously perhaps, an instance of displacement of the white woman's anger in face of the non-white enslaved woman's sexual attractiveness to white men. By including 1861 as a historical marker, Zambrana makes the point that, in this area, time has brought no change. Camila is caught between the rock of Carlos's unwanted desire and the hard place of Doña Josefa's undeserved displeasure. Her rejection of the Euro-Creole world is not, however, solid and unshakeable; her momentary attraction to Carlos's youthful magnetism, passion and good looks parallels Francisco's fleeting envy of what he perceives to be Carlos's social and physical advantage. But in the final analysis, this moment is merely part of the *de rigueur* suspense and complication of the Romantic plot. By mentioning but not developing this attraction, the author carefully ensures a swift abortion of the prospect of voluntary *rapprochement* between enslaver and enslaved.

Camila displays a kind of courage also apparent in Dorotea. Her imperious repudiation of Carlos is a more forceful version of her predecessor's stance against Ricardo. At one of the novel's most poignantly dramatic moments, Camila responds to Carlos's overtures with the words, "Go away! Whether as Francisco's wife or his widow I will hate you in the same way. Not one more word, not one more glance. Go away!" (*Vete; la mujer o la viuda de Francisco, te odiaré siempre lo mismo. Ni una palabra, ni una mirada. Vete!*)[32] In a subsequent show of resistance she vows to will her own death if Francisco is killed. Slaves, we are being induced to see, were as aware of their lack of control over life as they were conscious of their ability to control death. Camila also resembles Dorotea in her eventual capitulation to her master. As Suárez did before him, Zambrana features another side of this surrender; it is the voluntary price she pays to save her lover, recalling the sacrificial abortions, infanticide and self-poisoning of *petit marronage*. A sign of defeat, it is also a moment of heroism. Hence, while the masculine nuance of the chapter's title "El salvador" makes it seem to apply only to Francisco, who saves Carlos's life, it applies no less to Camila, who has saved him in his turn from certain death.

Zambrana is not unaware of slave rebellion as a more patent and radical statement, but for his dramatic purposes he allows evolution of his protagonists' antislavery consciousness to take place within limits set by their personal goals. His slaves are not radical maroons who defy their enslavers by escaping and establishing their separate community; *marronage* with its hardships has no appeal for these urban slaves. Yet the author does not conceive of his protagonists as mere victims. Zambrana's slaves express their discontent by contemplating a legal change of masters. Having them seek to improve their condition in this manner reiterates the thinking of the slave characters in Suárez's fictional world and goes some way to naturalizing this mode of resistance in urban slavery. Documents cited in Gloria García's *La esclavitud desde la esclavitud*, like Juan Francisco Manzano's autobiographical account, strengthen the impression created by these two authors that the slave's experience of house slavery was more likely to foster accommodation and less likely to inspire acts of *marronage*. Only when he ends up on the sugar estate does Zambrana's Francisco entertain any thought of becoming a fugitive, and not as a permanent solution but as a prelude to hoped-for placement with a more benevolent owner.

Added to the two slaves' disinterest in permanent escape is the disabling psychological consequence of their love. The author invests Camila, after her African conversion, with the potential to lead a slave revolt. She, however, is unconscious of her political promise, and her daring does not extend beyond strategies to free Francisco from torture. In like fashion, Francisco, who initially bears his bondage with dignity as part of the code of war, is driven to resent his master only as a personal rival. Although he finally comes to a fuller understanding of the systemic issues of power and powerlessness that determine his inferior position, he does not evolve beyond entertaining thoughts of retaliation against his rival. Feeling hard-pressed to wed political theme and Romantic drama, Zambrana makes his protagonists view their love as a solution for the misery of slavery. Far from diminishing them in the eyes of the reader, however, their selfish motivation is a measure of their humanity since, historically, not all slave resistance had a political motive. Flawed though they may appear, these two characters serve Zambrana's purpose well; his novel is not a sanitized tale of exemplary slave heroes but the enactment of a human drama in the theatre of slavery and all that it implies.

Zambrana patterns *El negro Francisco* on Suarez's novel by choosing the urban incidence of slavery as his first focus. Camila and Francisco are the classic house slaves; she finds favour with Doña Josefa as a surrogate daughter, while he is Carlos's protégé. However, where outside observers of the urban scene in nineteenth-century Cuba were taken in by this appearance of harmony, Zambrana unveils the conflict dormant beneath it. Any chance of real unanimity between the female slave and her owners (albeit her foster brother and surrogate mother) is ruled out by the racial and sexual politics of slave society.

Doña Josefa, a *costumbrista* type who exemplifies planter-class materialism, also dramatizes the ethnic and racial mediation of the enslaved–enslaver relationship. Her antipathy towards the unacculturated black slave Francisco is related to his ethnic Otherness; she prefers family slaves born, like her, in Cuba, not out of any sense of shared nationality but because such slaves, being presumably more tractable, present less of a threat to her supremacy. Her incorporation of the mulatto Camila into the family may be understood in similar terms. But even her ostensible maternal surrogacy is suspect; it lasts only as long as Camila's obedience and surrender of her free will. Apart from her disapproval of the slave's possible marriage to a negro, she will not allow her to form any other attachment. More importantly, with her obsessive need for her slaves to show respect and subservience, Doña Josefa embodies planter-class insecurity. With his pride and self-assurance, Francisco disturbs her sense of her superiority. Here Zambrana hints at the sugar planters' own psychic enslavement and their recognition of the inadequacy of brute force as an instrument of

absolute control. Doña Josefa's angry characterization of Francisco as inso-
lent[33] goes to the heart of this boomerang effect of slavery.

In both *Francisco* and *El negro Francisco* generational difference separates the slave mistress from her son. In the first novel the difference
favours the older generation. This situation is reversed in *El negro Francisco*, where Zambrana creates an impression of discord in the slave-owning ranks, with an older generation being challenged by a more liberally
inclined younger generation. Carlos's refusal to toe his domineering
mother's racist line is a symptom of this conflict. That Doña Josefa's outlook is to be regarded with disfavour becomes apparent in the collision of
her racist bigotry with her son's forceful assertion of the slave's positive
attributes. Carlos is not, however, free from ambivalence; though liberal
in theory and partial to Francisco as an individual slave, he is a creature
of the planter class and hence tolerant of slavery as a practice. Similarly,
although the impasse between Carlos and Camila attests to the same tan-
gled ideological web of sex and power evinced in *Francisco*, there is a hint
of more genuine *rapprochement* in Carlos's fantasy of marrying a mulatto
like Camila. Tempted by her, he is nevertheless constrained by the social
taboo against cross-racial marriage; hence his proposal of concubinage
with Camila under the cover of a legitimate, socially acceptable marriage
to a white woman.

Zambrana has captured both the surface and the subterranean levels of
power relations in slave society. The objection of Carlos and Doña Josefa
to the Camila–Francisco union is, on the one hand, a complicating feature
of the Romantic plot; on the other hand, it is shot through with complex
personal and ultimately political meanings. The enslavers' response is the
clearest pointer to their awareness of the accidentally subversive significance of the affair. It shows, moreover, how sex sullied master–slave interaction. Carlos's feelings towards Francisco turn sour only when both men
become rivals for Camila's love. The roots of these feelings grow deep
within the young slave master's psyche. He betrays his desperate intuition
of his slave rival's elusive sexual potency when he declares to Camila, "Me
or death. Francisco never . . . He will only live to see you in my arms. He
will see you in them or he will die a slow and horrible death at my hands"

(*Yo o la muerte. Francisco jamás . . . Él no ha de vivir sino para verte entre mis brazos. Te verá en ellos o lo mataré lenta y horriblemente*).[34] His compulsion to assert his will verbally over Camila and to have her acknowledge his authority is, similarly, the very sign of his precarious hold on power: "Here I am king, absolute king, am I not?" (*Aquí yo soy el rey y un rey absoluto ¿no es verdad?*)[35]

Carlos winces at the double blow the slave girl deals to his masculine pride by her refusal of his advances. On a deeper, subconscious level, her preference for Francisco inflames his social anxiety over the implicitly political defiance inherent in her "retrograde" step. Symbolically, the alliance between the civilized mulatto and the black savage undermines white Creole supremacy. In this outraged protest Carlos seems to articulate the Creole planters' nightmarish fear of a menacing negrification of the island: "You the wife of a black man! You the mother of black children! . . . I will never permit it!" (*¡Tú, mujer de un negro! ¡Tú, madre de negros! . . . ¡Jamás lo permitiré!*)[36] Tacitly this outburst also evokes memories of the proposed repatriation of African slaves and inundation of the country with white immigrants to redress the numerical imbalance that favoured non-whites in nineteenth-century Cuba.

The slaves' seeking to achieve happiness through an independent alliance is rightly seen by their enslavers as an act of free will. It translates into a hugely subversive gesture and a reminder of the limits of their power. Zambrana imagines this autonomy, no less than slave rebellion, as the gnawing threat that ironically keeps the enslavers in thrall to the enslaved. With his declaration "You need to love me very much" (*Es necesario que me ames mucho*),[37] Carlos appears pathetic, trying to achieve by diktat what Francisco has already achieved effortlessly. The author suggests that assimilation of mulattoes like Camila into the dominant culture (referred to by some black nationalists as a process of whitening) was an instrument of division. Francisco and Camila have sabotaged this process, albeit inadvertently. Power play in slave society, Zambrana seeks to show, was not a one-way street; it was tragic and it was also ironic. Entrenched in the tragedy of the master's (ab)use of his power to control the slave's body was the irony of the slave's power to arouse the master's deepest neuroses and frustrations, which he could try to appease only by violence.

In the corruption and conversion of Carlos lies one of the novel's core antislavery statements. At the outset the author's description exempts him from the typical vices of the youth of his time and class, which were defining traits of the young Fernando in Tanco's story. Although we do not witness the process of Carlos's transformation into an advocate of slave emancipation, the groundwork for his conversion has been carefully laid earlier in the novel through specific clues. Unlike his antecedent (the implacably evil Ricardo in Suarez's novel), Carlos, originally though not unequivocally, appears to be of a more progressive persuasion. His transgressive temperament is apparent in his choice of an African rather than a Creole slave as a coachman, and in his defence of Francisco, which goes against the conventional wisdom of advocates of slavery. His natural disobedience, seen further in his rejection of his mother's choice of a marriage partner, foreshadows his subsequent break with the ideology of his class, with the radicalization of his consciousness paralleling the radical turn taken by the War of Independence.

The subplot of Carlos's affair with the American Lucy is therefore integral to the narrative of Carlos's political transformation; her noxious influence arrests the development of the liberal potential and drives him to exact vicarious revenge for her betrayal by venting his venom on the innocent Camila. Attributing the cause of his degeneration to Lucy exonerates him, or at least mitigates his culpability. By shedding his ruthless image and recognizing the error of his ways, Carlos also pre-empts criticism by both author and reader. His redemption is a recuperation of his lost self; it involves both spontaneous confession and self-imposed punishment. By selecting this end for the story Zambrana has left the clearest sign of his optimism.

But poetic justice must take its course. At the end of this novel, like its predecessor, the slave protagonists have died after failing in their struggle to live autonomously. Ironically, however, like Christ the sacrificial lamb, their deaths become the catalyst for their oppressor's rebirth. Carlos survives but he does not triumph; though transformed, he must live with, and expiate, his guilt for the slaves' demise. His moral redemption will have both personal and political consequences; he will atone for his cruelty to the slaves by renouncing forever any prospect of happiness in a love relationship and by dedicating his life to the antislavery/abolitionist cause (albeit in the United States). More significantly, Carlos's redemption is the vicarious fulfilment of Suárez's dream, when he formulated the purpose of his novel in these terms:

> With regard to the aim of the work, it is undoubtedly to alleviate the miserable lot of the negroes by putting whites to shame. This will lead them to *repent* and to *mend their ways*. If only I could achieve such a grand objective! How happy I would be! [*en cuanto al fin de la obra, no le cabrá duda en cual sea aliviar la suerte desgraciada de los negros, sacando a la cara de los blancos los colores de la vergüenza. Porque de ésta viene el arrepentimiento y luego la enmienda ¡quién pudiera conseguir un objeto tan grandioso! ¡qué gloria para mí!*][38]

Carlos's new-found militant activism best expresses the author's faith in the programme and events of the War of Independence. This political engagement no doubt led him to envisage a positive role for white Creole slave masters in the emancipation process, a possibility still inconceivable to his predecessor in the 1830s.

The account of Carlos's conversion, though appended in an epilogue as an offstage development, represents a point of both convergence and divergence between the story and its model. Here Zambrana gives an even clearer indication of his debt to Suárez, in what in postmodern terms would be designated a metafictional moment. Drawing attention to his own novel's status as fiction, Zambrana makes his Carlos a parodic version of Suarez's Ricardo. Carlos appears no longer as an autonomous creature of Zambrana's imagination; he assumes the identity of the hypothetically "real" character whom Suárez (referred to by name) had cast as a fictional character in his story. Thus Zambrana merges the identities of the two characters while at the same time adding Carlos's reformation as a sequel and a twist to Suárez's story. In the epilogue Carlos diminishes the importance of the struggle against the metaphorical slavery of Cuba's colonial status. More critical in his view is the fight for abolition of the actual enslavement of Africans and their New World descendants. Here we find none of the reluctance of the gradualist approach to slave emancipation that was a strong current among even liberal whites at the time. Thus Zambrana grants emancipation in the political realm (independence from Spain) far less urgency than slave emancipation. In his view, redemption of the slave master does not obviate the need for abolition.

In *El negro Francisco* antislavery messages run the gamut of literary expression from drama to painting, from poetry to propaganda. They are communicated through overt means but also through less conspicuous detail. An active tension in the novel arises from the need to satisfy the competing demands of fact and fiction. In his introduction the author claims to be presenting the naked truth about slavery; art (*"fabricada mentira"*), he maintains, can never be as eloquent as nature (*"la verdad"*).[39] Accordingly, in the tradition of the best documentary fiction, the experience of slavery is presented at times by mere sprinklings of unembellished *costumbrista* detail. A casual reference, for instance, to the practice of generic naming is enough to underline the depersonalization of slave housekeepers. Some chapter titles, as well as the portrayal of both major and minor characters, serve a similar *costumbrista* purpose.

Scrupulously the author cites empirical sources, first-hand accounts and anecdotal evidence to instance the degradation of the slave. To establish the veracity of his account, he adduces historical facts such as the practice of dumping slaves at sea to escape English cruisers hunting slave ships. The second chapter of part 2 comprises a complete catalogue of the brutal regime of plantation slavery. Estate operations are described impersonally, but the author still feels beholden to artistic imperatives and compelled to rely on drama to expose slavery as lived experience. Casting the novel as drama assumes a non-intrusive author/narrator and transparent transmission of the message through events and actions. Pointed reminders that the characters are actors in a staged production are added to enhance this theatrical function. Dramatic exposition of the polemic on slavery is most famously executed in the studied dialogue between Doña Josefa and Carlos in the opening scene. This serves as an economical summary of the ideological conflict in slave society, with Carlos's more progressive views prevailing over his mother's intractable conservatism.

The risk of losing reality in the drama, however, is one that the author feels obliged to guard against. The novelist must maintain the fluidity of the boundaries between art and history. His aesthetic practice is inextricably implicated in, and constrained by, his social engagement. He resorts to horrific juxtaposition of culture and savagery to accentuate his point. After recounting in graphic detail the torture of a slave girl by her young mistress, the narrator characterizes the torturer as "a little girl, with satin skin and languid eyes and nervous look . . . an angel" (*una niña; de piel satinada, de ojos lánguidos, de aspecto nervioso . . . un angel*).[40] The tragedy of his fictional drama, he insists regretfully, is real and normal in slave society.[41]

Zambrana's initial promise merely to emphasize the facts proves difficult to keep. Time and again the political imperative asserts itself and the author yields to the urge to make tendentious editorial commentary. The story cannot speak for itself without direct authorial mediation. He violates the "bare-facts" approach with melodramatic outbursts and pithy, potent denunciations. Rising like a crescendo, the account of the breakup of slave families culminates in terse expressions of outrage at the end of successive paragraphs: "Horrific blasphemy! . . . Babylon in all its nakedness!" (*¡Horrible blasfemia! . . . ¡Babilonia sin mascara!*)[42] Plain-spoken statements combine with epigrammatic encodings of the author's meaning. The language in part 2 seesaws between drama and diatribe, between poetry and protest. Introspective techniques accentuate the suffering of the slave protagonists. Descriptions of Camila's hallucination and Francisco's jealous frenzy are worthy of the surrealist pen of Latin American writers such as the Guatemalan Miguel Angel Asturias, who took the stream-of-consciousness technique to a high point in the early twentieth century.

In the depiction of the sugar plantation, artistic stylizing combines with the bare-facts approach to advertise the themes of the paradox of the plantation as a whited sepulchre and of slavery as both a paradise of material gain for the sugar barons and a hell of human pain for the enslaved. Impersonal descriptions are complemented by lyrical denunciations of estate operations. A carefully orchestrated irony separates the superficial tourist's view from the insider-author's intimate understanding of the ugly truth of plantation slavery. The author repeatedly zooms in on the tranquillity and paradisiacal beauty of the natural landscape, but the ultimate aim of this Romantic accent is to underline slavery's nightmarish horrors through the use of deft counterpoint.

As the story unfolds, the author is drawn more and more towards polemic and the propaganda becomes more elaborate. Diatribe, not drama, is the dominant mode in the eighth chapter of part 2, "La derrota" (The Defeat). Here the author digresses into vehement antislavery preaching. Only a brief closing image of Camila witnessing the preparation of a grave for Francisco's imminent death contributes to the dramatic action. This image is preceded by a long preamble that forms the chapter's nub. In a dense paragraph the author launches a broadside against a Spanish journalist and detractor of the abolitionist cause. He gives the lie to proslavery arguments about New World slavery – the civilized West rescuing Africans from barbarism – by counterposing the horrors of the Middle Passage and the trauma of dispossession entailed in slavery. Persistent in his subversion of the myth of a savage Africa versus a civilized West, he declares his preference for "uncivilized" African ways. In a succinct manner he uses the principle of non-hierarchical cultural differentiation to vindicate the Africans' way of being, insisting on their desire for family, country and freedom – values they share with the rest of humanity.

One characteristic of art in the postmodern era is the artist's reflexive or self-conscious attitude towards artistic production and consumption. A version of this tendency is a commonplace in Cuban antislavery narrative, where forewords and introductions as well as textual self-insertions provide indispensable prisms for interpretating and deconstructing the narratives. Self-presentation (overtly or in disguise) is inseparable from representation in Zambrana's novel. He begins the process with the reference in his introduction to his adolescent susceptibility to the dominant belief system; he had imbibed the values of the slave society in which he had been born and bred. But the self-diminution of the reference to himself and others of his ilk as "mere storytellers"[43] is belied by a simultaneous and confident representation of their role as the moral conscience of an immoral society. Thus Zambrana establishes the validity of his antislavery posture in ethical rather than political terms.

With his novel Zambrana consciously subverts the literary establishment in practice as well as by precept. In the eighth chapter of part 2 the author reflects on the role of literature and the writer. He is bold and defensive in his criticism of the dominant tradition, which avoids dealing with "social aberrations" and prefers comic opera to tragedy.[44] More explicitly, he distances his writing from the *costumbrista* use of literature as mere entertainment, anchoring the justification for his approach in his faith in the power of art to influence public sensibility and action.

Hutcheon has noted the transhistorical tendency of parody to participate in the evolution of literary forms.[45] Aspects of Zambrana's picture of Camila prefigure the late-nineteenth-century transition from Romanticism to Modernism in Spanish-American letters, and most notably in the poetry of Rubén Darío. A Modernist tinge is added to Camila's otherwise Romantic portrait through the use of imagery from the graphic arts (painting and sculpture). In fact, the sensory highlights of her image recall the figure of Carolina in Darío's classic Modernist piece "Winter" ("De invierno").[46] But the parallel is merely formal; Zambrana subverts Modernism's exclusive concern with aesthetic effect and invests the slave's placement with social meaning. Camila is pictured lying like a cat at Doña Josefa's feet.[47] With this subtle pointer to her dehumanized status as a pet slave, the author has demystified the image of a unified family of enslaved and enslaver. And as if to further decry the slave/animal equation, the narrator creates a deliberately suggestive relationship between this first image and a subsequent snapshot of Carlos's pet dog, a Great Dane named Lucy, in a similar pose at her master's feet.

In addition to the chapter titles that bear the *costumbrista* stamp are others that mimic theatrical scenes or film sequences. In the opening chapter, strategies analogous to modes of filmic representation paint the slave owner's world. Moving from a brief focus on Doña Josefa and Carlos, the narrator's camera-like eye frames an image of Camila in a lengthy close-up. In the supreme moment of planter-class leisure, the mulatto slave is hardly distinguishable from her white owners, and with her elegant beauty she even appears to upstage them. However, as noted previously, the vision of the assimilated biracial Creole slave, of which this picture-perfect image is an apparent replica, vanishes upon closer observation.

Later the author resorts to filmic technique once again, this time to give a panoramic view of the sugar estate.[48] As in the opening shot of the family in Havana, a camera's-eye sweep gives the reader a tour of the estate and its operations. Quick sequences in a short paragraph show the frenzy of slave labour in the production process.[49] The tempo slows for a walking tour of the estate infirmary, where the camera shifts from a long pan across the room and its occupants to a close-up of an old slave.[50] Much of cinema's meaning, according to James Monaco, comes from an ongoing process of comparison of what we see and what we do not see.[51] This applies to one of the novel's most intense offstage moments.[52] First, a shot previewing the whipping post to which Francisco will be tied anticipates the whipping. Later, avoiding a gory description of the beating, the author records only the sounds and the counting of lashes as background for the primary visual image, Camila's distressed reaction. Such pictorial images are tentative signs of generic border-crossing, a straddling of the frontier between the literary and visual arts, a feature that Hutcheon sees as having come to characterize postmodern artistic expression.[53]

After 1871, Cuba's first independence war is said to have become unequivocally abolitionist.[54] This period of radicalization, which coincides with the composition of *El negro Francisco*, provided a propitious climate for Zambrana's liberal views to thrive, and separates his representation of both enslaver and enslaved from their equivalents in Suárez's novel. As Linda Hutcheon reminds us, however, because the model from which it deviates is included in parodic art as "backgrounded" material, "any real attack would be self-defeating".[55] Since a similar antislavery purpose is at the heart of both novels, any form of self-differentiation in Zambrana's story at his predecessor's expense would have been nothing short of suicidal. At the same time, recognition of this kinship does not provide licence to devalue Zambrana's achievement. If he cannot be easily judged a slavish follower of Suárez, neither does he exhibit a patricidal urge to free himself from his predecessor's influence.

*El negro Francisco* is neither mindless mimicry nor reckless rejection of *Francisco*. Zambrana's bond with Suárez brings to mind psychologist Judith Viorst's injunction in relation to the severing of family ties: "We stay in thrall to our parents as long as our way is simply whatever their way isn't. Our separation from them does not require repudiation. It requires free choices."[56] Zambrana likewise has opted to walk the path of postmodern parody rather than to take the route of unthinking imitation.

# ·6·

## ENSLAVING THE ENSLAVER

### *Tragedy, Irony and Dialogism in*
### *Cirilo Villaverde's* Cecilia Valdés

SOME FOUR YEARS after Antonio Zambrana published *El negro Francisco*, Cirilo Villaverde completed *Cecilia Valdés*. This novel would later come to be regarded as a literary *tour de force*, the mother of all nineteenth-century Cuban narratives and the standard by which other like-minded works are measured and found wanting. Although its genesis dates back to 1839, the novel's composition stretches over four decades of intermittent writing. Two earlier versions bearing the same title were published in 1839 and would later be incorporated into the definitive publication, which first appeared in New York in 1882.

Born in 1812 on the Santiago sugar plantation where he spent the first eleven years of his life, Villaverde was the son of the estate's doctor and a lawyer by training. He practised both journalism and teaching and was a prolific writer, authoring a variety of newspaper articles, textbooks and creative works. As a well-known activist agitating for Cuba's independence from Spain, he was imprisoned and sentenced to death for his involvement in the La Mina de la Rosa conspiracy in 1848. He escaped to the United States the following year, from where he continued his activism and where he was to remain for the rest of his life, except for a brief return to Cuba in 1859.

Although Villaverde's work commitments, political engagement, perse-

cution and exile conspired to delay its completion, the novel's long gesta-
tion period was not without its benefits. Spatial and temporal distance, as
well as intervening developments in local and international politics,
enabled the novelist's larger and longer view of slavery and of slave society.
Decreed by the Spanish metropolitan government in 1880, abolition
became a *fait accompli* only in 1886, four years after publication of the
definitive version of *Cecilia Valdés*. Understandably therefore, Villaverde's
novel, associated as it is with the period of transition from slavery to freedom, manifests neither the crusading zeal of Suárez's *Francisco* nor the
biting sarcasm of the novellas of Tanco and Calcagno. Another advantage
accrued to the late composition of the novel: as a founding member of the
del Monte circle, Villaverde was familiar with the work of predecessors
such as Tanco, Suárez and the slave poet Juan Francisco Manzano, and
he enjoyed the benefits and insights of the tradition they and others after
them had created. His was the challenge of giving his work a new impress
while dealing with old themes.

For most commentators, the final version of *Cecilia Valdés* is the one
that has legitimate claim to the antislavery label. On the question of its
political pedigree, however, there is no universal agreement. While Gordon
Lewis appears to endorse the view that the novel is "the most antislavery
in tone of them all",[1] Cuban critic Reynaldo González discounts its efficacy
as a denunciation of slavery and characterizes it instead, because of its
late publication, as a criticism of customs.[2] For William Luis, its opposition
to slavery is marginal to the main theme of the white man's exploitation
of the mulatto woman.[3] Displacement of the slavery theme from the
novel's centre has even led Richard D'Augusta to doubt its value as a
protest against slavery.[4] Such a perception is not surprising, given the standard of protest set by Suárez and Zambrana.

From a postmodern perspective, there is no compulsion to rank the
novel's antislavery value. *Cecilia Valdés* dissolves the distinction between
central and marginal themes, making indictment of slavery and slave society coextensive with other themes. The novelist pulls together the main
threads of earlier narratives, combines them into a synthesis and fills in
gaps left by his forebears in their literary accounts of slavery. Villaverde

deepens and widens the scope of his predecessors' work to reflect the complex human dynamics of the institution. And although the difference between the novel and its predecessors is striking, there are more parallels between them than first meet the eye.

It is equally true to say that to apply an unqualified antislavery label to Villaverde's novel is to run the risk of reducing it to only one of its many facets. Its singular contribution to the repertoire of colonial Cuban literature is the author's global vision of his society. Like a kaleidoscope, the picture Villaverde creates is composed of shifting images. With its variegated thematic threads, diverse voices and mix of actors, *Cecilia Valdés* is to Cuban nineteenth-century fiction what Nobel laureate García Márquez's *Cien años de soledad* is to the twentieth-century Latin American novel. Despite its all-inclusive scope, *Cecilia Valdés* did not constitute the last chapter in the antislavery story. Though it came long after the most important narratives, it still managed to be a pace-setter, inspiring later novels on a similar theme, most notably Martín Morúa Delgado's *Sofía* and Ramón Meza's *Carmela*, not to mention subsequent *telenovelas*, film adaptations, radio dramas, popular songs and ballets.

Over the years there has been no shortage of prescriptive judgements of *Cecilia Valdés*. The aspects that have found favour with literary reviewers include its impressive scope, its meticulous coverage of the local scene and the lucidity of its *costumbrista* vision. Its technical features have been the subject of rather less enthusiastic commentary. Some critics prefer to avoid the subject all together, while others (almost apologetically) have declared the work stylistically flawed and its author technically inept. Martín Morúa Delgado, the Afro-Cuban writer-politician who published his own novel, *Sofía*, in 1891 as a corrective to *Cecilia Valdés*, was one of Villaverde's sternest critics. He took the author to task for simplistic characterization as well as for linguistic and historical inaccuracies.

Reynaldo González's *Contradanzas y latigazos* is not only one of the most comprehensive Cuban studies of the novel to date but also especially valuable for its exploration of the ideological and political resonances of the novelist's representation of the life and mores of the time. While extolling its value as a historical document and a nineteenth-century classic,

González is confident in his assertion of the work's aesthetic deficiency, and cites various dimensions of the text in support of his theory. He uses this conviction to justify what he calls a "non-literary" reading – *"lectura no-literaria"*.[5] Such disabling comments on its alleged stylistic shortcomings do not encourage fair consideration of the author's representational strategies.

Slave characters are not the main focus of this novel, which tells the story of an incestuous love affair between Cecilia Valdés, a free mulatto who is the illegitimate daughter of the wealthy slave owner and slave trader Don Cándido Gamboa, and Gamboa's son, Leonardo. Nevertheless, an undeniable antislavery strain runs through the work. The differences between them notwithstanding, it is no less a denunciation of slavery than the narratives discussed in the previous chapters of this book. My concern here is to throw light on Villaverde's peculiar treatment of the themes on his liberal agenda from his location on the eve of emancipation.

Following in the footsteps of earlier writers, the author casts slavery as a tragedy for the enslaved. Like Tanco before him, he achieves his purpose through an intense focus on the enslaver and the use of irony as his prime subversive instrument. Villaverde expresses his meaning in *Cecilia Valdés* through a web of spoken dialogues between the characters, as well as subtle interchanges between the narrator and the reader as silent interlocutor. In addition, his representation of the ambivalent personalities and contradictory impulses of the actors in the theatre of slavery makes it difficult to identify any simple view of the world created in the novel. The ambiguity of Villaverde's fictional account, which is unacceptable to traditional tastes and might even seem to compromise the author's liberal pretensions, is less displeasing to the postmodern palate.

*Cecilia Valdés* is a *costumbrista* novel *par excellence*. Descriptions of social life, culture, leisure activities and different human types in the Havana scenario predominate, especially in the first two parts. The *costumbrista* essence of these sections may even appear to obscure the antislavery message, but like the proverbial needle in a haystack, subversive content is often concealed in the abundance of *costumbrista* details. Villaverde's choice of Cecilia as the title character of his novel, for example, is both a symptom of the author's interest in the life of the *gente de color* (mulattoes) and a reminder of one of the residual misfortunes of slavery. Though she is neither a slave nor the daughter of a slave, though she is as white as a mulatto can be, Cecilia bears the indelible "stain" of slavery in her mixed blood and the pathology of anti-black racism in her psyche. A slave connection, however remote, Villaverde implies, would continue to enthrall the free.

It is the near-whiteness of Cecilia's legendary beauty that is her passport to a love affair with the slave owner's son. Incest aside, it is equally her muted black taint – a throwback to her slave past – that precludes their marriage and permits only concubinage as the highest outcome of their relationship. This, then, is Villaverde's way of foregrounding, with critical intent, the persistent social consequences of slavery that his precursors, writing about the same period but according to different and more pressing imperatives, did not have the luxury of contemplating. As Villaverde saw it, the problem of slavery was not only legal but also social and psychological. Emancipation could change the slave's status under the law, but it could not cure the racial and social hangover of slavery's aftermath.

Moreover, Cecilia is only the egregious example of how slavery continued to inhabit the psychological world of the free mulatto. The racial anxiety of Uribe the master tailor stems from the same source. Uribe's pride in his pedigree is inseparable from his contempt for the descendants of slaves. He ascribes as much importance to his mother's non-African slave ancestry as to his father's white lineage. Other writers before Villaverde had focused almost to exhaustion on the racialized world of slavery during its heyday. From his late-nineteenth-century vantage point, Villaverde could look beyond the remedy of abolition to the deep-rooted and intractable mental maladies that had developed over centuries in a society organized around the inferiorization, subjugation and exploitation of an African-derived underclass by a European and European-descended elite and their collaborators.

Many episodes of this story are recounted in a manner that implies the author's understanding of the victimhood of slaves and his hostility to the practices of slavery. The horrific details of the Middle Passage journey (to which there are mere allusions in other narratives) and the tricks of the slave trade, as well as African complicity in the trade, all form part of the tragic picture painted by Villaverde's all-inclusive story. He foregrounds the vengeful acts of physical violence visited upon domestic and field slaves alike. Whenever slaves enter the picture in the first two parts of the novel, they do so primarily as objects of humiliation. The account of the domestic-slave experience centres on both physical and mental abuse. The whip is as handy a disciplinary tool for Leonardo, the young slave master, as it is for the *mayoral* on the estate.

In the first part of the novel the author carefully inserts small indices of the superciliousness of the slave owners and the subjection of the slaves. Don Cándido speaks to his coachman in imperious tones, while the latter responds appropriately with hat in hand. The recurring theme of the slave woman's lack of control over her body also appears in Villaverde's novel, but he avoids the narrative of ubiquitous sexual exploitation, making exploitation of her role as wet nurse his focal point. As in the case of Calcagno's *Romualdo*, whether he communicates his discontent by veiled allusion or through editorial intervention, the author/narrator puts ideological distance between his own viewpoint and his society's dominant perception. He activates this strategy, for example, when he underlines the slaves' status as virtual non-entities: "At nine in the morning . . . everyone was asleep in the Gamboa house. Here everyone includes only the owners, for the eight or nine family servants were not included" (*A las nueve de la manaña . . . todo el mundo dormía en casa de Gamboa. Hablamos aquí del mundo de los amos, en cuyo número no entraban los ocho o nueve criados de la familia*).[6]

Historical and sociological studies have postulated that urban slaves in domestic employ enjoyed an advantage over their rural counterparts, who were engaged in the more grueling fieldwork. Villaverde's novel seems to bear out this distinction, but only on the surface. In the first place, the gratuitous violence to which the male domestic slaves especially are submitted serves to diminish the difference between slavery in the two locations. Their low visibility in the first two parts of the novel is not fortuitous; it merely mirrors the slaves' real-world marginality as service providers, despite their placement in the bosom of the slave-owning family. Adding to their alienation, the slaves are shown to feel both self-hate and animus towards their peers. The hostility between two slave carriage-drivers is interpreted as a direct consequence of the hostility they are shown by their owners.[7] Forced to repress these feelings towards their enslavers, they displace them onto their peers – hostility begets hostility.

Yet another tragically divisive legacy of slavery that the novel exposes is the unbridgeable chasm created between black slave and free mulatto. The slaves' isolation is further exacerbated by the contempt of the upwardly mobile mulattoes in the free population, especially those belonging to the artisan class, to whom slave origins represent a curse. For this class, being a slave elicits not sympathy but reproach. When the mulatto craftsman wants to insult Dionisio, he dismisses him as his inferior, looking down on him not only because he is a cook but also because he is a slave. José Dolores Pimienta, the mulatto musician, also refers to Dionisio as a wretched slave, and there is hardly any difference between the stereotypical view of black slaves held by Cecilia and the views perpetuated by their enslavers.[8] This account of Dionisio's intrusion at the dance staged by the *gente de color* succinctly heralds the experience of social isolation marking the urban slave experience:

> Although he wore the appropriate clothes, his coat was too tight, his jacket too short, his stockings were old and discoloured, his shoes had no buckles, his shirt no frills and his collar was so high that it covered his ears. [*Aunque se vestía como se había dispuesto, el frac le venía algo estrecho, el chaleco se le quedaba bastante corto, las medias estaban descoloridas por viejas, carecían de hebillas sus zapatos, no tenía vuelos la camisa y el cuelo le subía demasiadamente hasta cubrirle casi las orejas.*][9]

With this emphasis on deficiency in dress, the slave's pariah status is confirmed. Clothes do not make the man, however. In a countervailing gesture of ironic distancing, the narrator directly interjects the parenthetical comment that Dionisio was no fool.[10]

Villaverde also discloses the reality behind the domestic slaves' marginalization. In the first place, their presence is palpable in their very absence, for it is their labour that enables the indolence and inactivity of the Gamboa women. Moreover, though located in the shadows, the slaves are forcibly implicated in the sordid conflicts that divide the family. This is the case with Don Cándido's displacement of his anger onto Tirso and Aponte, whom he expects to spy and inform on his son. The situation recurs in the episode of the jealous planter's wife who co-opts her coachman to report secretly on her husband's movements. The periphery of the household to which they are in theory relegated becomes in practice a position of privilege, which gives a subtle ironic twist to the domestic slaves' misfortune. Though not overtly so, these slaves are shown to be vigilant and perceptive; they study their owners' habits and anxieties and exploit the knowledge they gain to their benefit. Thus the novel provides more evidence of the failure of attempts to subjugate slaves and destroy their will.

Sugar plantation slavery (admittedly the most brutal manifestation of the institution) was the primary focus of earlier narratives. Villaverde is careful to juxtapose this variant for contrast with its coffee plantation equivalent. At the same time he is equally careful not to allow the differences between the two environments to obscure the uniformity of their aims. Being of opposite stripes, the two main slave-owning families in *Cecilia Valdés* preside over different practices of slavery. Whether in Havana or on the sugar estate, the Gamboa *modus operandi* is based on coercion – "treat 'em mean to keep 'em keen". On the other hand, the Illincheta family of the aptly named La Luz coffee plantation wields a soft form of power: they co-opt the slaves through good treatment, out of a shrewd sense that happy slaves yield more and are more easily controlled. The relationship between crime and punishment seems logical in this scenario, in which a supervisor or *mayoral* can be dimissed for brutal treatment of the slaves.

Isabel Illincheta is Villaverde's example of the most enlightened type of slave owner. Through her concern for her slaves' well-being she ensures the slaves' voluntary subordination. Rather than inspiring fear, she elicits their love and respect. In melodramatic excess, only Leonardo's ghastly gratuitous violence rivals Isabel's superlative compassion and tenderness.

The effectiveness of this ploy is corroborated by the slaves' behaviour. Isabel is a mythic figure in their eyes; more than a queen, she is regarded as a goddess. But the elaborate process of elevating Isabel and her practice of slavery is short-circuited by a skilful epigrammatic stroke. Insistently she forbids physical violence against the slaves, but only for the duration of the religious festival. Thus, by simultaneously reproducing and debunking the "good treatment" myth, Villaverde has erased the surface differences between these two modes of bondage. His account implies criticism of brute force and good treatment alike; both, he suggests, served the singular purpose of perpetuating the slaves' bondage and killing their desire for freedom.

For Villaverde it is as important to elicit sympathy for the enslaved as it is to induce revulsion for the enslavers. Viewed in this light, the former's repeatedly meek responses to abuse serve less to portray them as spineless than to shed an ugly light on their abusers. This line of attack on the practice of slavery is the purpose of the skilfully choreographed and grotesque image of the vicious whipping of Aponte by Leonardo, still dressed in his finery after an elegant social affair. Other indirect means are used to make the reader the author's accomplice and to discredit the Gamboa family. Mimicking the strategy used by Tanco, he reveals his ironic intent early in the novel by making a charade of the family's appearance of respectability. The immaculate cleanliness and luxury of their dwelling throws the unwholesomeness of the family situation into sharp relief.

By associating the Gamboa family with incest or near-incest, the author further erodes slave-owner prestige. The love affair between Leonardo and his half-sister Cecilia harks back to an egregious iniquity of slavery intimated in each of the earlier narratives: the potential for incest occasioned by the anonymity of mulatto children's slave-master fathers. But for Villaverde the incest trope has deeper roots within the family. It manifests first as Doña Rosa's sick love for her son, Leonardo, which befits a lover rather than a mother. Incest is also an undercurrent in the interaction between Leonardo and his legitimate sister Adela; they are barely restrained from being lovers by their biological relationship. Further reinforcing the incestuous overtones of this affinity is the subtle confusion of

Adela and Cecilia in Leonardo's eyes and his mind. Beyond its significance as a symptom of the absence of healthy love within the Gamboa family, incest becomes a compelling metaphor for the morbid self-centredness of a closed and impenetrable slave-owning class.

Villaverde also discloses ironies lying beneath the surface of the enslaved–enslaver power relationship. The paradox of the enslavement of the slave owner, which appears sporadically in earlier narratives, becomes one of his major themes. He challenges perceptions of the victimhood of the enslaved that imply the impunity of their enslavers. After allowing Leonardo to vent his fury on the slave coachman, the author – without losing sight of the significant difference between the two experiences – casts such violence as a psychological nightmare for both the tortured and his torturer. When the family visits the sugar estate, repeated bizarre references to the "music" of the whip are likewise a powerful comment on the psychological enslavement of the enslavers, who must live in perpetual unease, their sense of security contingent upon their continuous brutalization of the slave. Trapped in a vicious cycle, they rule by fear, but they are also fear's victims.

Like his predecessors, Villaverde is acutely aware of both the open signs and the hidden dimensions of friction between the enforcers of slavery and the enslaved. He shows how slaves inadvertently scored psychological points merely by managing to survive slavery and maintain their dignity and selfhood. This is the inference from the interaction between Liborio, the slave-supervisor, and two estate slaves, Tomasa and Julián. While they derive their happiness from their love for each other and positive engagement with their kin, Liborio can only satisfy his sadistic urges by inflicting pain on the two slaves. A perverted envy fuels Liborio's rage against Tomasa and Julián. Despite his superior power, the slaves' emotional fulfilment is a subliminal reminder to him of the sterility of his own life.

In his 1892 review of *Cecilia Valdés*, Martín Morúa Delgado remarked on what he deemed to be the unforgivable absence of a good character in the work, a view that he bases on Aristotelian-type poetics. The framing of Villaverde's character portraits is more in line with postmodern thinking; his characters are not contained neatly within the bounds of either virtue or villainy. Villaverde's main characters in the slave-owning camp appear static in the sense that they do not undergo dramatic change. Instead, their dynamic derives from their mercurial identities, the complexity of their personalities and the contradictions and ambivalence of their postures. Not only is such inconsistency not jarring to a postmodern sensibility, but it also facilitates the ironic estrangement of author from character. Neither slaves nor their masters, individually or as a group, can claim a unified identity. No other antislavery author captures this dissonance as Villaverde does.

Like Tanco before him, but more expansively, Villaverde's criticism of slavery finds its most robust expression in exposure of the psychology of the slave-owning class. Comparatively speaking, the slave owners play a larger role than the enslaved, especially in the earlier parts of the novel. Where the missionary impulse of earlier writers was directed at humanizing the slaves in order to contest proslavery arguments, Villaverde shows the humanity – or, to be more precise, the human vulnerability – of the enslaver, a strategy whose intent, nevertheless, cannot be mistaken for vindication. Goodness and evil no longer manifest as bipolar attributes of enslaver and enslaved. Villaverde replaces Tanco's unequivocal denunciation of the *nouveaux riches* peninsular sugar barons with more nuanced and complex insights into their thinking and being.

Don Cándido Gamboa, the novel's main slave owner, defies containment in a fixed category. Simultaneously sanctified and demonized, he is a prime example of unresolved ambiguity. Early in the novel he reveals the contradictory essence of his character when he appears incognito as the good father and guardian angel of his illegitimate daughter Cecilia and her family. Like Calcagno's Don Juan Castaneiro in *Romualdo*, this erstwhile womanizer has experienced a crisis of conscience and is fully repentant, candidly accepting blame for the sins of his reckless past. Throughout the novel he sows the seeds of his redemption as he tries to expiate his guilt by looking after Cecilia's material needs and expressing genuine concern about her moral conduct. His attitude to his son, Leonardo, though more complex, shows signs of a similar preoccupation, which makes him appear to be a more desirable parental influence than his overindulgent wife.

Paradoxically, in the same opening episode, the author also hints at Don Cándido's villainous other persona. When Cecilia's great-grandmother sees him, she inadvertently delivers a blow to his saintly image when she recoils in fear, believing him to be the devil. This reaction is reminiscent of stories of Africans' terrified response in their first encounter with white Europeans. As the story unfolds, the reader is exposed to this other Don Cándido, the rich, rapacious and ruthless business magnate who, as a clandestine slave trader and trader in other goods, reflects the concentration of wealth in slave-owning hands. Villaverde is unstinting in his condemnation of Gamboa in the slave-master role, unmasking without comment some of his most nefarious business dealings. Don Cándido rues the loss of a ship more than the loss of its cargo of slaves. His typical response to the horrors suffered by the slaves is callous. The glee with which he recounts his ghastly business endeavours removes him far from the saintly image of the novel's opening scene. Besides, though cognizant of the immorality of slavery, he cynically believes that slave owners cannot have moral scruples.

As a counterweight to his ostensibly secure privilege and power, Villaverde places the travails of Don Cándido alongside the tribulations endured by the slaves in his household. Despite his social and economic advantage, Don Cándido's psychological state is not the polar opposite of that of a slave; ironically, he is bound by cultural and personal shackles. Once an impoverished Spanish merchant, he has risen to become a sugar planter by marrying into the ranks of the Cuban Creole elite. Yet, never allowed to forget his beginnings, he wears his socio-economic origins like an albatross. The slaves' awareness of his inferior pedigree weakens his authority over them, and in the world of the slave-owning elite his social elevation is insufficient to compensate for his cultural limitations. To them he remains the classic country bumpkin, an upstart opportunist who has married into old money, and a mere businessman who lacks the education and finer social graces of the Creole elite. Another version of Tanco's "pig-rearing peasants", he covets the status of *hacendado* (owning property and slaves), which would elevate him above his standing as *comerciante* (trader), and he eventually buys a noble title from Spain. One cannot miss the traces of white Cuban Creole snobbishness in Villaverde's portrait of this species of slave owner. The inescapable subtext in the failure of Gamboa's attempts at "gentrification" is pride in the hereditary cultural superiority claimed by the class to which Villaverde belonged. An expression of anti-Spanish nationalism, this representation also suggests that such nationalism is the preserve of the colonial elite.

Hidden in Don Cándido's story is another, more tragic side: even though he makes provision for Cecilia's material needs and is concerned for her moral well-being, she repays him with neither respect, gratitude nor affection. In his family life Don Cándido is also a failure. His obsession with accumulating material wealth, his lack of education and his cultural deficiencies lead to a fractured relationship with his family. Present repentance and atonement notwithstanding, past peccadilloes vitiate his relationship with his wife, who, like Cecilia, misunderstands his motives. Hated by his son, he is also alienated from his daughters. Referring to their socio-political status as colonials, Reynaldo González reminds us of the precariousness of the power of the slave owners, whom he describes as "temporary owners of their own wealth" (*duenos interinos de su propias riquezas*).[11] For Villaverde this irony has not only a social but also a psychological resonance. The irony of Don Cándido's story is his self-created dilemma. As we saw in *El negro Francisco*, Zambrana imagined the emotional deprivation suffered by mulatto slave children because of the anonymity of their slave-owner fathers. Villaverde, in his turn, imagines the anxiety that beset these fathers. Don Cándido is doubly enthralled: in addition to being kept in a state of perpetual unease by his illicit business dealings, he is also dogged by the threat of incest hanging over his son's head.

Deepening his tragedy even further is Don Cándido's enslavement by his slave wet nurse María de Regla, the keeper of his most shameful secret – Cecilia's identity. At the level of metaphor, Villaverde once again reiterates the theme of the enslaver in bondage. Don Cándido is a slave to his past: "When he thought he was most free, he felt . . . the weight of the shackles tying him to the mysterious post of his original crime" (*Cuando más libre se creía, sentía . . . el peso de los grillos que le ataban al misterioso poste de su primitiva culpa*).[12] He too lives in a hell-world of psychological torment. Unlike Avellaneda's attempt to minimize the tragedy by glossing over the lived reality of slavery and appropriating the term as a metaphor for marriage, Villaverde, as we have seen, leaves no doubt about the distinction between rhetoric and reality.

The apparent impunity in the author's treatment of this character is a source of disquiet for Selwyn Cudjoe: "*Cecilia Valdés* leaves us with . . . the feeling that nothing has happened to the novel's most despicable character."[13] But Don Cándido cannot be said to escape poetic justice. Though not unredeemably despicable, in the end he (the man, as against the slave master) suffers emotional punishment commensurate with his transgressions: his investment in preventing an incestuous liaison between his legitimate son and illegitimate daughter comes to naught. His efforts at atonement are not sufficient to erase his transgressions. He survives with the noble title he has bought and the wealth he has accumulated, but also with responsibility for the story's tragic outcome. Justice has been served literarily.

Although in his portrayal of Don Cándido the author seems to echo Tanco's anti-Spanish sentiments, his perspective is nevertheless not a superior Cuban Creole's unequivocal deprecation of the Iberian Other. That the author wishes to set up a distinction between Cándido the person and Cándido the slave owner becomes evident when the narrator intervenes to exonerate him. In his defence the author/narrator notes that he has transcended his womanizing ways; his "good heart" compensates for his lack of good breeding, and even Doña Rosa is forced to admit that he is a dutiful husband. With this schizophrenic portrait, Villaverde shows that he has moved beyond Tanco's rank prejudice against the *nouveaux riches* Iberian sugar barons. In the final analysis, this slave owner is an inscrutable character; the reader's sympathetic response is induced by the tokens of his variable identity. The strategically placed final image of Don Cándido stricken by guilt for the tragedy precipitated by his actions ensures that sympathetic response. His self-exonerating words to his wife, "I'm not the wretch that your imagination has created" (*no soy el malvado que su imaginación la pinta*),[14] are not only his plea for her understanding and forgiveness but also the author's effort to pre-empt his reader's unqualified condemnation of this character.

Leonardo, the intended heir to the Gamboa fortune, exhibits signs of a similarly chameleonic personality. The author leaves no doubt about his savagery; the barbarity of his wanton abuse of the slaves is of caricaturesque proportions. Even his horse is shown to be capable of the compassion he lacks. But Leonardo is not monolithically monstrous; he is both sensitive and sadistic, debonair and devilish. Villaverde insists on the paradox of Leonardo's personality, a rough exterior hiding a soft and generous heart. While this is the aspect that prevails in his relationship with Cecilia, his seamless transition from gallantry and affection towards Cecilia to verbal and physical violence against his coachman makes an eloquent critical statement.

Through Leonardo, Villaverde develops the theme of an intergenerational rift in the slave-owning family like that which Zambrana broached in *El negro Francisco*. Implicated in this family conflict is the broader political division in the slave-owning class, involving separation of the superior Cuban Creole self from the Spanish *arriviste*. Like Carlos, Leonardo represents the younger generation of male slave owners, and his antipathy towards his father is expressed in both personal and ideological terms. He is but one example of the author's subversive use of insider voices. With stinging sarcasm he censures Don Cándido's involvement in illegal slave trafficking and his purchase of a noble title with the blood of the slaves. But like his antipathy towards his sister's Spanish suitor, Leonardo's criticism, though strident, is selective and carries weight as an anti-colonial rather than antislavery statement. Through his profound hatred of the Spanish, and especially the Spanish military authority in Cuba, Leonardo provides the white Creole version of the mulatto Sab's nationalism.

At the same time that Villaverde gives him this role, he signals his own ideological dissociation from the brand of nationalism espoused by the likes of Leonardo. To begin with, Leonardo is more vicious in his treatment of the slaves than the father he condemns. Moreover, though he resents Don Cándido and is critical of his slave-trading activities, these activities enable his profligate lifestyle. Without compunction he enjoys and even squanders the wealth generated by his father's illegal business, in the same way that he shares friendship with his Spanish peer O'Reilly but secretly desires his demise. Added to this is the fact that his anti-Spanish feelings are personal rather than principled and are informed by unthinking xenophobic prejudice. The anti-Spanish message might appear to coincide with Villaverde's own *independentista* politics, but it is sabotaged by the messenger's lack of moral authority. Without a grounding in anti-colonial political convictions, Leonardo's anti-Spanish feelings are gratuitous in Villaverde's eyes.

In her study of the British Caribbean experience, Barbara Bush notes that "the role and status of black women . . . [cannot] be satisfactorily analyzed without cross reference to the role of white women and the complexities of sex, class and race inherent in slave societies".[15] Villaverde's novel seems to respond to this concern by making the woman of the slave-owning class as well as the enslaved woman integral to the antislavery theme. Through her actions and the apparent schizophrenia of her attitudes, Doña Rosa exemplifies Villaverde's refusal to endow his characters with fixed identities. Condemnation of the cruel slave mistress that she represents does not stand in the way of acknowledgement of her virtues. She appears alternately cruel and charitable, demanding on one occasion that Dionisio be burnt alive for his recalcitrance and on another advocating good treatment of the slaves on the sugar plantation in the interest of positive self-presentation.

Where Villaverde is unforgiving is in his indictment of Doña Rosa's overindulgent relationship with her son, an area in which her husband seems less reprehensible. In exonerating Cándido, Villaverde blames his wife for being irrational and blinded by jealousy and pride. Like Leonardo, Doña Rosa serves Villaverde's expression of anti-Spanish politics. The author assigns the symbolic gesture of removing the runaway slaves' chains to this Creole lady, a member of the traditional slave-owning aristocracy. Taken in conjunction with her Spanish husband's lack of concern over how slaves are treated, this act translates into attribution of a more generous spirit to the Cuban Creole than to the Spanish colonist.

Since work was the province of slaves, white Creole women, from all historical accounts, lived a life of total leisure. Isabel Illincheta is, therefore, an unconventional member of this group. A coffee planter and slave mistress, she does not fit the mould of Romantic idol or delicate decorative object, as does Avellaneda's Carlota. Neither does she live a life of idleness like the Gamboa girls, for she manages the coffee plantation even though her father is alive. Having divested her of stereotypically feminine traits and invested her with a compassionate attitude, Villaverde prepares her to become the voice that criticizes the Gamboa way of being slave owners. By exploring her psyche he sets her up as the conscience of the slave owner. With her liberal inclination she stands as the author's surrogate, raising fundamental questions about the (im)morality of slavery. Yet, although her status as Leonardo's social equal lends credibility to her censure of his ways, her dissent can have no influence, since it is expressed only as an interior monologue.

Moreover, this favourable portrayal of Isabel is not sustained. In the final analysis, despite the difference in their motivations, she, like Doña Rosa, betrays the self-serving motive that inspires her ostensible altruism. Not only is her advocacy of good treatment based on her view of the slaves as "living capital",[16] but on a personal level she derives self-satisfaction from the fact that she is the object of their idolatry. Having failed to realize her revolutionary potential, she finally agrees to marry an unreformed Leonardo, thereby jettisoning her professed moral scruples. The alliance thus formed harks back to the incest motif in the Gamboa family relations, for in the end Isabel's class loyalty supersedes her ethical inclination. The author introduces a subtle foreboding of this turnabout in the episode where Isabel at first stoutly opposes the whipping of a horse during the trip to the Gamboa estate. Subsequently she allows her protest to be overruled and literally closes her eyes rather than be a witness to the cruelty. In like fashion, by eventually opting to marry Leonardo, she easily forgets his malevolence, and by this association she becomes guilty of the brutal practice of slavery. Like the repentant Carlos of *El negro Francisco*, Isabel breaks ranks with her class. But where he resolutely translates ideology into political action, a fickle Isabel ends up betraying her ideals. Thus, this novel seems to say, slave owners are irrevocably tied to the interests of their class. For this she is made to pay with Leonardo's death and her own retirement to a convent.

Mikhail Bakhtin, who has given the label "dialogism" to the multiplicity of voices that go into the making of a novel, explains the concept in this way:

> The novel orchestrates all its themes . . . by means of the social diversity of speech types and by the differing individual voices that flourish under such conditions. Authorial speech, the speeches of narrators, inserted genres, the speech of characters are merely those fundamental compositional unities with whose help heteroglossia can enter the novel . . . This movement of the theme through different languages and speech types, . . . its dialogization – this is the basic distinguishing feature of the stylistics of the novel.[17]

Bakhtin's dialogism implies an exchange of either complementary or competing voices. An author may create "independent" characters, that is, actors whose voices do not harmonize with that of their creator. The reader's task is to distinguish between characters from whom the author is separated and those who appear to speak for the author. This subtle distinction is important for decoding the text and offering an interpretation of the author's purpose. Villaverde uses the dialogic approach with varied intent, most conspicuously for articulation of the proslavery apologetic and as a means of revealing the perceptions of the defenders of slavery. In reading *Romualdo* the concept of surveillance was applied to the process by which the author/narrator creates an identity for the maroons. Slave identity is constructed in a similar manner in *Cecilia Valdés* by the slave owners and their surrogates. Throughout the novel, slaves and slavery are the subject of their conversations. But the advocates of slavery do not speak with one voice; instead, Villaverde casts their conversations as a trading of proslavery ideas.

In this world view, slave identity is unstable; each member of the group constructs it in a manner that serves his own purpose and arises from his own experience. Don Cándido's ethnology of African slaves, derived from trafficking, collides with Moya's first-hand experience as an estate supervisor. The priest offers a condescending view of the slaves as incapable of rational behaviour. Thus Villaverde conveys the idea of the fragmentation of slave identity that results from competing views, as well as the consensus among these views on the issue of slave inferiority. As in the case of the invisibility of domestic slaves, this use of talk not only shows the enslavers' failure to understand their slaves but also encodes the author's message about the slaves' powerlessness. The relationship between these voices and the author's voice is one of discord rather than unison.

One lengthy exposition that paints a picture of the slaves as soulless and inanimate is so outrageous that it smacks of satire. In the speaker's eyes a bundle of tobacco is a fitting analogue for a shipload of slaves.[18] The author is careful, however, not only to present misperceptions but also to enlist the reader's criticism through ironic distancing from such thinking. Long and laboured in exposing proslavery views, the novel is short and sharp in disputing them. The argument above is demolished with a parenthetical reference to the captive slaves as "the load, made up of *human beings, call them what he will*" (*la carga, compuesta de* seres humanos, diga él lo que quiera).[19] This reference is all the more powerful because of its terse and summary resonance and its calculated placement as the final words of the chapter. Interjection of similarly cryptic swipes causes the author/narrator's opposing view of slaves to prevail elsewhere in the novel.

Villaverde's sensitivity to gender dynamics is also embedded in the novel's dialogue on slavery. In this regard, the younger generation of women in the slave-owning group assume ironic importance. The exposé of proslavery views discussed above is attributed to male actors in the story. Though silenced under the dictates of their patriarchal society, white Creole female characters of the younger generation are nevertheless important interlocutors who represent a dissenting consciousness. Resisting the dominant ideology, they naturally extend their sympathies to the slaves. Like the slaves, their thoughts represent the untold story of opposition to slavery. Deftly Villaverde notes the silencing of female voices in this male-dominated dialogue. Their private meeting, ironically designated a "women's congress", is limited to talk of domestic affairs and presents no possibility for translating their subversive thoughts into political action.[20]

THE DEVIL IN THE DETAILS

The shortage of personal testimonies that could provide a complete psychographic profile of the enslaved has been noted in the historiography of Cuban slavery. By imagining the subjective world of his fictional slaves, Villaverde has presumed what he had no way of knowing in reality. To the pervasive talk about slaves and assumptions about their identity he counterposes their actions and their attitudes to their reality. If he is anxious to show the complexity and ambiguity of the enslavers' personalities, Villaverde is no less careful to depict the slaves in a similar manner. Although the covert dimension of their lives is not always developed, the author's sensitivity to its importance is telling.

An implicit acknowledgement of the discrepancy between slave subjectivity and outward appearance pervades the story. María de Regla, the domestic slave, harbours a perennial desire for freedom even while she cunningly disavows it when she finds herself in the presence of her owners. The ostensibly docile Dionisio secretly refuses the slave identity thrust upon him, declaring on one occasion that he was not born to be a slave all his life. Repeatedly the author shows the slaves' response as contingent upon their reading of the politics of the situation.

Despite his subjection to Leonardo's authority, Aponte the coachman carries within him the rebellious spirit of his historical namesake, José Antonio Aponte, who was executed for organizing the 1812 mixed-race abolitionist conspiracy. The coachman is also a fearsome figure to Reventos, the *mayordomo* (overseer). The author subtly dismantles the racist notion of slaves as simple-minded and meek by instancing Aponte's judgement and intelligence. This is also his purpose in juxtaposing the enslavers' condescending view of the enslaved with the shrewd actions of the foundation slave Goyo. He uses the leverage of his historical knowledge as well as his perceptive appraisal of their different personalities to intercede with Doña Rosa rather than Don Cándido on behalf of the returned fugitives and, more cunningly, to stoke the simmering conflict between the couple. Such details, taken together, constitute not fortuitous insertions but deliberate motifs in the novel's antislavery design.

In criticizing slavery as a social ailment, the writers of the period were not oblivious to slaves' efforts to use legal recourses to change their status or improve the conditions of their lives. Gloria García's study of historical records for the period shows that slaves made frequent use of legal provisions such as *coartación*, a system that allowed them to purchase their freedom. Other authors before Villaverde also invoke these options, but only to cast doubt on their efficacy; they bear no greater importance in the action than as strategies that the slave protagonists contemplate fleetingly.

In *Cecilia Valdés* Villaverde also instances these rights, but with cynical intent. With his incurable will to self-determination, Dionisio plans to work to buy his family's freedom. But the author erases any optimism to which contemplation of such a recourse might lead. As recounted in the anecdote involving Dolores Santa Cruz, even slaves who buy their freedom are still endangered; their lack of education makes them vulnerable to collusion between corrupt slave owners and their corrupt lawyers. María de Regla's story also demonstrates the distance between the theory of entitlements and the experience of real life. She receives a permit enabling her to escape Doña Rosa's animus and to become a hired slave, but she faces obstacles in finding alternative placement. These instances lend validity to the famous view that the "more humane provisions of Latin American slave law" were more often than not honoured in the breach.[21]

To demonstrate an extreme form of dissent, Villaverde turns to the sugar estate, where slave defiance reaches its climax. The rural slaves run away, withstand brutal beatings when caught and escape their bondage by committing suicide. Their staunchest show of resistance comes at the moment when physical punishment is at its fiercest. The classic punishment scenes, which are designed to evoke the reader's sympathy in Suárez's novel and which foster a view of the slaves as victims, are used here to different effect.

Taken at face value, Tomasa, the returned runaway slave, is an innocent victim because of her powerlessness. Yet the author/narrator does not claim sympathy for her victimhood; instead, he defines her as an agent for whom only admiration is permitted. The account of her whipping by her supervisor highlights this intent. The young, robust, defiant Tomasa stands without a moan as she is flayed in an orgy of blood. Refusing to be humiliated by the extreme pain, she utters not a moan nor begs her torturer for mercy or forgiveness. Her stance points us to a reversal in Villaverde's characterization strategy. Whereas it is the author/narrator who provides insight into the psychology of the outwardly compliant slaves, in the case of the captured runaways it is from their actions that one must deduce their dispositions. According to Ofer Zur, "The difference between victims and non-victims lies not in external factors, as is so often argued, but . . . in how they view themselves, the world around them, and their relationship to the trauma . . . The basic mode of operation of an adult victim is a feeling of helplessness and self-pity. The victim's locus of control is likely to be external and stable."[22] Like Pedro *briche*'s choice of suicide, Tomasa's response is testimony to her internal locus of control, which enables her to suffer this extreme physical abuse while still resisting the humiliation that was its ultimate aim.

Their secondary placement in the first sections of the novel led Martín Morúa Delgado to overlook the slaves in his comments on the inadequacy of the novelist's characterization strategies. This omission is understandable since, generally speaking, the enslaved in Villaverde's fictional universe do not acquire the individual status afforded their enslavers. The significant exception is the multifaceted María de Regla. Her function as a wet nurse has a double edge. As another form of forced labour, it epitomizes the awesome authority of the enslavers. It is equally a sign of the latter's dependence on those whom they hold in bondage.

Unlike her equivalents Camila and Dorotea, María is not primarily or only a sexual creature. In fact, sexual exploitation of the female slave – a core theme of other narratives – does not appear to be of major interest to Villaverde. Where other narratives distinguish the wet nurse from her more popular sex-object sister, Villaverde endows María de Regla with sexual and nurturing attributes in equal measure. Her self-narration gives her life story a tragic touch, but it also parodies incontinent white men's subjection to the slave woman's fabled magnetic attraction. In addition, María and her daughter, Dolores, capitalize on their sexual appeal as a resource to improve their situation. Dolores is flattered, not reviled like her predecessors, by the *mayordomo*'s sexual interest, and, more importantly, she avails herself of it to gain material and psychological satisfaction. Her mother consorts with the Biscayan carpenter on the estate for a similarly opportunistic reason.

The female slave's wet-nurse function (alluded to *passim* in earlier narratives) causes one of the novel's sustained conflicts and provides the key to a deeper understanding of the slave mistress's motives and anxieties. Her relationship with María opens a chink in Doña Rosa's supremacist armour. By ordering María to neglect her own daughter to nurse Adela, she seeks to exercise her right of ownership of the slave woman's body and to drive a social wedge between the slave child and the offspring of the slave owner. The author, however, infuses the incident with irony. Doña Rosa's efforts are doubly thwarted. María wilfully defies her and secretly nurses both babies simultaneously. Ultimately, however, Doña Rosa prevails over María; as punishment for her transgression she is demoted from her domestic position and banished to the sugar estate.

Nonetheless, María's subversion of her mistress's will to exploit her as a feeding machine is significant, though short-lived. She performs her role not with the soullessness of an automaton responding to a command, but as a deeply satisfying, nurturing experience. It might be argued that this unexpected turn of events implies the perverse notion that the enslaved woman benefited emotionally from a fundamental injustice of slavery. But another interpretation of this episode also suggests itself: the psychological victory that the enslaved woman scores over her enslaver is the author's pointer to unrecognized ways in which the ideological foundations of slavery were eroded.

More far-reaching still is the second, less tangible means by which Doña Rosa is defeated. Out of the experience of nurturing, Adela and her wet nurse develop a reciprocal mother–daughter attachment that finds no equivalent in Adela's relationship with Doña Rosa, her biological mother. Moreover, the genuine sisterly affection shared by María's Dolores and Doña Rosa's Adela puts a blight on the supremacy that Doña Rosa would preserve for her daughter, and, inferentially, on polarizing proslavery thought. Thus a sceptical shadow is cast on the frequent reports by travel writers of unproblematic sibling-like relationships between the children of domestic slaves and slave-owner children. In like manner, the secret camaraderie between María and the Gamboa girls serves to unsettle the racial separatism assumed by slave society.

In light of her demonstrated capacity for forgiveness and compassion, Doña Rosa's intransigence in refusing to pardon María's disobedience, even after many years, is well-nigh inscrutable. María is not a sexual rival to Doña Rosa like her fictional slave sister Petrona. But contrary to Martín Morúa Delgado's assertion that María has not offended Doña Rosa, one may read political symbolism in the tension in their relationship. As in the case of Petrona and Doña Concepción in Tanco's novella, María's strong constitution is a potent reminder to Doña Rosa of her inadequacy as a mother. It is the latter's visceral sense of her weakness that drives her implacable rancour. The punishment of exile that she imposes on María is conceived as a means of recovering from this blow to her ego and of reasserting her jealously guarded sense of superiority. Unwittingly the slave wet nurse has robbed the slave mistress of her peace of mind forever. María's relationship with Don Cándido reflects a similar erosion of power. As her owner, Don Cándido subjects her to his will by commanding her to serve as wet nurse for Cecilia. But this very act furnishes her with the key to the secret past that thereafter enslaves him, that he carries like a daily burden.

María is the novel's most ubiquitous slave character and the link between its different plots. She is also an eminent consciousness and eloquent purveyor of the novel's message. The slave wet nurse is a privileged insider and therefore a credible critical voice. As a figure of the acculturated slave, she is groomed for the role of pseudo-narrator that she comes to play towards the end of the novel. Her special location within the slave owners' world has enabled her to speak standard Spanish and to gain acceptance as racially but not culturally black. But lest her placement be thought to amount to co-optation, the author also makes her into a Caliban figure who uses her acculturation subversively.

A comparison of María's posture with that of her son and daughter, Tirso and Dolores, sums up the significance of her role. In the first part of the novel, Tirso and Dolores are mute fixtures in the background of family gatherings, acting out the classic role of perfect slaves. Like dumb animals, with eyes fixed on Don Cándido, they anticipate his every wish and satisfy it before it is expressed. As we saw in chapter 4, postcolonial discourse theory interprets the gaze of a self-appointed superior subject (the colonizer) as one means of confirming the inferiority of the subaltern Other (the colonized). *Cecilia Valdés* transposes the act of gazing to the master–slave interaction, reversing the viewing positions without altering the power dynamics: the literal gaze of these two slaves merely reaffirms their subjection to their enslavers.[23] In contrast, María's gaze, turned on the enslaver, is invested with authority. With her historical insider knowledge, she can disturb and ultimately disrupt the power relationship, for the enslaved woman is conscious of her power to undermine her master's prestige. The ascendancy of her voice towards the end of the novel is symptomatic of this dialogic shift.

As pseudo-narrator, María presents a view of events not available to others. Speaking openly and almost as an equal to the young female members of the Gamboa family, she tells of the secret strategies used by domestic slaves to delude their owners in order to survive. She uses a tongue-in-cheek expression of respect to veil her mockery of her owners; in a cunning game of speaking and unspeaking, she confronts the Gamboa daughters with uncomfortable truths about their family, retracting her sordid revelations but leaving their effect. Having reserved for María the task of tying up narrative loose ends, the author allows her voice to prevail for a long time. While the rebel slaves on the sugar plantation manifest one form of agency when they take their own lives, another form of slave agency is expressed through María, who lives to tell the tale. It is true that the voice she speaks with does not appear authentic or credible in a slave. But what is important is the role in which Villaverde conceives her. Bearing in mind that, as we have seen, the slaves feature mainly as a talking point for the slave owner, this use of María is a significant strategy for their vindication and rehabilitation of their image. By giving her this important literary purpose as well as a central thematic role, Villaverde has made the slave into a speaking subject rather than a talked-about object.

However, María de Regla's posture is not devoid of complication. As with the incestuous connections between Gamboa family members and the warped psyche of the mulattoes, the antislavery theme also finds expression through disclosure of the psychological malaise that afflicts her as a by-product of her bondage. María's preference for her mulatto son, Tirso, over Dolores, her black daughter, is an oblique endorsement of slavery's racist ideology resulting from her self-alienating proximity to the white world. Thus she is both a vocal critic of the dominant belief system and its unwitting creature who presents symptoms of the psychopathology of anti-black racism.

Although there is no denying the novel's antislavery tenor, the author/narrator's posture is prone to the very complexity and variability we have identified in his characters. On the one hand, his undeniably hostile view of Cuban slavery exists in symbiotic alliance with his *independentista* politics; each depends on and benefits from the other. For Villaverde, slavery describes both the condition of the African-descended labour force and Cuba's political standing as a Spanish colony. The voice of the *independentista* author resonates in his equation of the Creoles' failure to free the colony from subjection to imperial bondage with the young women's powerlessness to help the slave, who is described pointedly as "another victim of civil tyranny in his ill-fated country".[24] These issues are twinned linguistically when the narrator censures Leonardo for his lack of the political will needed to free Cuba from the shackles of colonial rule.

On the other hand, Villaverde is arguably the antislavery author who most consistently projects a Eurocentric view of Africa and Africans. In diagnosing Cuba's social ills, he shows keen sensitivity to the mulattoes' prejudice against black slaves and their preference for whites, but he is blind to his own racial and cultural bias. In his references to black slaves, he is the persistent voice of anti-black racism. Such bigotry recurs in characterizations such as the reference to "a slave *doubly* stupid because of his long years in slavery" (*un negro* doblemente *estúpido por sus largos años de esclavitud*),[25] implying that slavery merely exacerbated an original condition. Villaverde repeatedly labels his slave characters as savage or semi-savage, unwittingly discrediting his liberal pretensions. Where Suárez and Zambrana stoutly defend the integrity of African culture, Villaverde anachronistically reproduces the stereotype of Africa as a negative signifier and the site of savagery. In his view, the further removed characters are from their African roots – that is, the more they absorb European influence or conform to the Caucasian phenotype – the more acceptable they appear. He might even be said to be endorsing Doña Rosa's claim that transatlantic slavery benefited the slaves by bringing them out of the darkness of African barbarism into the light of European civilization.

The other side of his Eurocentric prejudice is Villaverde's elitist Creole loyalty and snobbery. Leonardo's behaviour, according to the author, is not absolutely uncouth but is unbecoming in a young white Creole of the slave-owning class. In singling out María de Regla as his stellar Creole slave character, he notes the civilizing benefits she has derived from interacting more with "decent" whites than with "ignorant" slaves. The author notes this privilege approvingly, oblivious to his self-sabotaging race and class prejudice. This undisguised chauvinism weighs heavily on judgements of the novel's antislavery efficacy. From a postmodern vantage point, however, Villaverde's racism can be viewed as coexisting, albeit in a dissonant relationship, with his antislavery objective. Each tempers but does not obliterate the other.

One of the strongest statements about the novel's defect appears in Selwyn Cudjoe's *Resistance and Caribbean Literature*. After an otherwise favourable appraisal of the work's empirical value, Cudjoe balks at its ending:

> We do know that Villaverde followed true-to-life incidents and people and we are indebted to him for an accurate and vivid presentation of Havana and plantation slavery. But real-life characters and incidents do not always make a good novel. What does make a good novel is a marshalling of all these elements into a creative work in an attempt to resolve some of the contradictions or paradoxes extracted from the real-life situation, to propose some concrete liberation for the oppressed characters and to convey a positive and important point arising from the confluence of historical data.[26]

He goes on to charge the author with violating Fanon's postcolonial proposal that, like a missionary, the colonized man who writes for his people ought to use the past with the intention of opening up the future, as an invitation to action and a basis for hope. This declaration speaks eloquently to the difference between the traditional and postmodern approaches to interpretation. In this prescriptive judgement Cudjoe craves closure and catharsis to enable the reader to experience slave heroism vicariously through the fictional characters. The author of *Cecilia Valdés*, for his part, seems unmoved by such idealistic imperatives.

In his novel Villaverde walks an ideological tightrope, maintaining a delicate and, some might say, precarious balance between condemnation of and compassion for the enslaver, and between the submissive and the subversive portraits of the slaves. As I have argued throughout, he tempers but does not tolerate the iniquity of his slave-owner characters at the same time that he redeems his slave victims without romanticizing them. If the novel does not satisfy the requirement for unqualified slave heroism, neither does it appease the desire for unequivocal slave-owner villainy. Similarly, the author's blindness to his own prejudice diminishes but does not completely destroy his antislavery project.

# CONCLUSION

CUBAN ANTISLAVERY NARRATIVES lend themselves to either confrontational or acquiescent readings. The question that arises, however, is whether interpretation should focus on where these narratives fall short or highlight what may be regarded as their constructive achievements. The postmodern answer is that it must do not one or the other, but both. Viewed in this light, the narratives appear tinged with different ideological colours; they are not easily reduced to either unproblematic liberalism or unequivocal conservatism. Increasingly, scholars who study the Caribbean are being called upon to generate a balanced appraisal of the region's history and cultural expression. Cuban historian María del Carmen Barcia Zequiera recently cautioned against historical accounts that fail to recognize that Cuban slaves did not constitute a homogeneous group. Noting the post-colonial tendency to focus on an exclusive metanarrative of slave rebellion and resistance, Barcia Zequiera calls for a slavery scholarship that avoids reductive and ahistorical dichotomies.[1] Her sentiments echo Antonio Benítez-Rojo's thinking about Caribbean cultural studies: "No perspective of human thought – whether premodern, modern or postmodern – can by itself define the Caribbean's complex sociocultural interplay . . . We need all of them at the same time . . . Every Caribbean person knows that the Caribbean is much more than a system of binary oppositions."[2]

Such thinking, as we have shown, bears directly on our view of the significance of Cuba's antislavery narratives. Neither as a corpus nor as individual works do these compositions satisfy the fundamentalist wish for a master narrative featuring chronically heroic slave rebels and terminally villainous slave owners. The authors were no doubt aware that slavery did not always present the enslaved with opportunities for heroism. In the postmodern age, flawed or modest heroes can find accommodation alongside exemplary ones. A postmodern optic can temper the prevailing view that these narratives promote humility and lack of a rebellious spirit in slaves. It enables us to retrieve the subversive value implanted in the frequently overlooked stories of controlled psychological resistance and the small triumphs embedded in the details of the slave characters' actions. The authors leave little doubt about the slaves' political consciousness and deep-rooted discontent, even where they lacked the ability to express it verbally or the opportunity to translate it into action.

All antislavery narratives are not one antislavery narrative. They are narratives of resistance and surrender, heroism and cowardice, adaptation and alienation, defeat and triumph. If their representations of the enslaved as submissive and weak are regarded as dubious antislavery statements, the authors' unflattering portraits of the enslaver qualify as a more unequivocal measure of antislavery value. And paralleling their careful insertion of minor signs of covert rebellion to relieve the bleak picture of slave passivity is their introduction of faint redemptive glimmers of light in the malevolent world of the slave owner.

We may choose to read only the tragedy of slavery in these narratives, or we may expand the lens we use to view them – not to minimize the tragedy but to show how the authors undermine the foundations of the institution through irony and paradox. The corollary of the powerless slaves' hidden strength is the veiled vulnerability and impotence of their enslavers. With its openness to dissonance, a postmodern reading is not compelled to either sanitize the stories or smooth over the contradictions of the antislavery effort. A postmodern world view is likewise unperturbed by the contradiction of a racist, conservative del Monte's providing a forum for incubation of radical antislavery views. It can also recognize the coexistence of residual prejudice and strong opposition to the practice of slavery in authors such as Villaverde and Zambrana.

Neither is one compelled to interpret these literary endeavours as either self-serving or altruistic; instead they may be qualified as both. Good survivors, Al Siebert notes, *"make the world a better place for themselves by devoting themselves to making it better for others. They are both selfish and unselfish at the same time . . . They act unselfishly for selfish reasons. They must, for their own good, take action to improve discordant situations. Actions that result in things working better lead to feelings of satisfaction and may be profitable as well."*[3] In a similar spirit, no code of silence need be imposed on the stories of slave passivity or submission; these stories exist side by side with others that tell of the slaves' struggle to maintain a human identity under a system whose aim was to dehumanize them. In a balanced critical enquiry, neither story will be allowed to eclipse the other.

In *La esclavitud desde la esclavitud* Gloria García has provided us with a valuable collection of letters and other documents that show how slaves used legal means to wage a tenacious struggle for their rights. She notes that these efforts were less spectacular than, but just as significant as, *marronage*. García claims that these records are useful for revealing the slaves' psychological profiles and, in particular, their determination to maintain their human dignity. This historian presents the legal documents as a corrective to traditional literary and historical representations, in which slaves appear as objects of benevolent concern and not as subjects who are able to understand their reality and to act in accordance with the challenges with which it confronts them.[4]

In a similar spirit Richard Jackson declares that "to really understand what it was like to be a slave in nineteenth-century Cuba, we should turn to the autobiographical account of a former slave who told his own story, edited and published in book form in 1966 by Miguel Barnet".[5] José Antonio Portuondo believes that only after 1880, when slavery had almost ended, did slave characters begin to assume the status of individuals in colonial literature.[6] These judgements should not lead us to discount the value of the outsider perspective of the writers of antislavery fiction, for it bears out an important extension of Siebert's theory of selfish altruism: "Wanting and needing to have things work well for everyone means that you must have an accurate understanding of what other people feel and think."[7] These narratives are testimony to the writers' capacity for empathy and their will to compensate for their limitations by imagining what slavery might have meant to the slave.

William Luis is mindful of the need for literary commentators to "reconstruct history and situate these narratives within the context of the past".[8] Gordon Lewis puts it more candidly:

> By bringing both the black and the mulatto to the forefront as figures worthy of literary comment and analysis, the novelists of the nineteenth century managed to compose a morally inspired social analysis critical of the slavery institution. To have asked them to have done more would be to assume on their part a supernatural ability to transcend the limitations of the time and the society in which they had to live and survive.[9]

These Creole authors had come a long way from the eighteenth-century European world view that fed Edward Long's belief that an orang-utan husband would not be a dishonour to a Hottentot woman,[10] and that necessitated the English abolitionist Granville Sharp's search for scientific evidence to prove that the African Negro was a human being and not an animal. With these perspectives in mind, one can better appreciate the importance of the Cuban novelists' disruption of the dominant ideology by making the theme of the slaves' humanity into their anthem. In dwelling at length on Francisco's feelings, Zambrana may be seen to do no more than follow the Romantic fashion of melodramatic sentimentalism. But his strategy also serves another ideological purpose. Investing Francisco with intense emotions recognizes the slave's humanity. According to psychologists Lambrou and Pratt,

> Emotions are a quintessential element of our humanity . . . Richly diverse emotions are a hallmark of the human condition . . . Our thoughts, senses, and emotions are the infinitely colorful and variable fibers of awareness and meaning of which our lives are woven . . . Our own particular set of emotional responses sets us apart as individuals, forming a vital part of the pattern we call our personality. Without emotions we would not be ourselves.[11]

Its shortcomings notwithstanding, one is hard-pressed to overlook the (albeit limited) revolutionary significance of the literary antislavery project in its time. In addition, when considered diachronically, the narratives tell a humanized version of Cuba's social and political history.

In a comment on the literary contribution to the antislavery cause in Cuba, Lewis bemoans the restriction of plots to "family domestic situations rather than general social-class or racial-caste situations", and he privileges Cirilo Villaverde's *Cecilia Valdés* for its "larger vision . . . of slavery as a moral cancer that invades all Cuban society and corrupts both black and white".[12] While this judgement may be defended, one needs to distinguish between sociological value and sociological method. Given the symbiotic relationship between the two, in representing family domestic situations the authors are ultimately representing the society. It is precisely their translation of sociological event into lived individual human experience that gives these narratives their literary purchase.

# NOTES

## Introduction

1.  Roberto González Echevarría, "*Cien años de soledad*: The Novel as Myth and Archive", *Modern Language Notes* 99, no. 2 (March 1984): 360.

2.  Digna Castañeda, "The Female Slave in Cuba During the First Half of the Nineteenth Century", in *Engendering History: Caribbean Women in Historical Perspective*, ed. Verene Shepherd, Bridget Brereton and Barbara Bailey (Kingston: Ian Randle, 1995), 143.

3.  Terry Eagleton, *Literary Theory: An Introduction* (Minneapolis: University of Minnesota Press, 1983), 8–9.

4.  Roberta Day Corbitt, "A Survey of Cuban *Costumbrismo*", *Hispania* 33, no. 1 (February 1950): 42.

5.  Richard Jackson, *The Black Image in Latin American Literature* (Albuquerque: University of New Mexico Press, 1976), 22.

6.  Eagleton, *Literary Theory*, 12.

7.  Linda Hutcheon, *A Poetics of Postmodernism: History, Theory, Fiction* (New York: Routledge, 1988), xi.

8.  Antonio Benítez-Rojo, *The Repeating Island: The Caribbean and the Postmodern Perspective*, trans. James E. Maraniss (Durham, NC: Duke University Press, 1996), 23.

9.  Mikhail Bakhtin, *The Dialogic Imagination*, trans. Caryl Emerson and Michael Holquist (Austin: University of Texas Press, 1981), 271–73.

10. Vera M. Kutzinski, introduction to *A History of Literature in the Caribbean*, ed. James Arnold (Amsterdam: John Benjamins, 1994), 16.

11. Benítez-Rojo, *Repeating Island*, 152.

12. Bakhtin, *Dialogic Imagination*, 259.

13. Ibid.

14. Ibid., 270–75.

15. Jill Netchinsky, "Engendering a Cuban Literature: Nineteenth-century Antislavery Narrative (Manzano, Suárez y Romero, Gómez de Avellaneda, Zambrana)" (PhD diss., Yale University, 1985), 6.

16. Carlos Alonso, *The Burden of Modernity: The Rhetoric of Cultural Discourse in Spanish America* (New York: Oxford University Press, 1998), 77.

17. Jackson, *Black Image*, 31.

18. Gordon K. Lewis, *Main Currents in Caribbean Thought* (Baltimore: Johns Hopkins University Press, 1983), 108.

19. H. Orlando Patterson, *The Sociology of Slavery* (London: Granada, 1973), 15.

20. Alonso, *Burden of Modernity*, 66.

21. Bruce King, "Caribbean Conundrum", *Transition* 62 (1993): 156.

## Chapter 1 *Petrona y Rosalía*

1. Félix Tanco y Bosmeniel, *Petrona y Rosalía* (1838; reprint, Havana: Editorial Letras Cubanas, 1980), 5–6.

2. Lewis, *Main Currents*, 6.

3. Tanco y Bosmeniel, *Petrona y Rosalía*, 17.

4. Lewis, *Main Currents*, 8.

5. Tanco y Bosmeniel, *Petrona y Rosalía*, 7.

6. Lewis, *Main Currents*, 7.

7. Ibid., 141.

8. Barbara Bush, *Slave Women in Caribbean Society, 1650–1838* (London: James Curry, 1990), 1–10.

9. Tanco y Bosmeniel, *Petrona y Rosalía*, 10.

10. Ibid., 18.

11. Sharon Romeo Fivel-Démoret, "The Production and Consumption of Propaganda Literature: The Cuban Anti-slavery Novel", *Bulletin of Hispanic Studies* 66, no. 1 (1989): 1.

12. Tanco y Bosmeniel, *Petrona y Rosalía*, 17.

13. Rómulo Gallegos, *Doña Bárbara* (Madrid: Ediciones Cátedra, 1997), 269.

14. Tanco y Bosmeniel, *Petrona y Rosalía*, 21.

15. Fivel-Démoret, "Production and Consumption", 5.

16. Lewis, *Main Currents*, 176.

17. Tanco y Bosmeniel, *Petrona y Rosalía*, 18 (my emphasis).

18. Ibid., 20.

19.  Ibid.

20.  Ibid., 11.

21.  Barbara Bush, "White 'Ladies', Coloured 'Favourites' and Black 'Wenches': Some Considerations on Sex, Race and Class Factors in Social Relations in White Creole Society in the British Caribbean", *Slavery and Abolition* 2, no. 3 (1931): 251–52.

22.  Tanco y Bosmeniel, *Petrona y Rosalía*, 12.

23.  Ibid., 7.

24.  Ibid., 10.

## Chapter 2 *Francisco*

1.  Alonso, *Burden of Modernity*, 66–67.

2.  Anselmo Suárez y Romero, *Francisco* (1839; reprint, Havana: Publicaciones del Ministerio de Educación, Dirección de Cultura, 1947), 217.

3.  Ibid., 23.

4.  Ibid., 31.

5.  Ibid., 220.

6.  Two noteworthy exceptions are Netchinsky, "Engendering", and Lorna V. Williams, *The Representation of Slavery in Cuban Fiction* (Columbia: University of Missouri Press, 1994), the second chapter of which explores various technical features of Suárez's novel.

7.  César Leante, "Dos obras antiesclavistas", *Cuadernos Americanos* 11, no. 4 (July–August 1976): 179.

8.  Suárez y Romero, *Francisco*, 77.

9.  Lemuel A. Johnson, *The Devil, the Gargoyle and the Buffoon: The Negro as Metaphor in Western Literature* (Port Washington, NY: Kennikat Press, 1971), 69.

10.  Bakhtin, *Dialogic Imagination*, 263.

11.  William Luis, *Literary Bondage: Slavery in Cuban Narrative* (Austin: University of Texas Press, 1990), 39.

12.  Suárez y Romero, *Francisco*, 54.

13.  Ibid., 145–46.

14.  Bill Ashcroft, Gareth Griffiths and Helen Tiffin, *Post-colonial Studies: The Key Concepts* (London: Routledge, 2000), 46.

15.  Ibid., 225.

16. Ibid.

17. Ibid.

18. R. Anthony Castagnaro, *The Early Spanish American Novel* (New York: Las Américas, 1971), 160–61.

19. Fivel-Démoret, "Production and Consumption", 3.

20. Suárez y Romero, *Francisco*, 93.

21. Lewis, *Main Currents*, 175.

22. Fivel-Démoret, "Production and Consumption", 5.

23. Suárez y Romero, *Francisco*, 63–64.

24. G.R. Coulthard, *Race and Colour in Caribbean Literature* (London: Oxford University Press, 1962), 12.

25. Suárez y Romero, *Francisco*, 49.

26. Bakhtin, *Dialogic Imagination*, 299.

27. Suárez y Romero, *Francisco*, 52.

28. Ibid., 28–29.

29. Castagnaro, *Early Spanish American Novel*, 160.

30. Ashcroft, Griffiths and Tiffin, *Post-colonial Studies*, 1.

31. Lewis, *Main Currents*, 163–65.

32. Coulthard, *Race and Colour*, 13.

33. Ashcroft, Griffiths and Tiffin, *Post-colonial Studies*, 13.

34. Suárez y Romero, *Francisco*, 56.

35. Orlando Patterson, *The Sociology of Slavery* (London: Granada, 1973), 179–80.

36. Fivel-Démoret, "Production and Consumption", 3.

37. Ashcroft, Griffiths and Tiffin, *Post-colonial Studies*, 12.

38. Suárez y Romero, *Francisco*, 138.

39. Ibid., 86.

40. Ibid., 139.

41. Lewis, *Main Currents*, 8.

42. Suárez y Romero, *Francisco*, 99–101.

43. Gloria García, *La esclavitud desde la esclavitud* (Havana: Instituto Cubano del Libro, 1996), 71.

44. Suárez y Romero, *Francisco*, 65.

45. Ibid., 176.

46. Sigmund Freud, *Civilization and Its Discontents,* trans. James Strachey (New York: W. W. Norton, 1961), 1.

47.  Netchinsky, "Engendering", 162.

48.  Coulthard, *Race and Colour*, 14.

49.  Fivel-Démoret, "Production and Consumption", 3.

## Chapter 3 *Sab*

1.  Catherine Davies, ed., *Sab*, by Gertrudis Gómez de Avellaneda (Manchester: Manchester University Press, 2001).

2.  Catherine Davies, "The Gift in *Sab*", *Afro-Hispanic Review* 22, no. 2 (Fall 2003): 46–53.

3.  See Debra J. Rosenthal, *Race Mixture in Nineteenth-century U.S. and Spanish American Fictions: Gender, Culture, and Nation Building* (Chapel Hill: University of North Carolina Press, 2004) and Richard C. D'Augusta, "Miscegenation, the White Aesthetic and the Cuban Antislavery Novel", *Revista de estudios hispánicos* 28, no. 1–2 (2001): 165–83.

4.  Fivel-Démoret, "Production and Consumption", 8.

5.  Stacey Schlau, "Stranger in a Strange Land: The Discourse of Alienation in Gómez de Avellaneda's Abolitionist Novel *Sab*", *Hispania* 69, no. 3 (September 1986): 495.

6.  William Luis, "La novela antiesclavista: Texto, contexto y escritura", *Cuadernos americanos* 236 (May–June 1981): 104.

7.  Brígida Pastor, "Symbiosis Between Slavery and Feminism in Gertrudis Gómez de Avellaneda's *Sab*?", *Bulletin of Latin American Research* 16, no. 2 (1997): 187.

8.  Edward Said, *Culture and Imperialism* (London: Chatto and Windus, 1993), 59.

9.  Williams, *Representation*, 118.

10.  Jerome Branche, "Ennobling Savagery? Sentimentalism and the Subaltern in Sab", *Afro-Hispanic Review* 17, no. 2 (1998): 12–23.

11.  Bakhtin, *Dialogic Imagination*, 261–63.

12.  Gertrudis Gómez de Avellaneda, *Sab*, ed. Mary Cruz (1841; reprint, Havana: Instituto Cubano del Libro, 1973), 135–36.

13.  Ibid., 177.

14.  Netchinsky, "Engendering", 198.

15.  Suárez y Romero, *Francisco*, 32.

16.  Jackson, *Black Image*, 26.

17.  Gómez de Avellaneda, *Sab*, 137.

18. Jackson, *Black Image*, 22–23. Pastor, "Symbiosis", and Branche, "Ennobling Savagery?", also proceed on the basis of this mistaken premise.
19. Davies, ed., *Sab*, 18–19.
20. Castagnaro, *Early Spanish American Novel*, 158.
21. Frantz Fanon, *Black Skin, White Masks*, trans. Charles Lam Markmann (New York: Grove, 1967), 69.
22. Ibid., 149.
23. Louis J. Pérez Jr, ed., *Slaves, Sugar, and Colonial Society: Travel Accounts of Cuba, 1801–1899* (Wilmington, DE: Scholarly Resources, 1992), 423.
24. Gómez de Avellaneda, *Sab*, 171.
25. Verena Martínez Alier, *Marriage, Class and Colour in Nineteenth-century Cuba: A Study of Racial Attitudes and Sexual Values in a Slave Society* (Ann Arbor: University of Michigan Press, 1989), 71.
26. Gómez de Avellaneda, *Sab*, 315.
27. Nara Araujo, "Raza y genero en *Sab*", *Casa de las Américas* 190, no. 19 (1993): 46.
28. Fanon, *Black Skin*, 8–11.
29. Ibid., 11.
30. Gómez de Avellaneda, *Sab*, 308.
31. Bush, "White 'Ladies'", 249–59.
32. Ibid., 257.
33. Gómez de Avellaneda, *Sab*, 293–94.
34. Ibid., 138.
35. Cruz, ed., in Gómez de Avellaneda, *Sab*, 33.
36. Gómez de Avellaneda, *Sab*, 142–43.
37. Ibid., 244.
38. Ibid., 313.
39. Ibid., 202.
40. Fanon, *Black Skin*, 145.
41. Netchinsky, "Engendering", 202–3.
42. Gómez de Avellaneda, *Sab*, 211 and 201.
43. Ibid., 133.
44. Ibid., 202.
45. See Pastor, "Symbiosis", and Schlau, "Stranger".
46. Davies, ed., *Sab*, 13.
47. Gómez de Avellaneda, *Sab*, 316.

48. Davies, ed., *Sab*, 5.
49. Gómez de Avellaneda, *Sab*, 302 (my emphasis).
50. Ibid., 306.
51. Bush, "White 'Ladies'", 256.
52. Ibid., 248–50.
53. Davies, ed., *Sab*, 28.
54. Gómez de Avellaneda, *Sab*, 227.
55. Despite Spain's 1835 agreement with Britain to outlaw slave trafficking, the practice continued in Cuba until 1865.
56. Gómez de Avellaneda, *Sab*, 264.
57. Ibid., 212.
58. Ibid., 257.
59. Ibid., 158.
60. Ibid., 127.
61. Ibid.

## Chapter 4 *Romualdo, uno de tantos*

1. Corbitt, "Survey of Cuban *Costumbrismo*", 41.
2. Rebecca Scott, *Slave Emancipation in Cuba* (Princeton, NJ: Princeton University Press, 1985), 19.
3. Francisco Calcagno, *Romualdo, uno de tantos* (1891; reprint in *Noveletas Cubanas*, ed. Imeldo Alvarez, Havana: Editorial de Arte y Literatura, 1977), 281.
4. Ibid., 280.
5. See Leviticus 25:44.
6. For a full discussion of this period in the history of Cuban slavery, see Scott, *Slave Emancipation,* and Franklin Knight, *Slave Society in Cuba during the Nineteenth Century* (Madison: University of Wisconsin Press, 1970).
7. Scott, *Slave Emancipation,* 40.
8. Ibid., 39–40.
9. Calcagno, *Romualdo,* 281.
10. Ibid., 299.
11. Ibid., 298.
12. Ibid., 279.
13. Ibid., 304.
14. Ibid., 292.

15. Ibid., 294.
16. Ibid., 279.
17. Scott, *Slave Emancipation*, 39.
18. Calcagno, *Romualdo*, 367.
19. Ibid., 295.
20. Ashcroft, Griffiths and Tiffin, *Post-colonial Studies*, 226–28.
21. Calcagno, *Romualdo*, 350.
22. Ibid.
23. Ibid.
24. Ibid., 372.
25. Ibid., 355.
26. A dish prepared from ground corn, water, salt and lard.
27. Calcagno, *Romualdo*, 373.
28. Ibid., 376.
29. Lewis, *Main Currents*, 159.
30. Ibid., 236.
31. Calcagno, *Romualdo*, 325.

## Chapter 5 *El negro Francisco*

1. Luis, *Literary Bondage*.
2. Netchinsky, "Engendering", 125–26.
3. Williams, *Representation*, 119–22.
4. Ibid., 158.
5. Pedro Barreda, *The Black Protagonist in the Cuban Novel*, trans. Page Bancroft (Amherst: University of Massachusetts Press, 1979), 86–87.
6. Linda Hutcheon, *A Theory of Parody: The Teachings of Twentieth-century Art Forms* (New York: Methuen, 1985), 36.
7. Ibid., 31.
8. Ibid., 36.
9. Ibid., 76.
10. Ibid., 75.
11. Ibid., 61.
12. Ibid., 65.
13. Ibid., 56–57.
14. Antonio Zambrana, *El negro Francisco* (1880; reprint, Havana: Editorial Letras Cubanas, 1979), 5–6.

15.   Ibid., 5.

16.   Ibid., 6.

17.   Ibid., 5.

18.   Ibid., 148–49.

19.   Ibid., 113.

20.   Suárez y Romero, *Francisco*, 15.

21.   Zambrana, *El negro Francisco*, 112–13.

22.   Ibid., 138.

23.   Ibid., 22.

24.   Ibid., 12.

25.   Suárez y Romero, *Francisco*, 53.

26.   Zambrana, *El negro Francisco*, 78.

27.   Ibid., 155.

28.   Ibid., 156.

29.   Williams, *Representation*, 124–26.

30.   Fivel-Démoret, "Production and Consumption", 8.

31.   Zambrana, *El negro Francisco*, 54.

32.   Ibid., 94.

33.   Ibid., 16.

34.   Ibid., 141–42.

35.   Ibid., 142.

36.   Ibid., 92.

37.   Ibid., 70.

38.   Suárez y Romero, *Francisco*, 216–17 (my emphasis).

39.   Zambrana, *El negro Francisco*, 6.

40.   Ibid., 116.

41.   Ibid., 54.

42.   Ibid., 26.

43.   Ibid., 58.

44.   Ibid., 151.

45.   Hutcheon, *Theory of Parody*, 35.

46.   Rubén Darío, "De invierno", in *Literatura Hispanoamericana*, ed. Enrique Anderson Imbert and Eugenio Florit (New York: Holt, Rinehart and Winston, 1966), 442. For a more extensive discussion of Modernist aestheticism in Zambrana's novel, see Barreda, *Black Protagonist*, chapter 5.

47.   Zambrana, *El negro Francisco*, 12. In addition to evoking Daréío's Modernist

poetics, the allusion to painting is reminiscent of similar placement of blacks in the paintings analysed by David Dabydeen in *Hogarth's Blacks: Images of Blacks in Eighteenth Century English Art* (Athens, GA: University of Georgia Press, 1987).

48. Ibid., 149–50.
49. Ibid., 147.
50. Ibid., 149.
51. James Monaco, *How to Read a Film: The World of Movies, Media, and Multimedia* (Oxford: Oxford University Press, 2000), 136.
52. Zambrana, *El negro Francisco*, 143–45.
53. Hutcheon, *Theory of Parody*, 9.
54. Scott, *Slave Emancipation*, 48.
55. Hutcheon, *Theory of Parody*, 44.
56. Judith Viorst, *Necessary Losses* (New York: Simon and Schuster, 1998), 229.

## Chapter 6 *Cecilia Valdés*

1. Lewis, *Main Currents*, 160.
2. Reynaldo González, *Contradanzas y latigazos* (Havana: Editorial Letras Cubanas, 1992), 42–43.
3. Luis, "La novela antiesclavista", 105–6.
4. D'Augusta, "Miscegenation",á 172.
5. González, *Contradanzas*, 28.
6. Cirilo Villaverde, *Cecilia Valdés* (1839 and 1882; reprint, Havana: Editorial Letras Cubanas, 2002), 179.
7. Ibid., 126.
8. The slaves' social isolation is not absolute; witness the alliance forged between Genoveva, a former slave, and the enslaved María de Regla, and that between Genoveva's stepson, the gangster Malangana, and María's husband, Dionisio.
9. Villaverde, *Cecilia Valdés*, 279–80.
10. Ibid., 280.
11. González, *Contradanzas*, 21.
12. Villaverde, *Cecilia Valdés*, 271.
13. Selwyn R. Cudjoe, *Resistance and Caribbean Literature* (Athens, OH: Ohio University Press, 1981), 100.

14.  Villaverde, *Cecilia Valdés*, 261.
15.  Bush, *Slave Women*, 245.
16.  Villaverde, *Cecilia Valdés*, 365.
17.  Bakhtin, *Dialogic Imagination*, 263.
18.  Villaverde, *Cecilia Valdés*, 189–90.
19.  Ibid., 190 (my emphasis).
20.  Ibid., 389.
21.  David Brion Davis, "Slavery and the Post–World War II Historians", in *Slavery, Colonialism, and Racism*, ed. Sidney W. Mintz (New York: Norton, 1974), 4.
22.  Ofer Zur, "Culture of Victims: Reflections on a Culture of Victims and How Psychotherapy Fuels the Victim Industry", http://www.zurinstitute.com/victim_psychology.html (accessed 12 July 2008).
23.  The position of the two slaves is reminiscent of the equation of slaves and animals in Hogarth's eighteenth-century paintings studied by David Dabydeen. See Dabydeen, *Hogarth's Blacks*.
24.  Villaverde, *Cecilia Valdés*, 353.
25.  Ibid., 350 (my emphasis).
26.  Cudjoe, *Resistance*, 100.

## Conclusion

1.  María del Carmen Barcia Zequiera, *La otra familia* (Havana: Casa de las Américas, 2003), 10–16.
2.  Benítez-Rojo, *Repeating Island*, 295.
3.  Al Siebert, *The Survivor Personality* (New York: Berkley Publishing, 1996), 42–43.
4.  García, *La esclavitud*, 3.
5.  Jackson, *Black Image*, 31.
6.  José Antonio Portuondo, "El negro, héroe, bufón y persona en la literatura cubana colonial", *Unión* 7, no. 4 (December 1968): 32.
7.  Siebert, *Survivor Personality*, 46.
8.  Luis, *Literary Bondage*, 64.
9.  Lewis, *Main Currents*, 236.
10.  Edward Long, *The History of Jamaica*, vol. 2 (1774; reprint, Kingston: Ian Randle, 2002), 364.

11.  Peter Lambrou and George Pratt, *Instant Emotional Healing* (New York: Broadway Books, 2000), 75–76.
12.  Lewis, *Main Currents*, 235.

# BIBLIOGRAPHY

Alonso, Carlos. *The Burden of Modernity: The Rhetoric of Cultural Discourse in Spanish America*. New York: Oxford University Press, 1998.

Araujo, Nara. "Raza y género en *Sab*". *Casa de las Américas* 190, no. 19 (1993): 42–49.

Ashcroft, Bill, Gareth Griffiths and Helen Tiffin. *Post-colonial Studies: The Key Concepts*. London: Routledge, 2000.

Bakhtin, Mikhail. *The Dialogic Imagination*. Translated by Caryl Emerson and Michael Holquist. Austin: University of Texas Press, 1981.

Barcia Zequiera, María del Carmen. *La otra familia*. Havana: Casa de las Américas, 2003.

Barnet, Miguel. *Biografía de un cimarrón*. Mexico: Siglo XXI, 1975.

———. "The Culture that Sugar Created". *Latin American Literary Review*, no. 8 (Spring–Summer 1980): 38–46.

Barreda, Pedro. *The Black Protagonist in the Cuban Novel*. Translated by Page Bancroft. Amherst: University of Massachusetts Press, 1979.

Benítez-Rojo, Antonio. *The Repeating Island: The Caribbean and the Postmodern Perspective*. Translated by James E. Maraniss. Durham, NC: Duke University Press, 1996.

Bertens, Hans. *The Idea of the Postmodern: A History*. New York: Routledge, 1995.

Bloom, Harold. *The Anxiety of Influence: A Theory of Poetry*. New York: Oxford University Press, 1973.

Bolland, Nigel. "Caribbean Cultures and Identities: Interpreting Garifuna Stories". 22nd Elsa Goveia Memorial Lecture, University of the West Indies, Mona Campus, Kingston, Jamaica, 29 March 2006.

Branche, Jerome. "Ennobling Savagery? Sentimentalism and the Subaltern in *Sab*". *Afro-Hispanic Review* 17, no. 2 (1998): 12–23.

———. "*Mulato entre negros (y blancos)*: Writing, Race and the Anti-slavery Question, and Juan Francisco Manzano's *Autobiografía*". *Bulletin of Latin American Research* 20, no. 1 (January 2001): 63–87.

Bueno Salvador. *El negro en la novela hispano-americana*. Havana: Editorial Letras Cubanas, 1986.

Bush, Barbara. *Slave Women in Caribbean Society (1650–1838)*. London: James Curry, 1990.

———. "White 'Ladies', Coloured 'Favourites' and Black 'Wenches': Some Considerations on Sex, Race and Class Factors in Social Relations in White Creole Society in the British Caribbean". *Slavery and Abolition* 2, no. 3 (1981): 245–62.

Calcagno, Francisco. *Romualdo, uno de tantos*. 1891. Reprinted in *Noveletas Cubanas*, edited by Imeldo Alvarez, 279–388. Havana: Editorial de Arte y Literatura, 1977.

Callinicos, Alex. *Against Postmodernism: A Marxist Critique*. Cambridge: Polity, 1991.

Castagnaro, R. Anthony. *The Early Spanish American Novel*. New York: Las Américas, 1971.

Castañeda, Digna. "The Female Slave in Cuba During the First Half of the Nineteenth Century". In *Engendering History: Caribbean Women in Historical Perspective*, edited by Verene Shepherd, Bridget Brereton and Barbara Bailey, 141–54. Kingston: Ian Randle, 1995.

Corbitt, Roberta Day. "A Survey of Cuban *Costumbrismo*". *Hispania* 33, no. 1 (February 1950): 41–45.

Coulthard, G.R. *Race and Colour in Caribbean Literature*. London: Oxford University Press, 1962.

Cudjoe, Selwyn R. *Resistance and Caribbean Literature*. Athens, OH: Ohio University Press, 1981.

Dabydeen, David. *Hogarth's Blacks: Images of Blacks in Eighteenth Century English Art*. Athens, GA: University of Georgia Press, 1987.

Darío, Rubén. "De invierno". In *Literatura Hispanoamericana*, edited by Enrique Anderson Imbert and Eugenio Florit, 442. New York: Holt, Rinehart and Winston, 1966.

D'Augusta, Richard C. "Miscegenation, the White Aesthetic and the Cuban Antislavery Novel". *Revista de Estudios Hispánicos* 28, no. 1í–2 (2001): 165–83.

Davies, Catherine. "Founding-Fathers and Domestic Genealogies: Situating Gertrudis Gómez de Avellaneda". *Bulletin of Latin American Research* 22, no. 4 (October 2003): 423–44.

————. "The Gift in *Sab*". *Afro-Hispanic Review* 22, no. 2 (Fall 2003): 46–53.

Davis, David Brion. "Slavery and the Post–World War II Historians". In *Slavery, Colonialism, and Racism*, edited by Sidney W. Mintz, 1–16. New York: Norton, 1974.

DeCosta-Willis, Miriam. "Self and Society in the Afro-Cuban Slave Narrative". *Latin American Literary Review* 16, no. 32 (1988): 6–15.

Eagleton, Terry. *Literary Theory: An Introduction*. Minneapolis: University of Minnesota Press, 1983.

Estevez, Francisco. *Diario del Rancheador*. 1837–42. Reprint, Havana: Editorial Letras Cubanas, 1982.

Fanon, Frantz. *Black Skin, White Masks*. Translated by Charles Lam Markmann. New York: Grove, 1967.

Fivel-Démoret, Sharon Romeo. "The Production and Consumption of Propaganda Literature: The Cuban Anti-slavery Novel". *Bulletin of Hispanic Studies* 66, no. 1 (1989): 1–12.

Freud, Sigmund. *Civilization and Its Discontents*. Translated by James Strachey. New York: Norton, 1961.

Gallegos, Rómulo. *Doña Bárbara*. Madrid: Ediciones Cátedra, 1997.

García, Gloria. *La esclavitud desde la esclavitud*. Havana: Instituto Cubano del Libro, 1996.

Giral, S. *El otro Francisco*. Havana: Instituto Cubano de Arte e Industria Cinematográficos, 1975.

Gómez de Avellaneda, Gertrudis. *Sab*. 1841. Reprint, Havana: Instituto Cubano del Libro, 1973.

————. *Sab*. Edited by Catherine Davies. Manchester: Manchester University Press, 2001.

González, Reynaldo. *Contradanzas y latigazos*. Havana: Editorial Letras Cubanas, 1992.

González Echevarría, Roberto. "*Cien años de soledad*: The Novel as Myth and Archive". *Modern Language Notes* 99, no. 2 (March 1984): 358–80.

Habermas, Jürgen. "Modernity versus Postmodernity". *New German Critique*, no. 22 (Winter 1981): 3–14.

Hutcheon, Linda. *A Poetics of Postmodernism: History, Theory, Fiction*. New York: Routledge, 1988.

————. *The Politics of Postmodernism*. New York: Routledge, 1989.

————. *A Theory of Parody: The Teachings of Twentieth-century Art Forms.* New York: Methuen, 1985.

Jackson, Richard L. *The Black Image in Latin American Literature.* Albuquerque: University of New Mexico Press, 1976.

————. *Black Writers in Latin America.* Albuquerque: University of New Mexico Press, 1979.

Johnson, Lemuel A. *The Devil, the Gargoyle and the Buffoon: The Negro as Metaphor in Western Literature.* Port Washington, NY: Kennikat Press, 1971.

Jung, Carl. *Man and His Symbols.* Garden City, NY: Doubleday, 1954.

King, Bruce. "Caribbean Conundrum". *Transition,* no. 62 (1993): 140–57.

Knight, Franklin W.S. *Slave Society in Cuba during the Nineteenth Century.* Madison: University of Wisconsin Press, 1970.

Kutzinski, Vera M. "Caribbean Theory and Criticism". In *The Johns Hopkins Guide to Literary Theory and Criticism,* edited by Michael Groden, Martin Kreisworth and Irme Szeman, 177–82. Baltimore: Johns Hopkins University Press, 2005.

————. Introduction to *A History of Literature in the Caribbean,* edited by James Arnold. Amsterdam: John Benjamins, 1994.

Lambrou, Peter, and George Pratt. *Instant Emotional Healing.* New York: Broadway Books, 2000.

La Rosa Corso, Gabino. "Félix Tanco, en el marco de la literatura cubana del siglo 19". *Revista de Literatura Cubana* 4 (July–December 1986): 34–59.

Leante, César. "Dos obras antiesclavistas". *Cuadernos Americanos* 11, no. 4 (July–August, 1976): 175–88.

————. *Los guerrilleros negros.* Havana: UNEAC, 1977.

Ledent, Bénédicte. "Caribbean Literature: Looking Backward and Forward". 19 January 2007. http://vetasdigital.blogspot.com/2007/01/caribbean-literature-looking-backward.html.

Lewis, Gordon K. *Main Currents in Caribbean Thought.* Baltimore: Johns Hopkins University Press, 1983.

Long, Edward. *The History of Jamaica.* Vol. 2. 1774. Reprint, Kingston: Ian Randle, 2002.

Luis, William. "*Cecilia Valdés*: The Emergence of an Antislavery Novel". *Afro-Hispanic Review* 3, no. 2 (May 1984): 15–19.

————. *Literary Bondage: Slavery in Cuban Narrative.* Austin: University of Texas Press, 1990.

————. "La novela antiesclavista: Texto, contexto y escritura". *Cuadernos Americanos* 236 (May–June 1981): 103–16.

Lyotard, Jean-François. *The Postmodern Condition: A Report on Knowledge*. Translated by Geoff Bennington and Brian Massumi. Minneapolis: University of Minnesota Press, 1984.

Manzano, Juan Francisco. *Autobiografía de un esclavo*. 1839. Reprint, Madrid: Ediciones Guadarrama, 1975.

Martínez-Alier, Verena. *Marriage, Class and Colour in Nineteenth-century Cuba: A Study of Racial Attitudes and Sexual Values in a Slave Society*. Ann Arbor: University of Michigan Press, 1989.

Meza y Suárez Inclán, Ramón. *Carmela*. 1886. Reprint, Havana: Editorial Arte y Literatura, 1978.

Monaco, James. *How to Read a Film: The World of Movies, Media, and Multimedia*. Oxford: Oxford University Press, 2000.

Morales, Jorge Luis, ed. *Poesía afroantillana y negrista (Puerto Rico, República Dominicana, Cuba)*. Río Piedras, Puerto Rico: Editorial Universitaria, 1976.

Morillas, Pedro José. "El Ranchador". 1864. Reprinted in *Noveletas Cubanas*, edited by Imeldo Alvarez, 23–44. Havana: Editorial de Arte y Literatura, 1977.

Morúa Delgado, Martín. *Sofía*. 1891. Reprint, Havana: Instituto Cubano del Libro, 1972.

Mraz, John. "Recasting Cuban Slavery: *The Other Francisco* and *The Last Supper*". In *Based on a True Story: Latin American History at the Movies*, edited by Donald Stevens, 103–22. Wilmington, DE: SR Books, 1997.

Mullen, E. *Afro-Cuban Literature: Critical Junctures*. Westport, CT: Greenwood, 1988.

Netchinsky, Jill. "Engendering a Cuban Literature: Nineteenth-century Antislavery Narrative". PhD diss., Yale University, 1985. (Published under the same title by Yale University Press, 1986.)

Ortiz, Fernando. *Los negros esclavos*. 1916. Reprint, Havana: Editorial de Ciencias Sociales, 1996.

Pastor, Brígida. "Symbiosis Between Slavery and Feminism in Gertrudis Gómez de Avellaneda's *Sab*?" *Bulletin of Latin American Research* 16, no. 2 (1997): 187–96.

Patterson, Orlando. *The Sociology of Slavery*. London: Granada, 1973.

Pérez, Louis J., Jr, ed. *Slaves, Sugar, and Colonial Society: Travel Accounts of Cuba, 1801–1899*. Wilmington, DE: Scholarly Resources, 1992.

Portuondo, José Antonio. "El negro, héroe, bufón y persona en la literatura cubana colonial". *Unión* 7, no. 4 (December 1968): 30–36.

Rosell, S. *La novela antiesclavista en Cuba y Brasil, siglo XIX*. Madrid: Editorial Pliegos, 1997.

Rosenthal, Debra J. *Race Mixture in Nineteenth-century U.S. and Spanish American Fictions: Gender, Culture, and Nation Building*. Chapel Hill: University of North Carolina Press, 2004.

Said, Edward. *Culture and Imperialism*. London: Chatto and Windus, 1993.

———. *Orientalism*. New York: Vintage Books, 1978.

Schlau, Stacey. "Stranger in a Strange Land: The Discourse of Alienation in Gómez de Avellaneda's Abolitionist Novel *Sab*". *Hispania* 69, no. 3 (September 1986): 495–503.

Schulman, Ivan A. "The Portrait of the Slave: Ideology and Aesthetics in the Cuban Anti-slavery Novel". In *Comparative Perspectives on Slavery: A Student Reader*, edited by Verene Shepherd and Hilary Beckles, 1077–86. Kingston: Ian Randle, 2000.

Scott, Rebecca. *Slave Emancipation in Cuba*. Princeton, NJ: Princeton University Press, 1985.

Siebert, Al. *The Survivor Personality*. New York: Berkley Publishing, 1996.

Suárez y Romero, Anselmo. *Francisco*. 1839. Reprint, Havana: Publicaciones del Ministerio de Educación, Dirección de Cultura, 1947.

———. *Francisco*. 1839. Reprint, Havana: Instituto Cubano del Libro, 1974.

Tanco y Bosmeniel, Félix. *Petrona y Rosalía*. 1838. Reprint, Havana: Editorial Letras Cubanas, 1980.

Villaverde, Cirilo. *Cecilia Valdés*. 1839 and 1882. Reprint, Havana: Editorial Letras Cubanas, 2002.

Viorst, Judith. *Necessary Losses*. New York: Simon and Schuster, 1998.

Waugh, Patricia. *Metafiction: The Theory and Practice of Self-Conscious Fiction*. London: Methuen, 1984.

Williams, Lorna V. *The Representation of Slavery in Cuban Fiction*. Columbia: University of Missouri Press, 1994.

Zambrana, Antonio. *El negro Francisco*. 1880. Reprint, Havana: Editorial Letras Cubanas, 1979.

Zur, Ofer. "Culture of Victims: Reflections on a Culture of Victims and How Psychotherapy Fuels the Victim Industry". http://www.zurinstitute.com/victim_psychology.html (accessed 12 July 2008).

# INDEX